# A Profile of the Software Industry

# A Profile of the Software Industry

## Emergence, Ascendance, Risks, and Rewards

Sandra A. Slaughter

business**expert**
Press

First published in 2014 by
Business Expert Press, LLC
222 East 46th Street, New York, NY 10017
www.businessexpertpress.com

ISBN-13: 978-1-60649-654-1 (paperback)
ISBN-13: 978-1-60649-655-8 (e-book)

Business Expert Press Industry Profiles Collection

Collection ISSN: 2331-0065 (print)
Collection ISSN: 2331-0073 (electronic)

Cover and interior design by Exeter Premedia Services Private Ltd., Chennai, India

First edition: 2014

10 9 8 7 6 5 4 3 2 1

Printed in the United States of America.

# Abstract

Software plays a critical role in today's global information economy. It runs the computers, networks, and devices that enable countless products and services. Software varies in size from vast enterprise and communications systems like SAP's enterprise resource planning system with hundreds of millions of lines of code to tiny apps like Angry Birds that run on mobile phones. Companies in the software industry produce and sell software products and related services. The industry is intensely competitive and has undergone a dramatic transformation from its roots in a handful of computer hardware mainframe producers in the 1960s to numerous large and small software companies today.

Understanding how the software industry works and how the industry is evolving are important. Since software runs the computers and networks that support the flow of information in the global economy, the software industry also affects companies in all other industries that use these products and services for their own competitive advantage.

This book offers a profile of the software industry and the companies in the industry. It describes the primary products and services produced in the industry; reviews the history of the industry; explains how the industry is structured; discusses its economics and competitive environment; and examines important trends and issues including globalization, workforce, regulation, and the emergence of new software business models.

# Keywords

computers, information technology management, intellectual property, network effects, offshoring, open-source software, outsourcing, software, software as a service, software business model, software copyright, software development, software ecosystems, software industry, software patent, software piracy, software platforms, software product, software security, software standards

# Contents

# Acknowledgments

This book is dedicated to my husband, Ron, who is my strictest critic, but my staunchest support, my very best friend, and soul mate. It is also dedicated to my Mom and Dad, who are with me in spirit always. Finally, it is dedicated to Lila, Sammie, Lucy, Baxter, Bonnie, Buford, and Peaches, who have always loved me, no matter what!

My sincere thanks to Chris F. Kemerer and Michael D. Frutiger for their feedback on earlier drafts of this book. Their comments and suggestions have been invaluable. I also thank Rajiv D. Banker and Gordon B. Davis, my PhD co-advisors, for encouraging me to study the software industry and for their wise counsel and advice throughout my academic career.

# Preface

## Introduction

Welcome to the software industry. Software is a place where great ideas thrive, but so do angry birds and super monsters and worms, viruses, and spam zombies. Vast fortunes have been won (and lost) in the industry.

From its conceptual origins in the 19th century England and early manifestations in humble Silicon Valley garages, the software industry has grown to a behemoth that generates more than a half trillion dollars in revenues. Companies in the industry produce and sell software products and services. As an industry, the software industry has competitive dynamics that make it truly unique. Entry and exit barriers are low, marginal costs of production are minimal, and product innovation occurs rapidly and disruptively. It is an industry where a 12-year-old can create a popular software app for a mobile phone,[1] a college dropout can become a billionaire, and a developing country can become an economic powerhouse. On the other hand, software is also an industry where companies can spend more on litigating over intellectual property than on creating the intellectual property and where products can be used to attack individuals and organizations or to launch cyber warfare.

Software is called a place where "dreams are planted but nightmares harvested."[2] Although the software industry is a powerful wealth generator, producing billions in revenues, countless new companies, numerous billionaires and millionaires, and innovative business models, there is a high rate of failure. Companies' competencies and strategies are critical for competitive advantage and survival.

Consider the fortunes of McAfee, Inc. and its founder, John McAfee. In 1987, John McAfee (a former software engineer at NASA, UNIVAC, Xerox, Computer Sciences Corporation, and Lockheed) founded McAfee Associates, a software company that produced software antivirus and security products. Acquired by Intel in 2011 for $7.7 billion,[3] the company today is one of the largest software antivirus and security companies in the world. It produces a wide range of software security products, such as antivirus software, firewalls, malware removal, software security products for cloud computing providers, data and network protection software, and parental software to monitor Internet use. In 2013, the company employed more than 7,600 and earned more than $2 billion in revenues.[4]

However, both McAfee (the founder) and McAfee (the company) have had numerous ups and downs over the course of their respective histories. With respect to the company, in 2006, the Securities and Exchange Commission filed a suit against McAfee, Inc. for accounting fraud (inflating revenues to investors from 1998 to 2000). The company paid a $50-million fine and settled a class action lawsuit brought by ex-employees to guarantee the value of their share options.[5] Subsequent problems have involved technical issues such as an erroneous virus definition file update by McAfee that caused millions of Windows XP computers worldwide to go offline; hackers identifying serious vulnerabilities in McAfee security software; and McAfee's home security software suffering outages and problems.[6]

With respect to its founder, after selling his stake in McAfee, Inc. in 1996, John McAfee became a multimillionaire. However, his personal fortune declined from $100 million to $4 million by 2009. In 2012, he was arrested (but released) for unlicensed drug manufacturing and possession of an unlicensed weapon in Belize.[7] He was later interrogated as a "person of interest" in the murder of his neighbor in Belize. He fled to Guatemala, seeking asylum, but his bid was denied. While awaiting deportation back to Belize he reportedly faked two heart attacks to delay his deportation, and he was ultimately sent back to the United States. He moved to Portland, Oregon, with his new 30-year-old wife (a former stripper) and is working on a biography.[8] Movies are being made about his life. He has been in the news recently on a number of fronts. He proposed a new device—called "Decentral"—that would allow Internet users to be anonymous and impervious to government surveillance and is working on putting together a start-up company to produce it.[9] And, he spurned a request from a U.S. House of Representatives committee to remedy HealthCare.gov because it "has no interest in fixing anything."[10]

McAfee is an example of the types of interesting companies and characters that populate the software industry.

This book will introduce you to the software industry. If you have an interest in the industry, but don't know much about it and you need a good book to read on a plane or train or in an afternoon, this is the book for you.

Even if you don't have an interest in the industry, you may still want to read this book. Why? Take a look around you … software is everywhere. Almost every man-made thing you see or interact with is powered by software or was made using software or both. Software helps stop and start your car, fly a plane, heat and air condition your home, power the stock market, entertain you on your cell phone, and run the businesses around you.

Understanding who creates software products and services and how they produce and market them is a key to understanding the software industry.

## How This Book Is Organized

This book tells the story of a dynamic and complex industry. The book provides a profile of the software industry, describes how the industry works, and identifies the main players in the industry. Each chapter introduces a particular topic of importance to the industry and ends with a brief summary of key takeaways.

Chapter 1 explains the basics of software—what it is and how it is created. It also defines the two primary types of software that define the software industry. Finally, it distinguishes between the kinds of firms that are included in the industry (and part of this book) and the kinds of firms that are not. After describing the key building blocks of the software industry, the book then turns to the roots of the industry in Chapter 2.

Chapter 2 describes the history of the software industry. It goes back more than 150 years to the first concepts of software and then moves to the start of the industry in the 1960s. The history of the software industry is intertwined with that of the computer hardware industry and the early days in the 1970s are often referred to as the mainframe era. The introduction of personal computers in the 1980s dramatically transformed the software industry, and the chapter tells the story of the intense competition for dominance in that era and the emergence of key firms such as Microsoft, Oracle, and SAP. The Internet came into prominence in the 1990s and 2000s and has dramatically changed the software industry again. Chapter 2 describes the innovative software products, services, pricing, and distribution methods enabled by the Internet.

After providing a historical perspective of the software industry in Chapter 2, Chapter 3 outlines the structure and competitive dynamics of the software industry today. It defines the different sectors and segments of the industry and profiles the major companies in the industry. The chapter then describes the software value chain: the different activities that are needed to produce and market software products. It concludes by identifying the unique economics of software and describes how these economics influence competitive dynamics in the industry.

Chapter 3 describes the market structure of the industry on a national scale, whereas Chapter 4 provides a global perspective of the software industry. Although the United States has historically dominated the industry, that situation is changing. In the 1990s software outsourcing and offshoring emerged and stimulated the growth of the industry around the globe. Vibrant software products and services industries have emerged in Europe, Asia, Australia, Africa, and Latin America. The chapter provides an overview of the software industry and profiles companies in key countries in these regions.

After describing the structure of the software industry in Chapters 3 and 4, Chapters 5 through 7 explore important trends, opportunities, and issues in the software industry including those relating to workforce, regulation, security, and the emergence of new software business models.

Chapter 5 discusses occupations in the software industry and workforce issues and trends. In contrast to other industries that manufacture a physical product, in the software industry, labor is the primary factor of production. The industry depends critically on human talent. This chapter identifies the major occupations in the software industry. It then discusses important workforce issues such as labor shortages, lack of gender and ethnic diversity in the industry, the global workforce, debates about the impact of the global workforce on the U.S. workforce, and other software workforce trends.

Chapter 6 examines regulation in the software industry. Given the unique economics of the industry, it is prone to monopolistic behavior.

This chapter describes the major regulations governing the industry. It also identifies the different types of intellectual property protections available to companies in the industry. The chapter concludes by considering problems with infringement of intellectual property in the form of software piracy and by examining the intensification of battles over software intellectual property being waged by companies in the industry.

Chapter 7 identifies key trends in the software industry. The chapter starts with a discussion of software security and privacy issues that are of increasing concern given the frequency and scope of attacks and the vulnerability and ubiquity of software. The chapter then reveals emerging software business models and innovative pricing and delivery schemes such as software as a service, open-source software, service-oriented architectures, and software platform ecosystems. The chapter concludes by envisioning the possible future of the software industry. It considers the possibility that companies in the software industry may be shifting to producing services rather than products and projects what that shift may mean for the structure and competitive dynamics in the industry.

For those who would like to learn more about the software industry, resources for further study on the software industry as well as a glossary of key terms and a complete set of references are provided.

# CHAPTER 1

# Software Basics

This book focuses on companies that produce and sell software—either for hire or for the mass market. Before you can truly understand the software industry and how it works, you really need to understand its key product: *software*.

This chapter is a bit technical, but important. It describes what *software* is and how it is created. It then describes the basic types of software products and related services that companies in the software industry produce and describes what types of companies the software industry includes (as the focus of this book) and what types of companies it does not.

## What Is Software

Computer software or *software* refers to computer instructions that control the functioning of computer hardware and direct its operations. Software includes two types of instructions: machine instructions (the binary code that turns certain electronic pulses on and off to communicate with the computer processor) and source code (more human-understandable instructions).

Since a computer can only understand machine instructions, software source code must be translated into machine code. This is accomplished using something called a *compiler*. For a hypothetical piece of code, Figure 1.1 visually illustrates the process by which a compiler translates human-understandable software source code into machine-understandable object code that can be executed by the computer processor.

A group or sequence of instructions is called a software *program*, which is written to perform a specific task with a computer. For example, a program could look up a customer number in a database to find the customer's past purchases. Another program could simply obtain and report

| Source Code | Compiler | Compiled "machine" code |
|---|---|---|
| Private Sub WebClass_Start()<br><br>'Write a reply to the user<br><br>With Response<br><br>  .Write "<html>"<br><br>  .Write "<body>"<br><br>  .Write "<h1><font face=""Arial"">WebClass1's Starting Page</font></h1>"<br><br>  .Write "<p>This response was created in the Start event of WebClass1.</p>"<br><br>  .Write "</body>"<br><br>  .Write "</html>"<br><br>End With<br><br>End Sub | | 10011010110101011100000111110000<br>10101010000000000011111111111110<br>10101010101010101010101010001011<br>11111000000001011111010000111111<br>11111111111111111111111111111111<br>11000000001010101010001000111000<br>11000110101010101010101010100000<br>00000000111100000000101010101000<br>11100111010101010100000000100000<br>00000000000000000000000011111111<br>11110101010101010101001001010101<br>01010101010101010101010101101010<br>10101010101000011110001100110010<br>10101110000000000101010101010110<br>00001110101010011010110101010111<br>00000111100001010101000000000000<br>11111111111101010101010101010101<br>1010101000011111111000000000010111<br>110100001111111110 |

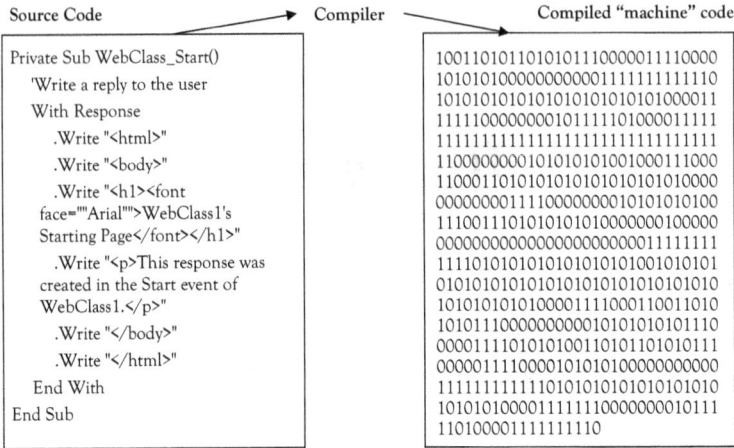

**Figure 1.1  Translation of software source code into machine code by a compiler**

Source: Freetutes.com (2011).
Note: The compiled machine code is not directly obtained from this code—it is illustrative only.

the current date and time. A grouping of related or connected software programs is called a *software system*. For example, a customer relationship management system includes programs to track, look up, and analyze customer purchasing history.

Software programs are typically written by computer programmers using programming languages, utilities, and other tools. A programming language is a specific set of notations used to write a software program. Examples of programming languages include Assembly, Java, COBOL, FORTRAN, and C++.

Programming languages are often described in terms of *levels* or *generations*.[1] Early or first-generation programming languages in the 1950s used machine language instructions and could only be executed on particular computers. The next- or second-generation programming languages were still machine specific, but were *mnemonic* and were known as assembly languages or *assembler*. Figure 1.2 shows an example of an assembly software code snippet that creates a clock to dynamically obtain and show the current time.[2] At the end of the 1950s, the language ALGOL was introduced and has influenced many other programming languages (such as Pascal, C, and Python).

```
Clock

CGROUP        GROUP VECTOR,CODESEG
VECTOR        SEGMENT AT 0H
        DB 6CH DUP(?)        ;FILLER
TIME_LO DW ?                 ;DOS TIME
TIME_HI DW ?                 ;DOS TIME
VEC_IP DW                    ;CLOCK UPDATE VECTOR IP
VEC_CS DW                    ;CLOCK UPDATE VECTOR CS
VECTOR        ENDS

CODESEG SEGMENT PARA
        ASSUME CS:CODESEG,DS:CGROUP
        ORG 100H
CLK     PROC FAR
        JMP SETUP            ;ATTACH TO DOS
INTRPT  LABEL DWORD
INT_IP  DW 0                 ;OLD UPDATE VECTOR IP
INT_CS  DW 0                 ;OLD UPDATE VECROR CS
TICKS   DW 0                 ;TICK COUNTER
SCR_OFF DB 0,0               ;SCREEN OFFSET IN BUFFER
CRT_PORT DW 0                ;SCREEN STATUS PORT
flag    db 0
TIME    DB 8 DUP(':',0BH)    ;TIME SAVE AREA
CLK_INT LABEL NEAR
        PUSH AX              ;SAVE REGISTERS
        PUSH CX
        PUSH DI
        PUSH SI
        PUSH DS
        PUSH ES
        PUSHF                ;AND FLAGS
        CALL CS:[INTRPT]     ;DO OLD UPDATE INTERRUPT
        MOV CX,0040H         ;GET SEGMENT OF DOS TABLE
        MOV DS,CX            ;PUT IN DS
        MOV CX,CS:TICKS      ;GET TICK COUNT
        INC CX               ;INCREMENT IT
        CMP CX,20            ;01F4H   ;HAS A MINUTE GONE BY?
        JB NO_MINUTE         ;NO, MOVE ON
        CALL UPDATE          ;YES, UPDATE CLOCK AND
        MOV CX,0             ; RESET TICK COUNTER
```

*Figure 1.2 Example of assembly code that obtains and shows the current time*

Source: Happy Codings (2013a).

```
NO_MINUTE:
        MOV CS:TICKS,CX      ;SAVE UPDATED TICK COUNT
        MOV CX,0B000H        ;GET VIDEO SEGMENT
        MOV ES,CX            ;PUT IN ES
        MOV DX,CS:CRT_PORT       ;GET CRT STATUS PORT ADDR
        MOV DI,WORD PTR CS:SCR_OFF ;GET SCREEN BUFFER OFFSET
        LEA SI,CS:TIME       ;GET DOS TIME
        MOV CX,16            ;SET UP TO MOVE 10 BYTES
        CLI                  ;DISABLE OTHER INTERRUPTS
WAIT1:  IN AL,DX             ;READ CRT STATUS
        TEST AL,1            ;CHECK FOR VERTICAL RETRACE
        JNZ WAIT1            ;WAIT FOR RETRACE LOW
        MOV AH,CS:[SI]       ;GET FIRST BYTE TO MOVE
WAIT2:  IN AL,DX             ;GET CRT STATUS
        TEST AL,1            ;CHECK FOR VERTICAL RETRACE
        JZ WAIT2             ;WAIT FOR RETRACE HIGH
        MOV ES:[DI],AH       ;MOVE BYTE TO SCREEN
        INC DI               ;INCREMENT INDEX
        INC SI
        LOOP WAIT1           ;MOVE NEXT BYTE
        STI                  ;ENABLE INTERRUPTS
        POP ES               ;RESTORE REGISTERS
        POP DS
        POP SI
        POP DI
        POP CX
        POP AX
        IRET                 ;RETURN FROM INTERRUPT
CLK     ENDP
UPDATE  PROC NEAR
        PUSH AX              ;SAVE REGISTERS
        PUSH BX
        PUSH CX
        PUSH DX
        PUSH DS
        MOV AX,0040H         ;GET ADDRESS OF DOS TABLE
        MOV DS,AX            ;PUT IN DS
        MOV AX,TIME_HI       ;GET HIGH BYTE OF DOS TIME
        mov flag,0           ;am flag
HOUR:   CMP AX,0CH           ;CONVERT TO HOURS
        JLE H1
        mov flag,1           ;set to pm
```

*Figure 1.2  (continued)*

```
            SUB AX,0CH
            JMP HOUR
H1:         AAM                     ;CONVERT TO ASCII
            ADD AX,3030H
            LEA BX,CS:TIME          ;GET ADDRESS OF TIME AREA
            MOV CS:[BX],AH          ;SAVE HOURS FIRST DIGIT
            MOV CS:[BX+2],AL        ;SAVE HOURS SECOND DIGIT
            MOV AX,TIME_LO          ;GET DOS TIME LOW BYTE
            MOV CX,8H               ;CONVERT TO MINUTES
            SHR AX,CL
            MOV DX,3CH
            MUL DL
            SHR AX,CL
            AAM                     ;CONVERT TO ASCII
            ADD AX,3030H
            MOV CS:[BX+6],AH        ;SAVE MINUTES FIRST DIGIT
            MOV CS:[BX+8],AL        ;SAVE MINUTES SECOND DIGIT
            MOV BYTE PTR CS:[BX+12],'A'
            CMP FLAG,0              ;IS IT AM?
            JZ GOAHEAD
            MOV BYTE PTR CS:[BX+12],'P'
GOAHEAD:
            MOV BYTE PTR CS:[BX+14],'M'
            POP DS                  ;RESTORE REGISTERS
            POP DX
            POP CX
            POP BX
            POP AX
            RET
UPDATE  ENDP
SETUP:      MOV AX,0                ;GET ADDRESS OF VECTOR TABLE
            MOV DS,AX               ;PUT IN DS
            CLI                     ;DISABLE FURTHER INTERRUPTS
            MOV AX,[VEC_IP]         ;GET ADDRESS OF OLD UPDATE IP
            MOV CS:[INT_IP],AX      ;SAVE IT
            MOV AX,[VEC_CS]         ;GET ADDRESS OF OLD UPDATE CS
            MOV CS:[INT_CS],AX      ;SAVE IT
            MOV VEC_IP,OFFSET CLK_INT ;PUT ADDRESS OF CLK IN
            VECTOR IP
            MOV VEC_CS,CS           ;PUT CS OF CLK IN VECTOR CS
            STI                     ;ENABLE INTERRUPTS
            MOV AH,0FH              ;READ VIDEO STATUS
```

*Figure 1.2  (continued)*

```
        INT 10H
        SUB AH,8            ;SUBTRACT 8 CHAR TIME FROM NCOLS
        SHL AH,1            ;MULTIPLY BY 2 FOR ATTRIBUTE
        MOV CS:SCR_OFF,AH   ;SAVE SCREEN TIME LOCATION
        MOV WORD PTR CS:CRT_PORT,03BAH ;SAVE MONO STATUS
        PORT ADDR
        TEST AL,4           ;CHECK FOR COLOR MONITOR
        JNZ MONO            ;IF MONO, MOVE ON
        ADD WORD PTR CS:SCR_OFF,8000H ;ADD COLOR OFFSET TO
        TIME OFFSET
        MOV WORD PTR CS:CRT_PORT,03DAH ;SAVE COLOR STATUS
        PORT ADDR
MONO:   CALL UPDATE                    ;DO FIRST UPDATE & PRINT TIME
        MOV DX,OFFSET SETUP            ;GET END ADDRESS OF NEW
        INTERRUPT
        INT 27H                        ;TERMINATE AND REMAIN RESIDENT
        DB 117 DUP(0)                  ;FILLER
CODESEG ENDS
        END CLK
```

**Figure 1.2 (continued)**

Third-generation programming languages (3GLs) were more *programmer friendly*, more abstract, and with instructions that were more understandable by humans. Examples of prominent 3GLs include FORTRAN, LISP, and COBOL. 3GLs were *portable* and could be implemented similarly on different types of computers that did not have the same machine code. Today, updated versions of these 3GLs are still used. Figure 1.3 shows an example of a COBOL software code snippet in which the current date and time are obtained and displayed.[3]

Subsequent languages (such as FOCUS and FOXPRO) called fourth- or fifth-generation programming languages (4GLs or 5GLs) were designed to reduce programming effort, the time it takes to develop software, and the cost of software development, by allowing such features as automatic code generation from a few higher level constructs.

The rise of the Internet has also inspired the development or refinement of programming languages such as Java and C++. Figure 1.4 provides an example of a software code snippet written in Java to display the current date and time.[4]

```
IDENTIFICATION DIVISION.
  PROGRAM-ID.dat.

ENVIRONMENT DIVISION.
  SOURCE-COMPUTER. IBM-PC.
  OBJECT-COMPUTER. IBM-PC.

DATA DIVISION.
  WORKING-STORAGE SECTION.
  01 cr-date1.
  05 yr pic 99.
  05 FILLER PIC X VALUE "/".
  05 mnth pic 99.
  05 FILLER PIC X VALUE "/".
  05 date1 pic 99 value 10.

  01 cr-date2.
  05 yr1 pic 99.
  05 mnth1 pic 99.
  05 date11 pic 99 value 10.

  77 jul-dy pic 9(6).
  01 tm.
  05 hh1 pic 99.
  05 mm1 pic 9.
  05 ss1 pic 99.
  05 fs1 pic 9.
  01 tm1 pic 9(10).
  77 dy-of-wk pic 9.

PROCEDURE DIVISION.
  ACCEPT cr-date2 FROM DATE.
  MOVE yr1 TO yr.
  MOVE mnth1 TO mnth.
  MOVE date11 TO date1.

DISPLAY cr-date1.
  DISPLAY "YEAR:" yr.
  DISPLAY "month:" mnth.
  DISPLAY "date:" date1.
```

*Figure 1.3  Example of COBOL code that obtains and shows the current date and time*

*Source*: Daily Free Code (2012)

```
    DISPLAY cr-date2.
    DISPLAY "YEAR:" yr1.
    DISPLAY "month:" mnth1.
    DISPLAY "date:" date11.

    ACCEPT jul-dy FROM DAY.

    ACCEPT tm FROM TIME.
    ACCEPT tm1 FROM TIME.
    ACCEPT dy-of-wk FROM DAY-OF-WEEK.

    DISPLAY "julian" jul-dy.
    DISPLAY "time" tm.
    DISPLAY "HH" hh1.
    DISPLAY "MM" mm1.
    DISPLAY "SS" ss1.
    DISPLAY "TM1" tm1.
    DISPLAY " day of week" dy-of-wk.

  STOP RUN.
```

*Figure 1.3  (continued)*

```
GetTheCurrentTime

package com.ack.j2se.date;

import java.util.Calendar;
import java.util.Date;

public class GetTheCurrentTime {
public static void main( String[] args ) {
        // one way
        long currentTimeInMillis = System.currentTimeMillis();
        Date today = new Date( currentTimeInMillis );
        System.out.println( today );

        // another way
        Calendar cal = Calendar.getInstance();
        today = cal.getTime();
        System.out.println( today ); }}  }
```

*Figure 1.4  Example of Java code to obtain and show the current date and time*

Source: Happy Codings (2013a).

It is important to understand programming languages for several reasons. One is that a programming language provides a standard way of describing the functions performed by the computer in a way that can be read, understood, and updated by other programmers. Another reason it is important to understand programming languages is that the effort (cost) to create or maintain software varies significantly by the type of programming language used to write the software code.[5] The earlier programming languages, especially those that are more machine specific, are very difficult and expensive to code.

Table 1.1 lists selected programming languages along with their estimated productivity rates (hours required to produce the same unit of functionality). The productivity rates are provided for a *function point*—a unit of measurement that expresses the amount of functionality provided to a user by the software.[6] Clearly, there are considerable differences in the effort to code in different programming languages. Thus, programming language is a critical factor determining the development and lifecycle cost for a software system.

To put things into perspective, it might help to understand just how large software systems are today. Since some of the first software systems were used to perform repetitive calculations in World War II, software systems have become increasingly complex.

*Table 1.1 Effort (hours) to code the same function in selected programming languages*

| Language | Lines of code for one function point | Hours to create one function point |
|---|---|---|
| Assembly | 340 | 79 |
| COBOL | 110 | 27 |
| Pascal | 40 | 10 |
| C | 130 | 32 |
| C++ | 50 | 12 |
| Java | 55 | 13 |
| Visual Basic | 30 | 7 |

*Sources*: Numbers in this table were created based upon Jones (1996); Boehm (1981).
*Note*: Capers Jones (1996) provides the lines of code for different programming languages corresponding to a function point. Boehm's (1981) COCOMO model for software effort estimation provides a formula to convert software lines of code to *man-months* of effort. Man months were converted into hours by multiplying by 22 work days and 8 hours per day.

For example, the first edition of the Unix operating system released in 1971 had 4,200 lines of code,[7] but the MS Windows XP operating system released in 2001 has more than 45 million lines of code.[8] The code for Visicalc (the first electronic spreadsheet program introduced in 1981) could fit in 27,520 bytes of storage,[9] whereas the code for the latest version of Microsoft's Excel requires orders of magnitude more storage. The *flame* computer virus that attacked Iranian computers in 2012 contained more than 250,000 lines of LUA code[10]—the same programming language used to create the computer game called *Angry Birds*. LUA is a Portuguese word that means "moon"; the programming language was created by developers in Brazil. SAP's enterprise resource system is believed to have 250 million lines of code.[11] A typical new automobile averages 100 million lines of code.[12]

Undoubtedly, today's software systems such as business-to-business electronic procurement systems are increasingly sophisticated and must meet more demanding requirements than in the past.

## How Software Is Created

The practice of developing software has also undergone major transformations as the nature of software systems has evolved. Originally, computer programs were written by scratch, ad hoc, and the early programmers had to use paper tape or punch cards to load the code onto the computer. Today, more sophisticated approaches and tools for developing software have emerged.

Developing software involves gathering requirements, analyzing and designing the system based on the requirements, creating the software source code for the system, testing the system to make sure it works, deploying the system, and supporting and maintaining it.

The first step in developing a software system involves collecting requirements. Requirements refer to the features and functions desired by current or potential customers. For example, the ability to compute an economic order quantity could be a functional requirement for an inventory management system. The ability to compute estimated sales tax could be a functional requirement for an order entry system. Vivid animation and quick response time could be technical requirements for a video game. Requirements can be gathered in a variety of ways, such as via customer focus groups, interviews, surveys, and observation. Sometimes, software developers create scenarios or user stories (use cases) to document requirements.

The software system's features, functions, and *look and feel* are designed based on its requirements. Software analysis and design involves creating rules and definitions (also called *specifications*) for how a software system should function. Software designs can be represented in abstract diagrams and models. An example of a software design diagram for a hypothetical online shopping system is shown in Figure 1.5. The diagram is called a

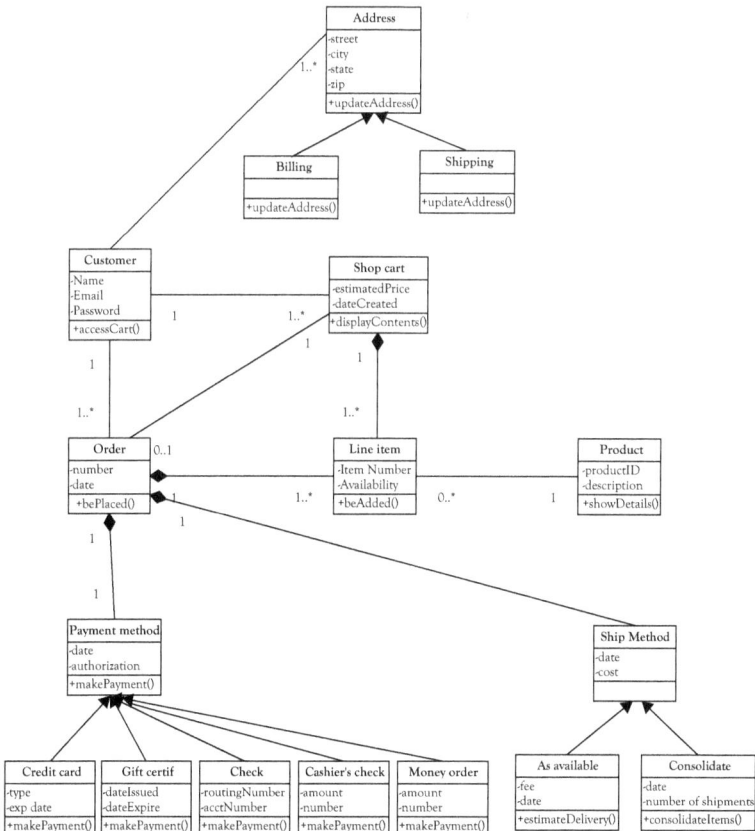

*Figure 1.5  A software design diagram for a hypothetical online shopping system*

*class* diagram, and it visually depicts the key classes or objects in the system such as the *shopping cart*, the *order*, the *item*, and the *payment method*.

Based on the analysis and design of requirements, the software code is created. Software programming involves writing the source code or computer instructions for a software system. As noted previously, in the early days of computing, programs were written by hand. Today, some programs are still written by hand, but there are also many tools available to help with coding tasks.

Sophisticated tools and development environments (such as computer-aided software engineering [CASE] tools or model-driven architecture [MDA] tools) can create software codes automatically, based on the design. These tools and others can also enable reuse of code. CASE includes a set of software programs that help automate the design, development, and implementation of a software system.[13] CASE includes tools to create visual diagrams and representations of the system; an information repository of software designs and components that can be reused; tools to design, generate, and test software codes; and other management tools. CASE can also include tools for helping the developer create the graphical user interface for the software. CASE tools are intended to help developers create software systems more easily and with fewer errors.

MDA is a recent approach to developing software that attempts to separate the design of the software from its physical implementation.[14] It involves creating design models of the functions and features to be implemented in the software and includes tools and techniques to help produce software code from those design models and diagrams. MDA approaches are intended to help developers more easily create software designs without worrying about how the software may be implemented in different environments.

Once the source code is written, developers use compilers to automatically translate the source code into machine code (as shown in Figure 1.1 earlier in this chapter) so that the program can be run on a computer. To make sure that the code works properly, developers test it. There are various types of tests that can be conducted, such as unit tests, integration tests, system tests, and acceptance tests.

*Unit* tests verify that the functionality of a specific part of the code works—these tests are typically conducted by the developer who created the code. *Integration* tests check whether the interfaces between connected programs work. *System* tests verify whether the system as a whole works properly. *Acceptance* tests are usually performed by the end user or customer who verifies whether the requirements are satisfied. Acceptance tests can include *alpha* tests (where internal staff play the role of a customer to test the software) or *beta* tests (where the software is released to the external customer for testing).

Software testing can also be *white box* (in which the internal workings of the software are tested) or *black box* (in which the tester examines the functionality of the software without considering how it is written).

After testing, the software is implemented—for off-the-shelf software, this is the point at which the software is made available for sale to the customer. For software created for hire, the software is installed at the customer site.

The software system then transitions to support and maintenance. In this phase, questions about software functionality are answered, bugs are fixed, the software is enhanced to add new features, and the software is upgraded to be compatible with new versions of computer hardware or systems. For many software systems, maintenance is the longest and most expensive phase of the lifecycle.

Companies use a variety of methodologies or approaches for developing software systems. Some of the primary methods include the waterfall, prototyping, spiral development, iterative and incremental development, rapid application development, object-oriented development, and agile development. These are briefly discussed next and illustrated with diagrams.

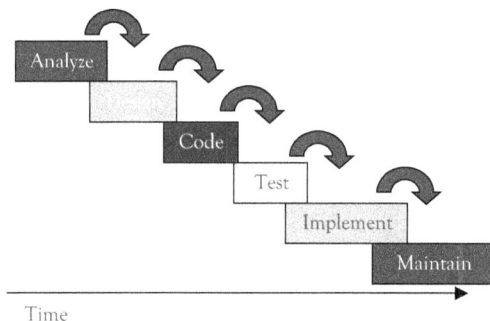

*Figure 1.6 Waterfall approach to software development*

One of the most common approaches to software development is called a *waterfall* method, illustrated in Figure 1.6. The waterfall approach is a step-by-step process in which developers create the software in phases by first understanding requirements, then designing the system, coding it, testing it, and finally implementing it. The process is sequential: Work in a subsequent phase cannot commence until the prior phase has been successfully completed. The waterfall process, although disciplined and straightforward to manage, suffers from problems such as long development cycles (it can take years to develop a system using this approach) and lack of flexibility (if a new requirement is found in the testing phase, it is difficult to go backward, i.e., *swim upstream* in the waterfall process).[15] Despite its disadvantages, the waterfall approach offers control and discipline of the process, and many companies use it to develop their software systems.

There are many alternative approaches to developing software systems that address some of the limitations of the waterfall process.[16]

*Prototyping* creates a *mock up* version of a system that is not fully functional, but can be developed quickly. It is useful for requirements determination, unfamiliar technologies, and complex interface design and can be used to manage risk as well as explore new ideas. Figure 1.7 depicts the prototyping process.

*Spiral development* is a method for developing software that is aimed at reducing the risks of software development projects.[17] A *spiral* starts with determining the objectives and requirements of the project, followed by a series of prototypes to reduce identified project risks. The effort then proceeds into detailed design, coding, testing, and release of the software. The effort is reviewed and the next spiral iteration is planned. Spirals continue until the project is finished. Spiral development can be useful

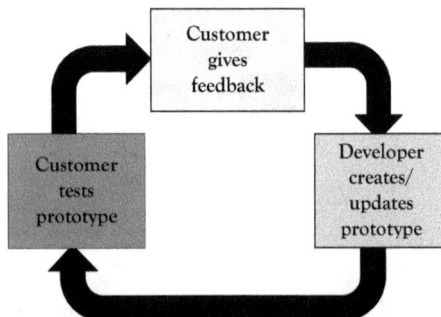

*Figure 1.7 Prototyping approach to software development*

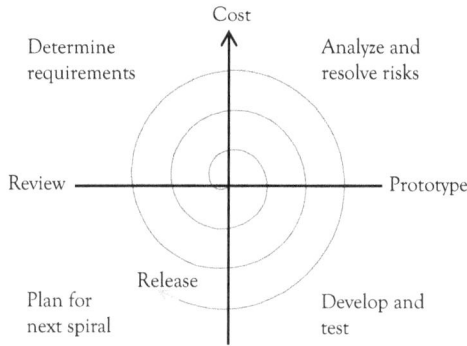

**Figure 1.8  Spiral approach to software development**

Source: Adapted by permission from Boehm (1988, p. 64) © 1988 by IEEE.

for very large, complex, and uncertain software projects, where there are major risks to be identified and resolved. Figure 1.8 illustrates the spiral approach to software development.

*Rapid Application Development* (RAD) approaches create *components* or small pieces of software systems that are fully functional and that can be built and installed within 60 to 90 days. A related approach is *Component-based Development* (CBD) in which the functions of the system are divided into small units or pieces. CBD includes defining, implementing, and composing the loosely coupled independent components into systems. The components are developed by separate teams, in parallel, and then integrated into a complete system. RAD-based approaches are very fast, but it can be difficult to separate a system into distinct pieces and it may be difficult to put the pieces together. Figure 1.9 provides a visual representation of the RAD process for software development.

*Object-oriented* approaches develop software by building self-contained modules (objects) that can be easily replaced, modified, and reused. Traditional approaches to software development structure programs into two distinct elements: code and data; the code includes the methods through which the data are processed. In contrast, an object-oriented approach integrates the code and data using the concept of an *object*. Object-oriented approaches to software development model elements as a collection of discrete objects that correspond to real-world objects. An object is an entity (person, place, or thing) that has data (attributes) and that does things (provides services or has methods). For example, a book is an object. The book object has attributes such as title, author, and

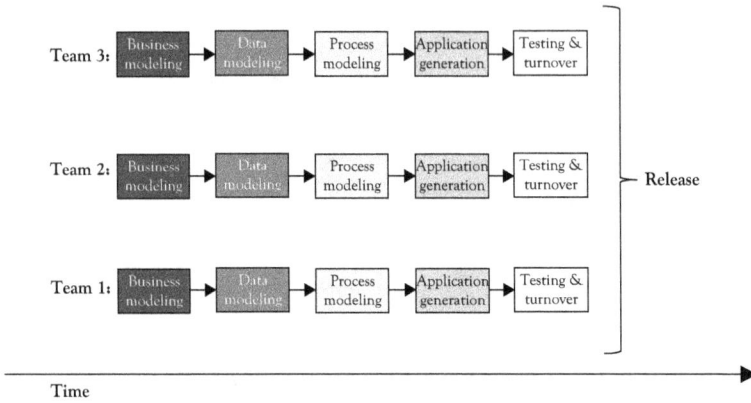

*Figure 1.9  Rapid Application Development (RAD) approach to software development*

chapter, and it performs services such as be Ordered and be Shipped. In the object-oriented approach, an object *encapsulates* (includes and pro-tects) its attributes; attributes can only be accessed via methods. Objects (more generally called *classes*) are organized into class hierarchies. For example, a *book* class may be at the top of a hierarchy that distinguishes between different types of books at the next level, such as *mystery, romance* or *history* or *hard cover* versus *ebook*. Each of these different types of books may not only have unique attributes or methods but also *inherits* attributes and methods defined for the more general book class. Figure 1.5 (shown earlier in this chapter) visually illustrates a class diagram for an online shopping system that was created using object-oriented approaches. As can be seen in this figure, some of the classes in the system include Order, Customer, Item, and Product. Each class has attributes (such as order number and order date for Order) and methods (such as be Placed for Order). Because attributes and methods do not need to be defined for each class in a hierarchy and because objects correspond to things in the real world, object-oriented systems are thought to be easier to develop, understand, and maintain.

The unified approach (UA) is a methodology for object-oriented anal-ysis and design. The UA combines best practices, processes, and guide-lines with the Object Management Group's Unified Modeling Language (UML).[18] The UML is a set of notations and conventions used to describe and model an object-oriented system. The OMG (object management group) agreed to make UML a standard for object-oriented analysis and design in 1995. The current version of UML is version 2. Examples of object-oriented programming languages include C++, Java, Smalltalk, Python, and Ruby. Figure 1.4 earlier in this chapter shows an example of Java code. Many companies have shifted to object-oriented approaches. Object-oriented approaches can also be used in combination with other approaches to software development.

*Iterative and Incremental Development* (used by many large software companies) combines traditional and modern approaches, whereby a system is repeatedly developed and delivered in increments, versions, or releases. The initial release is the core product. Updates and extensions to the core product are made in subsequent increments, versions, or releases. The system is developed via repeated iterations in small increments. This allows software developers to learn and improve the system as they are developing it. Figure 1.10 illustrates the incremental development approach to software development.

Finally, *agile methodologies* are becoming an increasingly popular way to develop systems. Agile methods break down software development into small pieces or increments that can be completed within a short time frame (time boxes) that typically last from one to four weeks. A small, cross-functional team works on an increment, and at the end of the iteration, a working product results.

Popular agile methodologies include eXtreme Programming (XP) and Scrum. XP promotes small, frequent releases of software after short development cycles.[19] Among other elements, it involves programmers

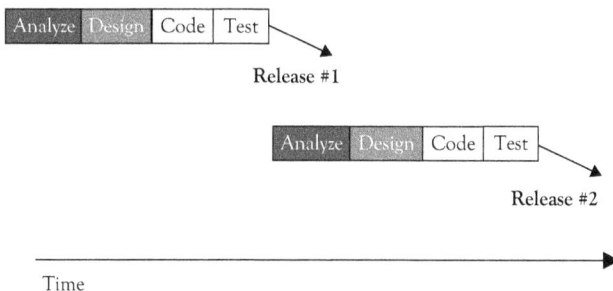

*Figure 1.10  Incremental approach to software development*

working in pairs, extensive communication with customers, limited management, frequent code reviews, and comprehensive unit tests. The approach gets its name from the idea that the best practices for software development (such as communication and code reviews) are taken to the extreme.

Scrum is a development approach in which the developers work as a team to achieve a common goal.[20] It encourages team colocation and communication. Like XP, Scrum methods are set up to accommodate changes in requirements. Scrum involves three primary roles: the product owner (or customer), the development team, and the scrum master (who enforces Scrum rules and makes sure the development team can be effective). Figure 1.11 shows the Scrum process. As shown in Figure 1.11, each development effort is referred to as a sprint, which is scoped to last between one week and one month. The input to the sprint is the backlog of requirements for the product (which are prioritized by the customer). From the backlog, the goal for the sprint is identified and the requirements relevant to the sprint are collected. The team then works on coding and testing the requirements for the sprint, meeting daily with short scrum meetings to communicate progress and identify impediments to progress. When the sprint is finished and a working piece of software has been created, a final review meeting is held, and the software is released.

Agile methodologies can increase the flexibility and speed of software development, while building in quality. However, the methodologies can be intense for the participants and require close collaboration, which

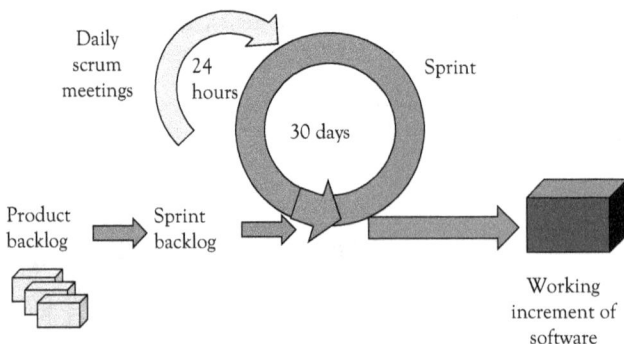

*Figure 1.11 Scrum approach to software development*

Source: Adapted by permission from Schwaber (2004, Figs. 1–3, p. 9).

may be challenging in some settings (such as where team members are geographically dispersed). In addition, the flexibility of the approach can make it difficult to control the scope of the product.

If a company does not want to use its own staff to develop the software for its product, the company can *outsource* the software development by hiring another firm to create the product using the development approaches and tools previously described. Software companies can even *purchase* software capabilities by acquiring a company that created an application and merging the application with their own product offerings. For example, in 2000, Microsoft acquired Visio Corporation—a Seattle company that developed the Visio diagramming application, for $1.5 billion in stock; Microsoft then integrated Visio within its suite of business productivity products.[21]

## Types of Software Products and Services

Companies in the software industry produce software products and software-related services. A software product is a set of one or more computer software programs that a company offers for sale. Examples of software products include a spreadsheet, a word processing program, or an antivirus software tool.

Software products can be organized into two broad categories: systems software and applications software. As explained in Chapter 3, the software industry is segmented by these broad categories of software.

Systems software runs the computer system. It controls, integrates, and manages the individual hardware components so that other software and the users of the system do not have to worry about the lower level details such as reading or transferring data from memory to disk or onto a display. Generally, system software consists of an operating system and utilities such as file managers, display managers, text editors, user authentication (login), security and systems management tools, and networking and device control software.

Applications software is used to accomplish specific tasks other than just running the computer system. Application software may consist of a single program, such as an app to verify a credit card number or to check a password. A group of programs or a *software package* works closely together to accomplish a task, such as an architectural rending package like AutoCAD. A group of software programs can also be called an *application software system*, such as an accounts receivable system, which is a collection of fundamental programs that may provide some service to a variety of other independent applications. A larger group of programs or software suite includes related, but independent, programs and packages that have a common user interface or shared data format, such as Microsoft Office. The Microsoft Office suite consists of an integrated word processor, spreadsheet, database, presentation software, and other programs. The largest grouping of application software can also be referred to as a systems of systems such as enterprise resource planning systems that are a collection of interdependent systems. Figure 1.12 visually illustrates the different levels of software applications, and Table 1.2 shows examples of each type of software product.

| Instruction | Program (App) | Package (System) | Suite (System of systems) |
|---|---|---|---|
| $Instruction_{11}$ | $Program_1$ | $Package_1$ | $Suite_1$ |
| $Instruction_{12}$ | | | |
| ... | | | |
| $Instruction_{21}$ | $Program_2$ | | |
| $Instruction_{22}$ | | | |
| $Instruction_{23}$ | | | |
| $Instruction_{24}$ | | | |
| ... | | | |
| $Instruction_{31}$ | $Program_3$ | $Package_2$ | |
| $Instruction_{32}$ | | | |
| ... | | | |
| **EXAMPLE** | | | |
| **Instructions** | **Programs (Apps)** | **Packages (Systems)** | **Suite (System of systems)** |
| Draw a line | Draw a rectangle | Create diagrams with shapes | Create documents and diagrams with shapes |
| Connect a line | | | |
| Draw a curved line | Draw a circle | | |
| Draw a line | Draw an arrow | Create documents with shapes | |
| Draw an endpoint | | | |

*Figure 1.12 Levels of software*

*Table 1.2  Examples of types of systems and applications software products*

| Systems software | Applications software |
|---|---|
| Operating systems (e.g., MS Windows, Linux, Unix, DOS) | Office productivity suite (e.g., MS Office) |
| Device drivers (e.g., graphics drivers and firmware) | Game software (e.g., World of Warcraft) |
| Compiler or Debugger software | Enterprise resource planning software (e.g., SAP) |
| Utility software (Network utilities, data compression or encryption software, antivirus software, disk defragmenters, archive utilities, etc.) | Graphics software (e.g., Adobe) |
| | Database management systems (e.g., SQL Server, Oracle database management system) |

In addition, software products can be organized into software product lines. A software product line is a set of software programs that share common features that satisfy the needs of a particular market segment. Programs in a software product line are developed using a common or shared set of software functions and tools. A software product line might distinguish between types of users and include the products that fit the needs of the users in a particular segment. For example, one software product line might include software security products for corporations while another software product line could include software security products for noncorporate, individual users.

As described earlier, producing software products involves a variety of related activities. A software service includes the different tasks associated with producing a software product, such as design, programming, testing, documentation, deployment, training, and support. Companies can sell one or more of these services to customers.

## Companies in the Software Industry in This Book

The software industry accounts for a significant market share of the information technology (IT) industry overall. Figure 1.13 shows the global spending on IT products and services projected by Forrester for 2013.[22] Forrester estimates a total of $2.069 trillion in spending on products produced by the IT industry in 2013, of which $542 billion was spent on software products and services, and $389 billion was spent on IT consulting and systems integration services.

Global spending on IT products & services in 2013

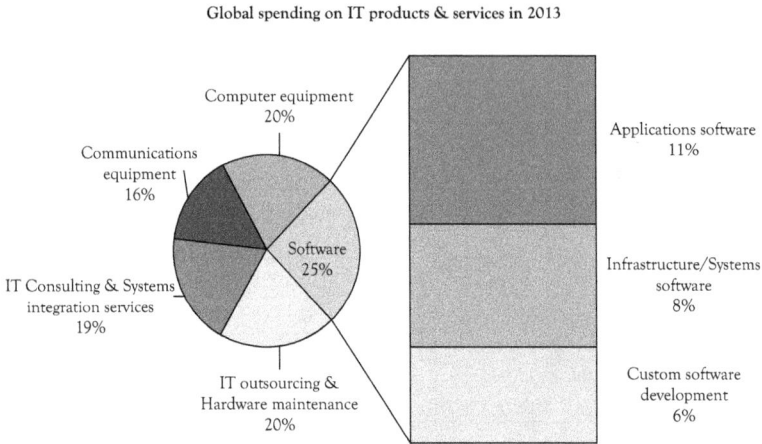

*Figure 1.13  Projected sales of IT industry products and services, by major segment*

*Source*: Lunden (2013).

As can be seen in Figure 1.13, the IT industry produces and sells computer and communications equipment (which together comprise 36 percent of IT industry sales); IT outsourcing, systems integration, and consulting services (which together make up 39 percent of the IT industry); and software products and services which account for 25 percent of IT industry sales. Within the software product segment, there are three major types of products: applications software products, infrastructure/systems software products, and custom software development services, of which applications and systems software products account for 75 percent of the projected 2013 sales in the software segment of the IT industry.

From the U.S. government's perspective, software is classified as a business service (Standard Industrial Classification Code[SIC],73) and is further described in industry group SIC 737: Computer Programming, Data Processing, and Other Computer Related Services. This industry group includes companies who provide a variety of computing products and services, ranging from computer hardware repair to custom programming. Table 1.3 shows the SIC 737 industry group and subgroups, relating them also to their respective North American Industry Classification

*Table 1.3 SIC 737 industry subgroups for computer programming, data processing, and other computer-related services*

| SIC Code | NAICS Code | Title | Description |
|---|---|---|---|
| 7371* | 541511 | Computer programming services | Companies primarily engaged in providing computer programming services on a contract or fee basis. Companies in this industry perform a variety of additional services, such as computer software design and analysis; modifications of custom software; and training in the use of custom software. |
| 7372** | 511210 | Prepackaged software | Companies primarily engaged in the design, development, and production of prepackaged computer software. Important products of this industry include operating, utility, and applications programs. Companies in this industry may also provide services such as preparation of software documentation for the user installation of software for the user; and training the user in the use of the software. |
| 7373*** | 541512 | Computer integrated systems design | Companies primarily engaged in developing or modifying computer software and packaging or bundling the software with purchased computer hardware (computers and computer peripheral equipment) to create and market an integrated system for specific application. Companies in this industry must provide each of the following services: (1) the development or modification of the computer software; (2) the marketing of purchased computer hardware; and (3) involvement in all phases of systems development from design through installation. |
| 7374 | 514210 | Computer processing and data preparation and processing services | Companies primarily engaged in providing computer processing and data preparation services. The service may consist of complete processing and preparation of reports from data supplied by the customer or a specialized service, such as data entry or making data processing equipment available on an hourly or time-sharing basis. |

*(continued)*

*Table 1.3 SIC 737 industry subgroups for computer programming, data processing, and other computer-related services (continued)*

| SIC Code | NAICS Code | Title | Description |
|---|---|---|---|
| 7375 | 514191 | Information retrieval services | Companies primarily engaged in providing on-line information retrieval services on a contract or fee basis. The information generally involves a range of subjects and is taken from other primary sources. |
| 7376*** | 541513 | Computer facilities management services | Companies primarily engaged in providing on-site management and operation of computer systems and data processing facilities on a contract or fee basis. |
| 7377 | 532420 | Computer rental and leasing | Companies primarily engaged in renting or leasing computers and related data processing equipment on the customers' site, whether or not also providing maintenance or support services. |
| 7378 | 811212 | Computer maintenance and repair | Companies primarily engaged in the maintenance and repair of computers and computer peripheral equipment. |
| 7379*** | 334611, 541512, 541519 | Computer-related services, not elsewhere classified | Companies primarily engaged in supplying computer-related services, not elsewhere classified. Computer consultants operating on a contract or fee basis are classified in this industry. |

*Source*: U.S. Department of Labor (2013).

*Note*: Subgroup SIC 7371 performs custom software development for hire. The book covers companies in this subgroup as the primary service involves software development.

** *Note*: Subgroup SIC 7372 is a focal industry segment that is covered in this book.

*** *Note*: Firms in subgroups SIC 7373, 7376, and 7379 that provide software-related services are covered in this book.

System codes (NAICS), a more recent classification system of industries introduced in 1997.[23]

Given the complexities of the types of products and services offered by the companies in the SIC 737 industry group, it is important to clarify the focus of the software industry profiled in this book.

*As noted at the beginning of this chapter, this book examines companies that make and sell applications software products, systems software products, or their related software services.* This includes the subsegments within the software segment of the IT industry shown earlier in Figure 1.13 (i.e., applications software, systems software, and custom software development). Companies producing IT consulting and systems integration services are also relevant to the extent that the services are software related. This also corresponds to companies that list their primary SIC code as 7371, 7372, 7373, 7376, or 7379.

Companies producing software for the mass market are included in SIC 7372 or the NAICS number 511210. This segment is frequently referred to as the *packaged* or *prepackaged* software industry. As noted in Table 1.3, companies in the prepackaged software industry SIC 7372 are primarily engaged in the design, development, and production of prepackaged computer software. These companies create and market software products that perform functions such as desktop productivity suites, enterprise resource planning systems, customer relationship management systems, business intelligence tools, video games, statistical software, operating systems, and security software. Such products generate about $400 billion in annual sales worldwide.[24] Companies in this industry also carry out operations necessary for producing and distributing their software products, such as designing, providing documentation, assisting in installation, and providing support services to software purchasers. Prominent companies in this industry include Microsoft, Oracle, Salesforce. com, Adobe, and Intuit.

Companies listed in SIC 7371, SIC 7373, SIC 7376, and SIC 7379 (NAICS codes 541511, 541512, or 541513) also perform software development but produce custom software for hire on a contract or fee basis or provide software-related services such as systems integration. Although a primary focus of this book is on companies that produce software for sale in the mass market, the custom software development services sector has become increasingly important, especially in the global software industry. For example, Infosys, a large consulting and software services company that is headquartered in Bangalore, India, is listed in SIC 7371. Custom software development generates over $130 billion in sales worldwide, while IT consulting and systems integration services generate $389 billion in global sales.[25] In addition to Infosys, prominent companies in this industry segment include IBM, Hewlett-Packard, Computer Sciences Corporation, and Accenture.

This book does NOT cover companies that operate in other sectors within the SIC 737 industry that are hardware or data related—including companies providing data preparation and processing services (SIC 7374), information retrieval services (SIC 7375), computer rental and leasing services (SIC 7377), and computer maintenance or repair services (SIC 7378). The services provided by companies within these subsectors do not involve producing software products or software services for sale.

It should also be noted that this book does not cover Internet retailing companies (such as amazon.com) whose primary product for sale is not software, nor does it consider companies that are primarily computer equipment manufacturers (such as Advanced Micro Devices or AMD whose primary SIC code is 3674, semiconductors and related equipment). These companies do not list themselves as belonging in the software industry and may not sell the software if they create it (or such sales may be a minor part of their business).

Finally, it is important to note that companies may produce their own software, internally for their own use, but do not sell it, and such internal software activities are not considered part of the software industry (and are not covered in this book).

## Key Takeaways

The software industry profiled in this book focuses on companies that produce and sell software and software-related services for hire or for the mass market. The software industry is dynamic and constantly evolving. It is high risk but also high reward for the participants. Thus, it is very important to understand some fundamental concepts that define the industry.

The main *product* is software and related services. As described in this chapter, software does not have a physical component. It is just a set of instructions that tells a computer what to do. Software is created by programmers using different languages, development approaches, and tools. These languages have evolved over the last 50 years and have generally become easier and less expensive to use. There are many approaches to software development, with more recent approaches focused on developing software more quickly and easily, in smaller increments. Software can be as small as a tiny app or program with a few thousand lines of code running on a mobile phone or as large as an enterprise-wide system of systems with hundreds of millions of lines of code.

Companies in the software industry make either systems software products or applications software products (or both) or provide software-related services, and the industry is segmented by these products. This book examines companies that primarily make packaged software products for sale or custom software development for hire and that provide related services. Computer hardware manufacturers that do not produce software or software services for sale, Internet retailers, and companies that develop software for their internal use are not included.

The next chapter—Chapter 2—explores the history of the software industry. Chapter 3 includes a more detailed discussion of the companies in the software industry and how they compete. While Chapter 3 has a U.S. focus, Chapter 4 takes a global perspective of the software industry.

# CHAPTER 2

# History of the Software Industry

The software industry has experienced many ups and downs, with not only innovations and breakthroughs but also some dead ends. To understand where the software industry is today, and how it got there, it helps to look at its history. This chapter considers the origins of software and the software industry and reviews the evolution of the industry into its current state today.

## Software in Concept—the Early Days (19th Century)

The history of the software industry is intertwined with that of the computer hardware industry. This should not be surprising, given the mutual interdependence of computer hardware and software. However, what may be surprising is that the first software program existed before the first computer was built and that the first programmer was a woman.

The concept of computing was developed more than 150 years ago, often attributed to Charles Babbage in 19th century England.[1] Charles Babbage (born 1791) was the son of a wealthy London banker and was a brilliant mathematician, philosopher, inventor, and mechanical engineer. Among other things, Babbage was interested in developing mechanical devices that could automatically compute numerical tables. He conceived of two interesting devices—a Difference Engine and an Analytical Engine—which were supposed to solve mathematical problems. The Difference Engine was more of a mechanical calculator and was actually partially constructed by Babbage and fully built by Babbage's son, Henry. The Analytical Engine was closer to modern conceptions of a computer, but it was never assembled. It could theoretically be programmed by the use of punched cards.

Augusta Ada King (born 1815), Countess of Lovelace and daughter of the poet Lord Byron, met Charles Babbage and became interested in his work. Lovelace collaborated and corresponded with Babbage and, at his request, translated his ideas on the Analytical Engine, elaborating with her own notes. Among her notes is *Note A*, which described how the Analytical Engine could act upon numbers:

> *The distinctive characteristic of the Analytical Engine, and that which has rendered it possible to endow mechanism with such extensive faculties as bid fair to make this engine the executive right-hand of abstract algebra, is the introduction into it of the principle which Jacquard devised for regulating, by means of punched cards, the most complicated patterns in the fabrication of brocaded stuffs. It is in this that the distinction between the two engines lies. Nothing of the sort exists in the Difference Engine. We may say most aptly that the Analytical Engine weaves algebraical patterns just as the Jacquard-loom weaves flowers and leaves... In enabling mechanisms to combine together general symbols in successions of unlimited variety and extent, a uniting link is established between the operations of matter and the abstract mental processes of the most abstract branch of mathematical science. A new, a vast, and a powerful language is developed for the future use of analysis, in which to wield its truths so that these may become of more speedy and accurate practical application for the purposes of mankind than the means hitherto in our possession have rendered possible.[2]*

Her Note G included a description of an algorithm specifying how the Analytical Engine could derive Bernoulli numbers. These notes are regarded by some as the world's first computer program, written in 1842.

Lovelace's notes are important in the early history of computing. However, some see her primary contribution not in the program described in Note G (around which there are questions as to the extent of her contributions) but rather her ability to see the potential for computing. She articulated a vision of the capability of computers to go beyond mere calculations of numbers. For example, her notes describe her conviction that

Babbage's Analytical Engine could be programmed to act upon objects other than numbers, providing an example of how the engine might compose music.[3] Although she died an early death in 1852, Lovelace lives on in her namesake software programming language—Ada—created by the U.S. Department of Defense.

With respect to Babbage, his Numerical and Analytical Engines have significantly influenced the subsequent thinking and design of computers. He is considered a father of the computer, and his engines are among the first numerical computers.[4] A copy of his Numerical Engine, built by his son, Henry, was donated to Harvard University and is thought to have inspired the design of the IBM Mark I (International Business Machines) computer in 1944 by Howard Aiken.[5]

One other key innovator in the early history of computing whose ideas are significant for the software industry is Alan Turing. Turing was a gifted mathematician from England, who, during World War II worked for the British government to help develop techniques to break German ciphers, particularly the German Enigma Machine.[6]

Before the War, Turing proposed a hypothetical device later called the Turing Machine and proved that this hypothetical machine could perform any conceivable mathematical computation if it were representable as an algorithm. Turing's work has been acknowledged as providing the central concept of computation and his concepts of symbols and operations are considered the essence of software programming.[7]

## The Origins of Modern Computing (1940s and 1950s)

The first modern computer is generally accepted to be the ENIAC (Electronic Numerical Integrator and Computer) developed in the World War II era. The ENIAC was designed in 1943 by John Mauchley and J. Presper Eckert of the University of Pennsylvania to calculate artillery ballistic tables for the U.S. Army.[8] Completed in 1947, the ENIAC used 17,468 vacuum tubes[9] and weighed almost 30 tons! It was programmable using IBM punch cards, and a team of six women did most of the programming.[10] As described in Chapter 1, programming in the early days of computers was quite arduous. Early programmers flipped switches to execute commands by manually changing electrical signals within the computer. Paper tape and punch cards were also used. According to accounts of the ENIAC, it took weeks to determine how to map a problem into a program, a full month to get the program into ENIAC and additional days to verify and debug it.[11] As it turns out, the first programs run on the ENIAC were calculations for the hydrogen bomb rather than for artillery tables and required one million punch cards.[12]

A famous mathematician by the name of John von Neumann consulted on early versions of the ENIAC as well as its successor—the EDVAC (Electronic Discrete Variable Automatic Computer). One of the key insights of von Neumann was that computer instructions and data could be stored together in the same memory unit in a computer, referred to as the *stored program technique*.[13] The stored program technique enabled complex software programs to be developed and debugged in days rather than weeks, because the programs could be changed in memory rather than requiring a new paper tape or new punch cards to be created every time the programmer changed an instruction. The technique also enabled frequently used programs to remain in memory, which greatly increased the processing speed of the computer. von Neumann's stored program technique (commonly called the von Neumann architecture) became the basis for modern computer design and was used in the ENIAC and the EDVAC. The von Neumann architecture is still used today.

After World War II, Mauchley and Eckert commercialized the ideas behind the ENIAC, in the form of a machine called the UNIVAC (Universal Automatic Computer), which was designed for general purpose business use. Their small company was bought by Remington Rand (the large office machine company), and the first commercial UNIVAC was installed for use in the U.S. Census Bureau in 1950. The UNIVAC became *famous* when it correctly predicted the results of the 1952 U.S. presidential election after analyzing just one hour's worth of votes.[14] A total of 50 UNIVAC machines were sold.

The 1950s saw many improvements in computing technology and spawned the advent of the computing industry. By the end of the 1950s, there were dozens of companies in the computer industry in the United States such as Remington Rand (now Sperry Rand), RCA, Honeywell, General Electric, Control Data, and Burroughs. A significant event in the development of the industry involved a company called IBM, which was awarded a large contract by the U.S. government to build a real-time air defense system called Semi-Automatic Ground Environment (SAGE) for use during the Cold War.[15]

Although there were computers and computing companies in the 1950s, and the computers ran software, there was no software industry at that time. Software was bundled together with the hardware and was not sold separately from it. Software was also specific to a machine and could not run on different computers.

The first actual occurrence of the word *software* is attributed to a Princeton mathematics professor by the name of John Wilder Tukey, who wrote in a 1958 article:

> *Today the 'software' comprising the carefully planned interpretive routines, compilers, and other aspects of automative programming are at least as important to the modern electronic calculator as its 'hardware' of tubes, transistors, wires, tapes, and the like.*[16]

As noted earlier, the first computer programmers were women, as many men were fighting in the war. One of the most famous of these early female programmers was Grace Murray Hopper—a mathematician who joined the U.S. naval reserve during the war and eventually became an Admiral. Hopper joined Mauchly and Eckert's UNIVAC Company and developed code for the machine. She also became determined to promote the concept of automatic programming and programming languages that were closer to English. At the time Hopper was advocating for simpler ways to program computers, the world's first higher level computer software programming language—Formula Translator (FORTRAN)—was being developed at IBM.[17]

For the first time, the FORTRAN language allowed programmers to program computers using simple English-like instructions, not machine code. The development and release of FORTRAN in 1954 led to the development of other languages such as Common Business-Oriented Language (COBOL) in 1959, which was strongly influenced by Hopper. COBOL was based on a compiler-based programming language called FLOW-MATIC, created by Hopper and her team when she worked on the UNIVAC.[18] Languages such as Algorithmic Language (ALGOL), programming language 1 (PL/1), Report Program Generator (RPG), and Beginner's All-purpose Symbolic Instruction Code (BASIC) also became popular.

## The Origins of the Software Industry (1960s)

An important event in the early history of the software industry was the release by IBM in 1964 of the IBM System 360 family of computers. The models in this family had a similar architecture. Today, it is quite common to see families of computers, but the idea was revolutionary in the 1960s. The development of the IBM System 360 (S/360) was the largest Research and Development (R&D) project ever undertaken by a nongovernment company.[19] The reason the IBM S/360 is so important is that its architecture enabled compatibility, both upward and downward, among the 360 computer family of machines. This means that the software could run on multiple models in the family as they shared the same architecture.

A book called *The Mythical Man Month* written by Frederick P. Brooks who led the project to develop the operating system software for the IBM 360 computer (the OS 360), became an early classic on software development.[20] The OS 360 project involved more than 1000 programmers; the system was delivered years late and millions of dollars over budget and was never free of defects.

In the late 1960s, the threat of antitrust suits by the U.S. government led IBM to unbundle its systems software from its hardware, and the first piece of software to be sold by IBM was its transaction processing system called Customer Information Control System (CICS) in 1968.

The unbundling of computer hardware and software is pivotal for the software industry as it sparked a market for other software companies to compete against IBM and led to the emergence of software contractors and service suppliers. This market became the early software industry.

By 1965, there were about 50 major companies that provided software and programming services and numerous small companies.[21] Many of the large companies—such as Computer Sciences Corporation (CSC)—were performing custom software development for the U.S. government and major computer manufacturers.

Early software products included one created by Applied Data Research, a custom software development company, that was apparently the first to offer a software product for sale—called Autoflow (a diagramming tool for programmers); Martin Goetz, the product manager for Autoflow, holds the first software patent, granted in 1968.[22] A company called Informatics offered an early database program called Mark IV in the late 1960s, which was offered for sale at the price of $30,000 (more than $180,000 in today's dollars).[23]

The profession of software engineering came into being during this era. The profession traces its origins to two conferences sponsored by the NATO Science Committee—the first conference on Software Engineering was held in Garmisch, Germany in 1968[24] and the second conference on Software Engineering Techniques was held in Rome, Italy, in 1969.[25]

## Evolution of the Software Industry in the Mainframe Era (1970s)

The software industry grew and thrived in the 1970s as the decision by IBM to unbundle the Systems 360 software inspired the creation of software companies, many of which were formed to supply software for IBM and IBM-compatible mainframe computers.

By the mid-1970s, there were thousands of software services companies and hundreds of software companies producing and selling application software packages which could be bought off-the-shelf. Examples of such packages include payroll, inventory management, and accounting systems. Prominent companies that sold application software packages included McCormack and Dodge, Management Science America (MSA), Pansophic, and Oracle.

There were also companies that sold systems software, such as for network management, tape backup, security, and other utilities, typically for the IBM 360 mainframe computer. Prominent systems software companies included Compuware and Computer Associates (started by Chinese immigrant Charles Wang in 1976).

Database management systems emerged in the 1970s, with the invention of the relational database by a researcher at IBM called Edgar F. Codd in 1970.[26] Codd's notion of how data could be stored in tables of related rows and columns was revolutionary at that time, and relational databases are still the most popular databases today. Although the idea of relational databases originated at IBM, a company called Relational Technology was first to market with a database product called Ingres, followed by a company called Relational Software with its product—Oracle. Both companies eventually renamed themselves after their famous products.

Programming services companies also entered the software industry and provided custom programming for large organizations, such as the U.S. government. Computer programmers were expensive and difficult to find in the early years of the industry, so companies with programming needs often preferred to rely on service firms. Software contractors such as Thompson Ramo Wooldridge Inc. (TRW), MITRE Corporation, and CSC offered services in software system integration and programming. Other large software service companies were in the industry such as Automatic Data Processing (ADP) and Electronic Data Systems (EDS). These companies provided a range of services to large companies, from programming of custom applications in inventory management and customer information systems to automation of more mundane record-keeping tasks, such as payroll. This work was done on a contract basis.

Improvements in hardware technology in the 1970s sparked further innovation and growth in the software industry. IBM introduced the Systems 370 in 1971 with new hard disk technology that significantly increased the performance of online disk storage and the response time of time sharing systems.

Another significant development was that of the minicomputer. Digital Equipment Corporation (DEC) and other companies such as Data General, Wang Laboratories, Apollo Computer, and Prime Computer developed minicomputers for use in distributed computing applications. Although mainframe computers typically cost more than $1 million in 1970 dollars (more than $6 million in today's dollars) and had the processing capacity to run large enterprise transaction processing systems, minicomputers cost less than $25,000 in 1970 dollars ($150,000 in today's dollars), had at least 4K in memory, and could run programs in higher level languages like FORTRAN and COBOL.[27] Minicomputers were often used as front ends for mainframes, in data communication systems, and in process control systems. Given the diversity of use of the

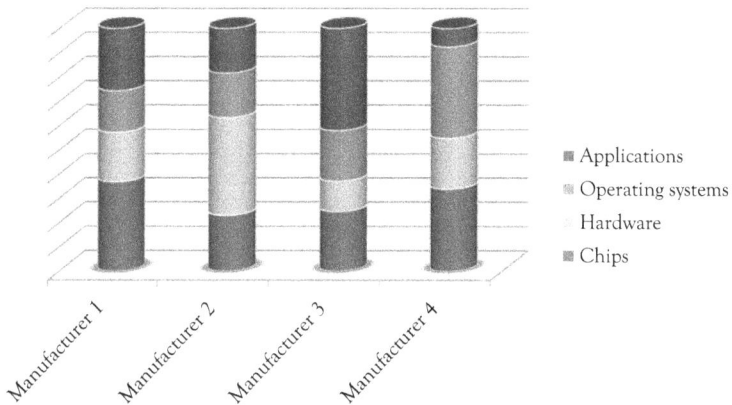

*Figure 2.1  The stovepipe structure of the computing industry in the 1970s*

*Source:* Grove (1996) refers to and diagrams the vertical structure of the software industry in the 1970s.

minis, the software applications for these computers were quite varied, and the market for these applications was fragmented.

Mainframe software package applications dominated the market, accounting for more than 70 percent of applications.[28] Despite the proliferation of minicomputers (the installed base of minis significantly outnumbered that for mainframes), minicomputer software application packages accounted for a small percentage of the total software applications on the market.

Figure 2.1 shows a diagram illustrating the general structure of the computing industry in the 1970s. As can be seen in this diagram, in the 1970s, the industry was organized vertically (in stovepipes) by major mainframe computer manufacturers.[29] Computer manufacturers or licensed software vendors developed and sold software applications developed to run on the manufacturer's mainframe computers. Packaged software applications were tied to particular computer hardware.

The software industry grew significantly in this decade: Sales of software products expanded by a factor of six during the decade; the software industry generated less than $500 million in revenues from the sales of software products in 1970, but by 1980, it was generating more than $2.8 billion in sales ($1.3 billion in 1970 dollars).[30]

The 1970s also experienced emerging problems with software development productivity and quality and these issues continued and expanded in the 1980s.

## Evolution of the Software Industry in the Era of Microcomputers and Personal Computers (1980 to 1995)

The packaged software industry was transformed in the 1980s with the advent of the microcomputer and the personal computer. Microcomputers were small, relatively inexpensive computers with microprocessors as their central processing unit (CPU). Early models—such as the Altair 8800—were distributed as kits to be assembled by users and had a capacity of 256K Random-Access Memory (RAM).

Microcomputers were produced by Apple computer, Tandy Corp, Atari, and Commodore. The Commodore 64—the first cheap home computer for the masses—was one of the most popular microcomputers of its era, and the best-selling model of home computers of all time, despite the fact that 80 percent of them were returned to the manufacturer for repairs.[31] Small companies were entering the software industry to write software applications for these computers. In 1979, Visicalc, the first spreadsheet computer program, was developed by Dan Bricklin and Bob Frankston in two months' time on a $500 budget and was introduced for the Apple II. The idea for the electronic spreadsheet program came from Bricklin who, while a student at Harvard Business School, observed the laborious process of a professor who created a financial model on a blackboard and had to erase and rewrite the model every time he found an error or wanted to change something.[32] Visicalc was revolutionary in concept, although not easy to use.

In 1981, IBM entered the microcomputer market and introduced its version of the microcomputer, which it called a *personal computer* (PC) to distinguish it from competitors. Except notably for Apple, many other computer manufacturers made their computers compatible with IBM's PC, which meant that software running on one manufacturer's PC could also run on other compatible manufacturers' PCs. IBM's PC was highly successful, and the market for personal computers grew rapidly; by 1984, personal computer sales accounted for more than other computer markets, and the installed base of PCs grew to 23 million.[33]

A momentous event in this phase of the software industry was IBM's decision to hire Microsoft to develop a disk operating system (called PC-DOS) for the IBM PCs. Microsoft was a start-up company created in 1975 by Bill Gates and Paul Allen in Albuquerque, New Mexico, to develop an implementation of the programming language BASIC for the Altair 8800. The company was originally called Micro-soft and its early products were variants of the Microsoft Basic programming language. Since Microsoft didn't have an operating system, Bill Gates bought an operating system called QDOS (Quick and Dirty Operating System) from a small company called Seattle Computer Products for $30,000, renamed it, and licensed it to IBM.[34] In 1979, the company moved to Bellevue, WA, and eventually incorporated as Microsoft, Inc. in 1981.[35]

The entry of IBM into the PC market, the standardization of other computer manufacturers on IBM's PC using Microsoft's DOS, and the fact that IBM allowed Microsoft to market PC-DOS to other companies as MS-DOS were significant events that changed the entire dynamics of the software industry. These events de-coupled the PC hardware and operating system in a way that had not been done and sparked a market for independent software providers. The development of software applications for PCs increased dramatically, and many new companies entered the software industry. Over 21,000 software packages were available for PCs as early as 1983, and sales in the packaged software industry were booming: growing at a rate of nearly 50 percent each year.[36]

By the end of 1983, Microsoft was earning $69 million in sales of its software.[37] Other companies entered the industry and were enormously successful. For example, Lotus Development Corporation introduced its 1-2-3 spreadsheet software package in 1983, selling $53 million and tripled its revenues to $256 million by the end of 1984.[38]

In 1984, Apple introduced the Macintosh—the first popular computer to use a graphical user interface (GUI). Microsoft countered in 1985 with its release of Windows—a GUI that ran on its MS-DOS.

There was intense competition in the software industry in the mid-to-late 1980s, with many different software packages for spreadsheets, word processing, databases, and graphics. For example, there were an estimated

300 word processing packages for the IBM-compatible PC alone![39] Software prices were heavily discounted, and large software companies began offering collections or suites of programs at a discount.

By the late 1980s, the market for packaged software for PCs was starting to mature and sales growth was starting to slow. Microsoft dominated the software applications and operating system market. The market for PC software resembled that of publishing and companies used similar methods for promotion and distribution as the book and record industries. For example, independent distributors emerged who could provide popular software on demand for *hit* software products (later referred to as *killer apps*). Software applications like Lotus 1-2-3 and WordPerfect were some of the killer apps in the 1980s. Software packages were available from retail distribution channels and mail order suppliers as well as via direct sales from the producers.

The cost dynamics in the packaged software tended to favor companies who offered a leading product. The relatively fixed costs of software development R&D and the even larger costs of advertising, promotion, and marketing could be recovered by sales to millions of users. Therefore, companies earning significant revenues could fund significant R&D expenditures to continually enhance their product offerings, creating a virtual cycle. The huge size of the market and the unique cost dynamics introduced elements of monopolistic competition into the packaged software industry. Major producers like Lotus Development and Microsoft, for example, enjoyed impressive gross margins (81 percent and 74 percent, respectively, in 1989).[40] That said, the industry experienced significant churn in products and companies, as *hit* products emerged and former hit products faded. In 1980, the company Visicorp (which produced the popular Visicalc) was earning $40 million; by 1985, the company disappeared, acquired by another. In 1984, Micropro's WordStar had 23 percent market share of word processing software with sales of more than 300,000 copies and Word Perfect had one percent; by 1989, WordStar had essentially disappeared and Word Perfect was a market leader.[41]

Aggregate sales in the U.S. domestic packaged software industry grew to over $30 billion by the end of the decade and reached almost $50 billion by 1995 ($11 billion in 1970 dollars).[42] The structure of the industry by the end of the 1980s was such that there were a few main players, some second-tier companies, and thousands of very small companies. The success of the PC market spurred complementary developments in computer hardware and peripherals, which in turn, sparked the development of software applications such as for file utility management, desktop publishing, and graphics display.

The explosion of demand for application software outpaced the efforts of in-house programmers to develop applications from scratch. PCs did not have the power or capacity to replace mainframe computers, and companies struggled to develop their own applications. There was significant concern about the lack of software development productivity and quality, especially for these custom application development efforts. Best practices for software development emerged. For example, in 1987, the Software Engineering Institute at Carnegie Mellon University introduced a five-level Capability Maturity Model for Software [now called the CMMI® (Capability Maturity Model Integration)] that described how companies could transform their capability for building software by focusing on software process improvement.[43] Firms at the lowest level of the CMMI® are considered to be ad hoc in their software development processes; firms appraised at levels 2, 3, or 4 are considered to have software development processes of increasing maturity that are defined, repeatable, and quantitatively managed, respectively, whereas firms appraised at level 5 are considered to be optimizing and operating at the highest level of software development capability. Such best practices and maturity models were deployed in companies to increase the performance of their internal software development efforts. For companies that did not wish to develop their own applications, computer services companies such as CSC and EDS and an outsourcing industry emerged to fill the niche in the development of large-scale applications for governments and major corporations.

A fourth generation of programming languages as well as application code generating tools (called, collectively CASE [Computer Aided Software Engineering] tools) also emerged to address software productivity and quality issues. However, for a variety of reasons, these tools and languages were not fully successful.[44]

As the demand for application software increased, the software development and integration services segment of the software industry grew accordingly and provided an attractive alternative to in-house programming. In addition to EDS and ADP, other software services companies such as Informatics and System Development Corporation (SDC) became more prominent. Some of these companies, such as SDC, had already been providing software services to the U.S. military. In fact, SDC is considered by some to be the world's first computer software services company.[45] When IBM was unable to provide software development for the U.S. military's SAGE system in 1955, the SDC systems engineering group was formed at Rand Corporation to create the code for the air defense ground system. RAND spun off SDC in 1957 as a nonprofit organization that provided expertise for the U.S. military in the design, integration, and testing of large, complex systems, and in 1969, the company became a for-profit concern and offered programming services to other types of organizations than the U.S. military.[46] It was acquired by Unisys in the 1980s.

Ultimately, as more effective software packages came to market in the 1990s, companies moved to buying off-the-shelf packages for their major applications. Personal and desktop productivity software (e.g., Microsoft Excel and Access) also allowed noncomputing professionals to develop their own *quick and dirty* applications and decision support systems.

Figure 2.2 shows a diagram illustrating how the computing industry was structured in the 1980s. As can be seen in this diagram, in the 1980s the industry was organized horizontally in a layered structure, and different companies could offer different hardware and software products as there was some standardization around the IBM PC and MS-DOS operating system.[47] As long as the computers were compatible with the IBM PC and MS-DOS operating systems, applications that could run on MS-DOS could run on different vendor's computers. There were also many different channels for sales and distribution of products. This is a distinct contrast to the stovepipe structure of the software industry in the prior decade.

At the end of the 1980s and in the early 1990s there were intense battles for control of the operating system market for PCs. The operating system was seen as a key to success in the industry because application software was tied to particular operating system platforms. In addition to Microsoft, there were a number of major players who were hoping to

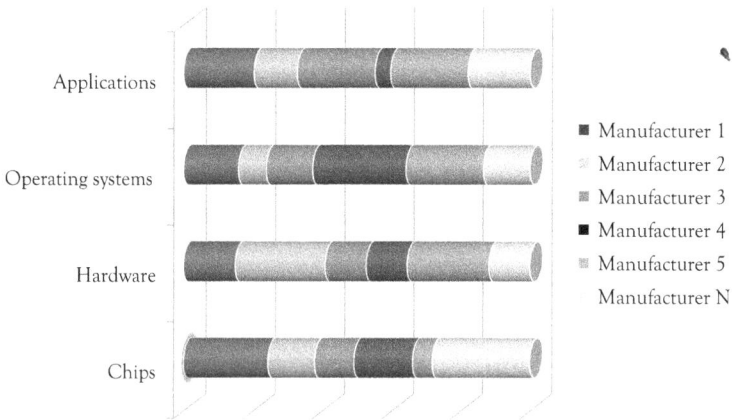

**Figure 2.2** *The layered structure of the computing industry in the 1980s*

*Sources:* Grove (1996) refers to and diagrams the horizontal structure of the software industry in the 1980s.

dominate this market. IBM spent an estimated $ 2.5 billion in R&D, plus outlays in advertising and marketing in developing its own operating system—OS/2.[48] However, IBM's OS/2 was not attractive to customers as it required the purchase of relatively expensive hardware. IBM's third generation of PCs, named PS/2, was released in 1987 and offered a number of technical innovations such as the VGA video standard for PCs, but it was expensive. Also, other computer manufacturers were reluctant to create compatible hardware as IBM demanded royalties on a per-machine basis. Given the pricing and licensing strategies, IBM's PS/2 was largely unsuccessful with the consumer market.

Apple's Macintosh and Sun's Unix (a common operating system on workstations) were also competitive, but, for various reasons, Apple crashed. Unix, originally developed by AT&T for telecommunications networks, was gradually becoming a standard operating system on high-end scientific and technical workstations. Unix had great power and stability but lacked standardization, and few versions were available outside the science and engineering market. Novell bought Unix in 1992 in an attempt to compete with Microsoft, and in 1993 a number of major Unix companies (among them IBM, HP, and Sun) agreed on a standardization scheme and released new versions of Unix. These efforts failed to dislodge Microsoft from its dominant position.

A key element of Microsoft's success was its release of Windows 3.1 in 1992 and Windows NT in 1993. Windows NT ("New Technology") was a powerful, high-level language-based, processor-independent, multiprocessing, and multiuser operating system with features comparable to Unix.[49] It included novel Internet technologies. By the mid-1990s, Microsoft was dominant in the operating systems market for PCs.

## Evolution of the Software Industry in the Era of the Internet (1995 to Today)

Several trends re-shaped the software industry in the mid-1990s and beyond. One significant trend in the software industry in this time period was the growth in enterprise resource planning (ERP) systems. ERP systems connected what were, heretofore, largely independent applications (e.g., order management, inventory management, accounting, human resource management), under a common interface. Despite their size, ERP systems were sold off-the-shelf, but often required significant customization, training, and other services to be useful. Many ERP vendors emerged in the 1990s, including the German company Systems, Applications and Products in Data Processing (SAP), Peoplesoft, Baan, and Oracle. ERP systems were difficult to implement and often associated with huge cost overruns, lawsuits, and disasters. For example, Hershey Foods spent $112 million on SAP's R/3 ERP system in 1999, but ran into difficulties in implementing it. Issues prevented orders for $100 million of candy to flow through the system. As a result the company's profit was off 19 percent that quarter and its stock price dropped 8 percent.[50]

Other trends in the software industry were sparked by a path-breaking new technology called the *Internet*.

In the early 1990s companies were engaged in connecting PCs into extensive networks. For the most part, these networks were internal. However, a major disrupter of the software industry was about to emerge: the Internet. The origins of the Internet can be found in the late 1960s when the U.S. Department of Defense expressed a desire to connect computers at various universities and research institutions with its own computers. An agency called Advanced Research Projects Agency (ARPA) hired a small company in Boston by the name of Bolt, Beranek and Newman

Technologies (BBN) to implement a new technology called packet switching for this network. In October 1969, the first Internet message was sent from the University of California at Los Angeles (UCLA) to Stanford University, and two other universities later joined them in a network called the ARPAnet. Given the difficulties of using this network, its early usage was restricted to academia and the military, until in 1982 a standard called TCP/IP was developed by ARPA to simplify use. With the introduction of this standard, the concept of a worldwide network of interconnected TCP/IP networks, called the Internet, was introduced. In 1989, Tim Berners-Lee created the concept of the World Wide Web and devised a language called HTML as well as a communications protocol called HTTP, which allowed people to move easily between locations on the Internet. The development of the first browser software for the Internet in 1992 and 1993—called Mosaic—by Marc Andreessen and Eric Bina, spurred use of the Internet significantly, and by the end of 1993, there were already over a million users.[51]

Figure 2.3 shows the number of Internet users per 100 inhabitants from the mid-1990s to 2014, based on data from the International Telecommunication Union (ITU). As can be seen in this graph, the popularity of the Internet has skyrocketed since the introduction of Internet browsers in the mid-1990s.

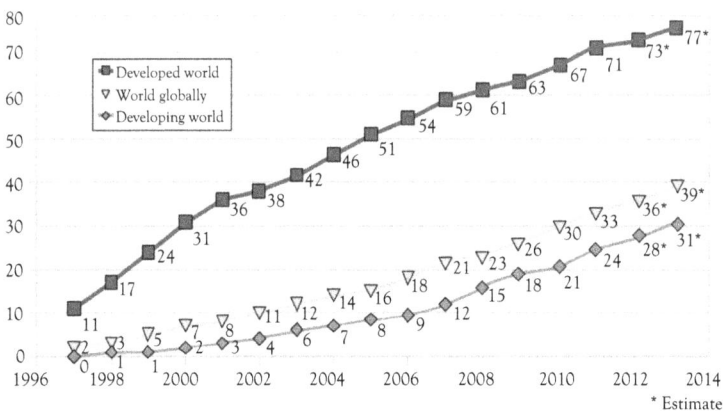

*Figure 2.3 Internet users per 100 inhabitants, 1996 to 2014*

Source: Ogden (2013)
Note: This diagram was created by Jeff Ogden based on data from the ITU (2013). No changes were made to the diagram. It is licensed under the Creative Commons Attribution Share-Alike 3.0 Unported license.

For the software industry, the Internet has been radical in its impact, and there are still many ripple effects felt today.

First, the Internet has spawned the creation of new types of software applications. The first commercial Web browser software—Netscape Navigator—was released in 1994, as a free download, and within a year, Netscape controlled 80 percent of the browser market.[52] Other companies, many of them start-ups, entered the software industry during the dot.com boom in the mid-to-late 1990s and created and marketed software for Internet tasks like managing e-mail, browsing new sites, and authoring web pages.

Microsoft, of course, responded, and in 1995, the company launched its own browser—Internet Explorer, given away online and free with other Microsoft programs. The early version was *clunky* and seen as inferior to Netscape. However, Microsoft partnered with America Online (AOL) in 1996 who agreed to feature Internet Explorer as AOL's preferred browser. Microsoft's clout in the market prevailed, and it went on to capture 40 percent of the browser market share in 1998 and 80 percent by 2000, peaking at 95 percent in 2002.[53] Note that in 2013, Internet Explorer holds about 50 to 60 percent of the browser market share.[54]

Second, the Internet has enabled innovative models for software development. In 1992, a Finnish university student by the name of Linus Torvalds developed a version of Unix, called Linux. Linux was developed using a new model of software development called open source. Under this model, instead of being developed within a company by paid programmers, open-source software is posted to the Internet. Any developer can improve it, and post changes for review and acceptance by the community of developers. A critical aspect of open-source software is that the source code is available. If you remember the discussion in Chapter 1, the source code for software contains the instructions that are understandable by humans. Therefore, having access to source code is extremely important, if you wish to change the software. If you buy software from a vendor, such as Microsoft, you will not obtain the source code (only the compiled code) and you therefore cannot change it. Open-source software is also free to users, although if users need support (such as training, installation, or help), such services are typically not freely available. Thus, companies such as RedHat have emerged to provide support services around the open-source application.

The open-source movement has its own manifesto—The Cathedral and the Bazaar, written by Eric Raymond.[55] The manifesto criticizes the traditional method of developing software (formal, closed, precise, planned, like building a cathedral) to the open-source approach, which is more democratic and informal like a medieval bazaar of developers and users. Raymond argues that by opening up the development process, more eyes are on the software, which helps to improve its quality and usability.

There are many types of open-source applications available today. Table 2.1 summarizes some of the major open-source projects.

These projects and others have thousands of open-source applications and utilities that anyone can download for free. For example, there are open-source databases (e.g., MySQL) and even open-source enterprise resource planning (ERP) packages (e.g., Compiere). The Apache web server has become extremely popular and is more widely used than its commercial competitors. Although the Apache web server got off to a slow start in the mid-1990s, it emerged as a leading contender in

*Table 2.1  Some major open-source projects*

| Name | Website | Description |
|---|---|---|
| Linux | www.linux.org | An operating system inspired by Unix. RedHat provides user support for the system. |
| Apache | www.apache.org | A web server that evolved from a series of patches written by NCSA (i.e., a patchy server). Includes HTTP server software, Jakarta, Perl, and PhP languages, among others. |
| Mozilla | www.mozilla.org | A web browser that uses the source code from Netscape's Navigator browser, which was released in 1998. |
| Source Forge | www.sourceforge.net | A hosting service for open-source development projects. Includes 3.4 million developers who work on 324,000 projects having more than 46 million users and 4 million downloads per day. |
| Fresh Meat (now freecode) | www.freecode.com | Has the Web's largest index of Linux, Unix, and cross-platform software, and mobile applications. |

global usage market share for web server software in the 2000s, significantly outpacing Microsoft's IIS and other competitors. In recent years, Apache's global usage market share has hovered between 40 and 60 percent.

Of course, the open-source movement, and Linux in particular, appear to have posed a significant challenge to Microsoft's dominance. IBM has endorsed Linux and sponsors it to the tune of several million dollars per year, in paid contributors. According to IDC, in 1999, Linux became the #2 operating system behind Microsoft's Windows NT. From 2000 to 2004, Linux shipments grew at a rate of 28 percent from 1.3 million in 1999 to 4.7 million in 2004—and its market share grew by almost 30 percent.[56]

Some software companies (including Microsoft) have seen the open-source movement as a threat to capitalism. Various executives from Microsoft have called open-source anti-American, and Microsoft's operating systems chief, Jim Allchin, called open-source an intellectual-property destroyer in 2001.[57]

That said, open-source products have not turned out to pose a real threat to Microsoft's dominance in the desktop operating system market: according to data from netmarketshare.com on global usage, as of June 2013, Microsoft's operating systems hold over 90 percent global usage market share, followed by Apple's OS X at seven percent and Linux at just over one percent market share.[58]

However, in the mobile operating system market, open-source software has proved more competitive. In terms of global usage market share (based on website visits), according to data from netmarketshare.com, Apple' iOS dominates with 58 percent of market share, followed by Android (a Linux-based operating system for smart phones and hand-held devices) at 25 percent, Java ME (an operating system for embedded systems available as open source) at 11 percent, and Symbian (an open-source platform for mobile phones developed in 2009 by Symbian Foundation) at 2.5 percent market share.[59] Overall, in the mobile operating system market, open-source products altogether hold almost 40 percent global usage market share.[60]

Figures 2.4 and 2.5 display the relative market share (based on worldwide usage, not sales) of closed-source and open-source operating systems

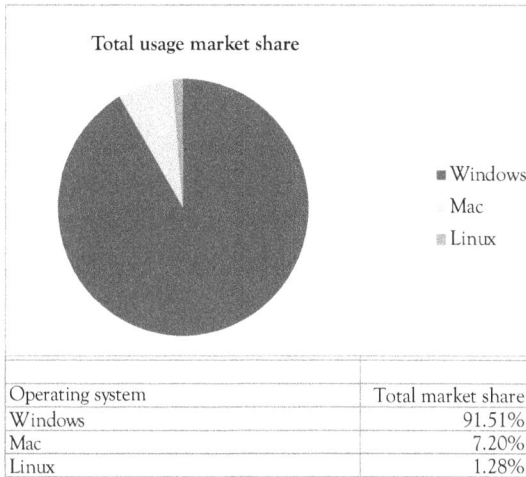

| Operating system | Total market share |
|---|---|
| Windows | 91.51% |
| Mac | 7.20% |
| Linux | 1.28% |

*Figure 2.4  Desktop operating system market share based on usage*

*Source:* Data provided by Net Market Share (n.d.)

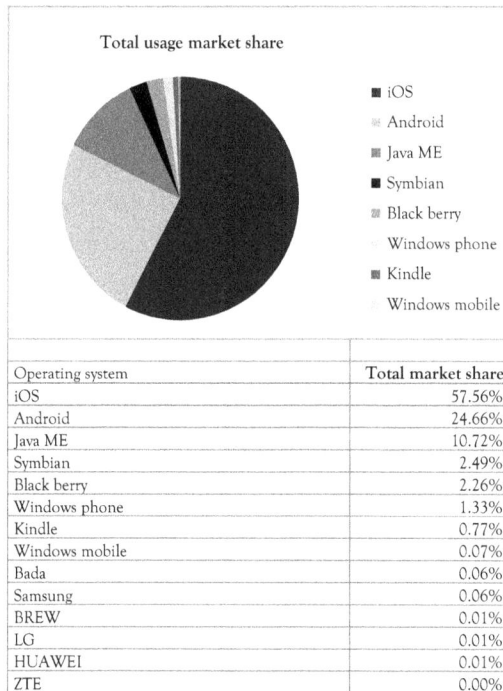

| Operating system | Total market share |
|---|---|
| iOS | 57.56% |
| Android | 24.66% |
| Java ME | 10.72% |
| Symbian | 2.49% |
| Black berry | 2.26% |
| Windows phone | 1.33% |
| Kindle | 0.77% |
| Windows mobile | 0.07% |
| Bada | 0.06% |
| Samsung | 0.06% |
| BREW | 0.01% |
| LG | 0.01% |
| HUAWEI | 0.01% |
| ZTE | 0.00% |

*Figure 2.5 Mobile/tablet operating system market share based on usage*

*Source:* Data provided by Net Market Share (n.d.)

for desktop computers and for mobile/tablet devices, respectively, as of June 2013.

Although the Internet has opened up new opportunities, it has also presented new threats by creating new access points from the outside into companies. In 2002, more than 7,000 new viruses, Trojan horses, and computer worms were reported, but by 2012 the number of new malicious computer programs has grown exponentially, with reports of 200,000 new viruses detected every day![61] Thus, security has become a popular topic, and sales of security software products such as firewall applications, encryption, and antivirus programs have taken off. Middleware software, such as that used to connect older legacy applications to the Internet for e-commerce has also become popular. Chapter 7 discusses software security and privacy issues.

Finally, the Internet has significantly impacted how software can be supplied to customers. Instead of distributors mailing copies of software applications to customers or stores carrying inventories of disks with the applications, it is possible for software companies to offer their applications directly to customers via a simple click to download via the Internet. By shifting software distribution and hosting to the Internet, this new delivery mechanism has the potential to completely eliminate the "middle man"—that is, sales distributors and resellers. The Internet has also opened up new options in software pricing and release strategies such as software renting, which are discussed later in this book in Chapter 7.

The software services segment of the industry also grew very rapidly in this time period as companies needed computer applications and systems to help generate greater internal efficiencies and to conduct business over the Internet. In particular, there was a surge in growth in demand for software services due to Year 2000 compliance (Y2K) concerns. The Y2K (or Year 2000) problem occurred at the roll over from 1999 to 2000, for computer systems that abbreviated and stored the year in a date as two digits instead of four digits. Storing only two digits could cause problems with date sequencing, leap year calculation, and other issues. Thus, firms worldwide had to update their computer systems to fix this issue before the year 2000. Y2K significantly increased the demand for programming services to help companies remediate their legacy systems. The Y2K problem also spurred millions of dollars of spending on new enterprise software like ERP systems as many companies preferred to buy new systems rather than spend money to fix old systems.

The need for programming services was also driven by strong demand for web-based applications, e-commerce, and the dot.com bubble. By the late 1990s, there were more than 32,000 companies in the United States (the vast majority with less than 50 employees) providing custom programming services.[62] Industry revenues more than tripled during the decade, estimated at $21 billion in 1990 ($8.3 billion in 1970 dollars) in the United States, and reaching a peak of $69.4 billion in 2000 ($21 billion in 1970 dollars).[63] The passing of the year 2000, and the dot.com crash in 2001 negatively impacted this segment of the software industry, and the segment did not start to recover until the mid-2000s. The 1990s and 2000s also saw the emergence and growth of a global industry for software services provision, with programming services companies coming to prominence in India, Ireland, and other parts of the world. The next chapter (Chapter 3) discusses the structure and competitive dynamics in the software industry today. Chapter 4 discusses the globalization of the software industry, in which the software services segment plays a particularly significant role.

## Key Takeaways

The software industry is dynamic and ever-changing. Changes in the industry are driven by new technologies that shake up the status quo. The concept of software was present more than 150 years ago, but the first modern computer and computer program were created in the 1950s. Women played an important role in the software industry, serving as some of the first programmers in the 1950s.

Software, as an industry, did not exist until the late 1960s when IBM was forced by federal legislation to separate its software from its hardware for the S/360. In the 1970s, mainframe computers dominated, and packaged software applications for mainframe computers held most of the market share. In the 1980s, the software industry experienced a major shake-up with the introduction of PCs, and shifted from a vertical silo structure in which major vendors developed software for particular mainframe computers (and marketed, sold, and distributed the software) to a horizontal structure with many players in which software applications could work on many PCs that were compatible. IBM's PC was most popular in this era. The 1980s is an important era in the software industry: It saw the rise of major software companies such as Microsoft and Apple that sold software for end-user productivity, as well as companies such as SAP that sold enterprise resource planning systems for companies. By the mid-1990s, Microsoft was the dominant software company in the industry.

In the mid-1990s and 2000s, the Internet emerged and changed the industry again. The Internet sparked the development of new types of applications for the web and the advent of *browser* wars. Although Netscape was an early leader, Internet Explorer attained almost all of the market by 2002. The Internet also made possible a new form of software development called *open-source* software. Open-source software was freely available to users, who could download the source code from the Internet. Major open-source communities emerged who created popular open-source products. Security software such as firewalls and antivirus tools became popular with an exponential increase in malicious software delivered over the Internet. The Internet also changed the software delivery mechanism as companies could easily distribute their products directly to customers over the Internet. This era also saw a surge in growth in software services companies in the United States and abroad to fulfill the demand for Y2K compliance and Internet commerce applications.

# CHAPTER 3

# Structure and Competitive Dynamics of the Software Industry

The software industry has a unique structure and intense competitive pressures. A few companies tend to dominate segments within the industry, and there are thousands of smaller companies. Although almost any talented individual with a computer can enter the industry, there is a very high rate of failure. For example, from 1995 to 2007, 16 percent of companies in the software industry failed, whereas only 11 percent in the computer hardware industry and 5 percent in the pharmaceutical industry failed during the same time period.[1]

Consider Visicalc. Remember Visicalc? Visicalc was the first electronic spreadsheet. Personal Software (later renamed Visicorp), the company that introduced and marketed Visicalc in 1980, earned almost $23 million from Visicalc by 1982. However, after Lotus Development introduced Lotus 1-2-3 in 1983, Visicalc lost money and Visicorp did not survive. In 1984, Visicorp was acquired by a company, called Paladin software and did not retain its name.[2] This example is not unique. Indeed, the software industry is highly dynamic with many entrants and exits. Figure 3.1 shows the number of companies entering and leaving the software industry from 1995 to 2007.[3] Note the spike of new entrants into the industry in 1998, during the dot.com boom, and the relatively high exits in 2001 during the bust.

Given the high rates of failures and new entries, the set of particular companies present in the software industry can change frequently. A few companies have been present for many years; some companies completely exit the industry; and others merge or are acquired. Merger and acquisition activity is very high in the software industry. According to Ernst

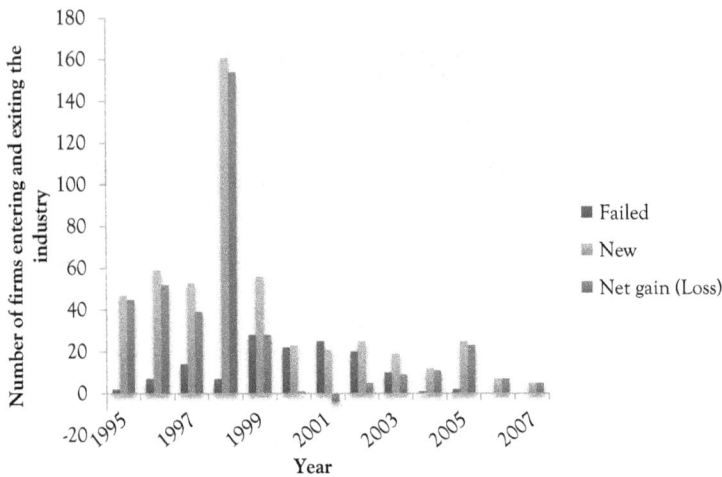

*Figure 3.1 Entries and exits in the packaged software industry (1995–2007)*

Source: Li, Shang, and Slaughter (2010).

and Young, in 2011, software companies accounted for 36 percent of the 2,689 mergers and acquisitions in the computing industry, and 34 of the deals were valued at more than $1 billion each.[4]

Sales in the software industry also experience booms and busts, given disruptive innovations in computing technology, the popularity of hit applications, and the ups and downs in economic cycles. In the 1980s and 1990s, the software industry experienced double-digit annual growth rates, but during the dot.com bust in 2001/2002, the industry experienced its first-ever decline. Since then, strong growth has resumed. Figure 3.2 shows U.S. domestic sales of packaged software from 1970 to 2015 (projected), both in nominal dollars and in inflation-adjusted dollars.[5]

Given the interesting and unique dynamics of the software industry, it is important to understand how it works. This chapter will begin by first describing the types of products and services provided by companies in the software industry and will identify the major companies in the industry. Then the software value chain and the economics of software production will be described. Finally, the chapter will turn to the competitive forces in the industry, identifying the primary customers, suppliers, competitors and other important stakeholders, and their relative power.

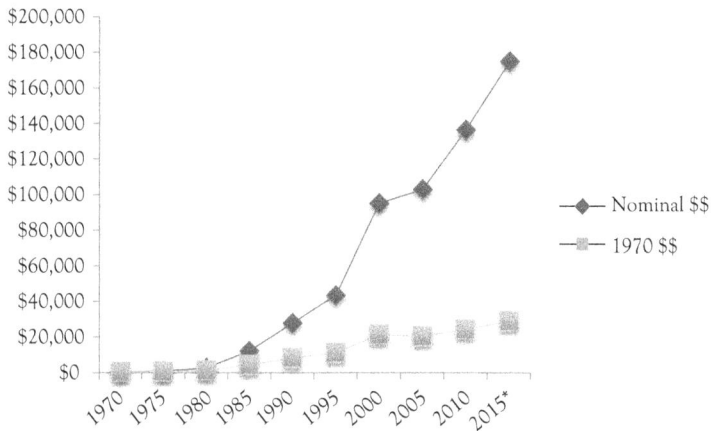

*Figure 3.2  U.S. domestic sales of packaged software*

*Sources:* Steinmueller (1996) and OECD (2002).

## Software Products and Services

Companies in the software industry produce and sell software applications and related systems and services. As noted in Chapter 1, the software industry is organized into major segments that correspond to the two primary types of software: system infrastructure software and applications software, with different product types within those groups. Another important segment is software services. The competitive dynamics differ considerably in the different segments. Some segments are mature and only one or two firms dominate, whereas other segments are emergent with a number of players. Figure 3.3 shows the types of products and services in the industry.

*Applications software* performs specific end user functions. The industry includes different subsegments that focus on different types of applications such as visual applications (e.g., video games, graphics, and entertainment systems) and traditional decision support applications (e.g., enterprise resource planning systems, customer relationship management, statistical analysis, financial reporting, and word processing). Examples of best-selling application software products include World of Warcraft, TurboTax, AutoCAD, Adobe, MS Word, and PeopleSoft.

*Systems software* includes the basic systems needed to operate the computer hardware and networks, including operating systems, data

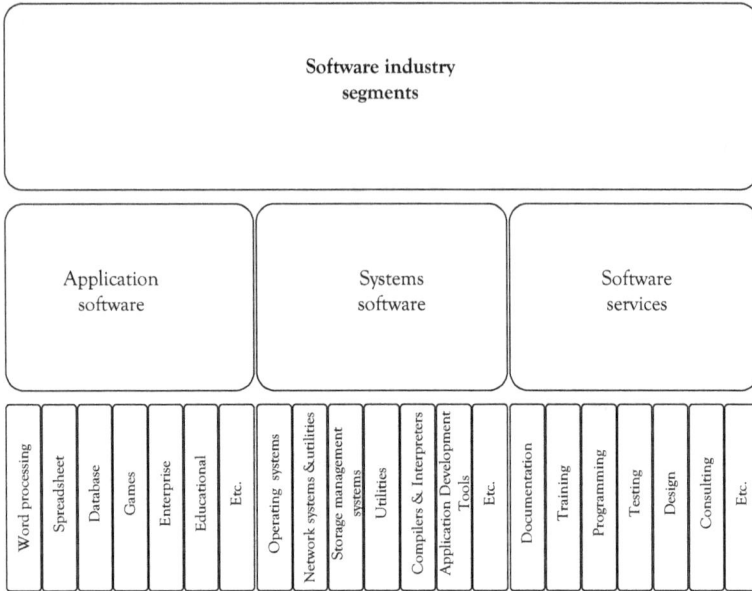

*Figure 3.3 Types of products and services in the software industry*

management tools, network software, application design and development tools, application life-cycle management, application development platforms, and middleware. Some examples of systems software products include Microsoft Windows, Unix, Boa Constructor, IBM Rational Application Developer, NetBeans, RadRails, Ping, and SQL Server.

*Software-related services* include services provided directly to customers for documentation, training, custom programming, testing, design, and others. Many of these services are offered directly to customers via the Internet.

## Major Companies in the Software Industry

Table 3.1 shows the top 30 companies in the world that supply software, in terms of worldwide software revenues and market share (as of 2012).[6] Note that the revenues reported are for software sales. Some companies— such as IBM, Hewlett-Packard (HP), and EMC—provide hardware as well as software, but the numbers reported in this table are for their software sales (based on data from IDC). The table distinguishes overall rank, rank for companies that primarily supply software, and rank for

Table 3.1 Top 30 suppliers of software as of 2012 (worldwide)

| Overall rank | Rank for software company | Rank for U.S.-based software company | Company | Revenues (in $$ millions) | Market share (%) | Cumulative market share | Major products/services | Country of headquarters |
|---|---|---|---|---|---|---|---|---|
| 1 | 1 | 1 | Microsoft | 58,454 | 17.06 | 17.06 | Operating Systems and Office Applications | U.S. |
| 2 | | | IBM | 29,129 | 8.5 | 25.56 | Computer Hardware | U.S. |
| 3 | 2 | 2 | Oracle Corp | 27,826 | 8.12 | 33.68 | Enterprise applications and database systems | U.S. |
| 4 | 3 | | SAP | 16,989 | 4.96 | 38.64 | Enterprise applications | Germany |
| 5 | 4 | 3 | Symantec | 6,423 | 1.88 | 40.52 | Security and storage software | U.S. |
| 6 | | | Hewlett-Packard | 5,513 | 1.61 | 42.13 | Computer Hardware | U.S. |
| 7 | | | EMC | 5,140 | 1.5 | 43.63 | Computer storage and retrieval devices | U.S. |
| 8 | 5 | 4 | Adobe | 4,337 | 1.27 | 44.9 | Desktop publishing software | U.S. |
| 9 | 6 | 5 | CA Technologies | 4,304 | 1.26 | 46.16 | Enterprise applications and systems software | U.S. |
| 10 | 7 | 6 | Vmware Inc. | 4,253 | 1.24 | 47.4 | Systems software | U.S. |
| 11 | | | Fujitsu | 3,131 | 0.91 | 48.31 | Computer Hardware | Japan |
| 12 | 8 | 7 | Salesforce.com | 2,825 | 0.83 | 49.14 | Internet-based applications and platforms | U.S. |
| 13 | 9 | 8 | SAS | 2,666 | 0.78 | 49.92 | Software for business analytics | U.S. |
| 14 | 10 | 9 | Intuit | 2,465 | 0.72 | 50.64 | Accounting applications software | U.S. |
| 15 | 11 | 10 | Infor | 2,464 | 0.72 | 51.36 | Enterprise applications | U.S. |
| 16 | | | Siemens | 2,455 | 0.72 | 52.08 | Computer hardware and manufacturing systems | Germany |

(Continued)

*Table 3.1 Top 30 suppliers of software as of 2012 (worldwide) (Continued)*

| Overall rank | Rank for software company | Rank for U.S.-based software company | Company | Revenues (in $$ millions) | Market share (%) | Cumulative market share | Major products/services | Country of headquarters |
|---|---|---|---|---|---|---|---|---|
| 17 | 12 | | Dassault Systemes | 2,269 | 0.66 | 52.74 | Computer aided design and manufacturing systems | France |
| 18 | 13 | 11 | Autodesk | 2,263 | 0.66 | 53.4 | Computer aided design software | U.S. |
| 19 | 14 | 12 | Citrix Systems | 2,099 | 0.61 | 54.01 | Network software applications | U.S. |
| 20 | | | Cisco | 2,000 | 0.58 | 54.59 | Computer Hardware and Networks | U.S. |
| 21 | 15 | 13 | BMC | 1,983 | 0.58 | 55.17 | Enterprise systems software | U.S. |
| 22 | | | Hitachi | 1,980 | 0.58 | 55.75 | Computer Hardware, networks, electronics | Japan |
| 23 | | | NEC | 1,942 | 0.57 | 56.32 | Computer Hardware | Japan |
| 24 | 16 | | Sage Group | 1,790 | 0.52 | 56.84 | Enterprise applications | U.K. |
| 25 | 17 | 14 | Synopsys | 1,721 | 0.5 | 57.34 | Electronic design automation software | U.S. |
| 26 | | | Intel | 1,675 | 0.49 | 57.83 | Semi-conductors | U.S. |
| 27 | | | Apple | 1,601 | 0.47 | 58.3 | Computer Hardware | U.S. |
| 28 | 18 | 15 | Activision | 1,580 | 0.46 | 58.76 | Video game software | U.S. |
| 29 | 19 | 16 | SunGard | 1,393 | 0.41 | 59.17 | Financial and investment systems | U.S. |
| 30 | | | McKesson | 1,332 | 0.39 | 59.56 | Healthcare applications and systems | U.S. |

*Source:* Based on data from Coffey (2013).

U.S.-based companies that primarily provide software. The table further distinguishes market share, major products and services, and country in which the company is headquartered.

As can be seen in Table 3.1, the top 30 companies that supply software account for almost 60 percent of the global revenues from software sales. These companies produce software that is representative of the different market segments described earlier: applications such as enterprise resource planning, accounting, desktop publishing, games, and healthcare applications; and systems software such as network software, security software, operating systems, and data management and storage systems.

The software industry is largely dominated by U.S. companies. Microsoft alone represents 17 percent of the worldwide market share for software sales. Twenty-three of the top 30 companies are based in the United States and account for more than half of the global revenues from software. The top five, U.S.-based companies that primarily supply software are Microsoft, Oracle, Symantec, CA Technologies, and Adobe. A brief profile of each company follows.

### Microsoft

Microsoft, of course, has figured prominently in the history of the software industry, and its history is discussed in detail in Chapter 2. The company's major products include operating systems (Windows) and office/desktop productivity applications (Word, Excel, Access, Powerpoint), although the company offers other products as well—such as Microsoft Dynamics ERP—an enterprise resource planning system.

### OracleCorp.

Oracle was founded in 1977 by Larry Ellison, Robert Miner, and Edward Oates in Santa Clara, California, as Software Development Laboratories.[7] Inspired by Codd's paper on relational database systems (refer to Chapter 2), the company's flagship product was a relational database called Oracle Database. The product was very successful, and in 1982, the company renamed itself after it. In addition to its database management system, the company today offers a variety of products, including enterprise systems, customer relationship management software, supply chain software, middleware, collaboration software (called Beehive), and others. As shown in Table 3.1, in terms of revenues, Oracle is the second largest software company in the world (and second in the United States).

### Symantec

Symantec was founded in 1982 by Gary Hendrix in Mountain View, California, with a National Science Foundation grant.[8] Symantec was originally focused on artificial intelligence-related projects, and its first employees were hired from Stanford University. One of these employees was Barry Greenstein who was a professional poker player and who developed the software for the Q&A product. Over the years, the company was acquired (but retained its name) and performed its own acquisitions, and its product line evolved to include the popular Norton antivirus software and Internet security tools. It is the fourth largest software company in the world and third in the United States in terms of revenues.

### Adobe Systems, Inc.

Adobe (named after a creek near its founders' homes) was established in 1982 in Mountain View, California, by John Warnock and Charles Geschke.[9] Warnock and Geschke had left Xerox PARC to develop and sell PostScript—the company's first product. Sales of PostScript took off when Apple licensed it for use in its LaserWriter printers in 1985. Adobe introduced its flagship product—Photoshop—in 1989. In the early 1990s, the company introduced Adobe Acrobat and the Portable Document Format (PDF), which is now an international standard for electronic documents. Adobe offers a range of desktop publishing and enterprise software products and is the fifth largest software company in the world (fourth in the United States).

### CA Technologies

Rounding out the top five U.S.-based software companies is CA Technologies (formerly Computer Associates International, Inc.). It is also known as CA and was founded by Charles Wang and Russell Artzt in 1976, in Islandia, NY.[10] CA came into being when IBM was forced to unbundle sales of its operating systems software from sales of its hardware. Wang and Artzt created a company to develop and sell IBM mainframe software. Their initial success occurred when they acquired the rights to distribute a product called CA-Sort. CA-Sort was a data management utility that allowed mainframe computers to efficiently sort, merge, and copy data and was originally developed by a Swiss company named Computer Associates, founded by Sam Goodner and Max Sevcik several years earlier. Wang and Artzt partnered with Computer Associates and called their joint company—Trans-American Computer Associates (later Computer Associates International). The company grew rapidly through acquisitions and has become the sixth largest software company in the world and fifth in the United States in terms of revenues. Its products include enterprise management software tools and utilities.

As is clear from Table 3.1, a number of major companies selling software are actually computer hardware manufacturers such as IBM and HP. These companies produce and sell software that is compatible with their hardware, but software is not their primary business. Still, the sales from their software products are quite significant. IBM, for example, although ranked second in the world in its sales of operating systems and systems software, is not primarily in the software business (its software sales represent just 24 percent of the company's total revenues).[11]

Despite being primarily computer hardware manufacturers, both IBM and HP are among the top sellers in the software industry and have had a significant influence on it, and thus merit discussion.

## IBM

International Business Machines—nicknamed Big Blue—is headquartered in Armonk, NY. IBM's history dates back to the 19th century when three companies—the Tabulating Machine Company (founded by Herman Hollerith), the International Time Recording Company, and the Computing Scale Company merged. Among the wide range of products offered by the merged company was punched card equipment based on Hollerith's innovations. During the World Wars, IBM enhanced punched card technology, producing an electric key punch and its own design of the punch card, and was selected by the U.S. Government to maintain employment records for all U.S. citizens after the 1935 Social Security Act. The company produced 5 to 10 million punched cards per day in the 1930s and built the Harvard Mark I—the first large-scale electro-mechanical calculator for the U.S. Navy.[12]

As described in Chapter 2, during the 1950s IBM was named the primary computer hardware manufacturer for the SAGE air defense system by the Department of Defense. These government partnerships, combined with innovative computing technology and a series of commercially successful products enabled IBM to emerge from the 1950s as the world's leading technology firm. As mentioned in Chapter 2, a major event in the late 1960s was IBM's development of the System/360, and the subsequent decision (under pressure from the U.S. Justice Department) to unbundle its computer hardware and software and sell each separately. This key decision spawned the software industry in the 1970s. Although the company underwent turbulent times in the late 1980s and early 1990s and lost billions when its forays into the personal computer market were less successful than hoped, in the 1990s IBM made a number of transformations that have shaped the current company's strategy and products. IBM focused on high-end super- and mainframe computing (e.g., producing supercomputers such as Deep Blue, Blue Gene, and most recently—Watson) and on becoming a global services business, moving away from unprofitable hardware products and becoming more brand agnostic. The company also invested in developing and selling middleware (software that connects applications to operating systems), not applications software.

The company has continued to invest heavily in Research and Development (R&D): spending almost $6 billion a year in research, development, and engineering.[13] In 2010, IBM was awarded almost 6,000 patents, more than any other company.[14] IBM employees have earned five Nobel Prizes, four Turing Awards, five National Medals of Technology, and five National Medals of Science.[15] Today, the company has almost a half million employees worldwide in more than 170 countries and is one of the largest and most profitable of information technology companies. It is ranked second, behind only Microsoft, in worldwide software revenues.

### Hewlett-Packard

HP was founded by Stanford University classmates, William Hewlett, and David Packard in 1939 in a garage in Palo Alto, California, with an initial investment of $538.[16] One of the company's earliest products was an audio oscillator that was purchased by Walt Disney Productions for use in the movie *Fantasia*.[17] The company manufactured a number of electronic products and test instruments. In 1966 it entered the computing industry with the HP 1000 series of minicomputers, and produced a desktop calculator that was referred to by *Wired Magazine* in 2000 as the first personal computer—the HP 9100A.[18] In the 1970s and 1980s, the company manufactured more advanced minicomputers, as well as programmable handheld calculators, inkjets, and laser printers. In 1999, HP spun off its original instrument and test equipment business to a company called Agilent—the largest initial public offering at that time ($2.1 billion in 1999 dollars or $3 billion in today's dollars) in the history of Silicon Valley.[19] Today, HP provides computer hardware, software, services, and consulting. The merger with Compaq in 2002, and the acquisitions of Electronic Data Systems (EDS) in 2008, 3Com in 2009, and Palm, Inc. in 2010 have enabled HP to offer a wide range of computing hardware, software, and services to its customers. The company employs about 350,000 worldwide, and in 2012 HP was the world's largest personal computer vendor in terms of unit sales, shipping over 48 million PCs.[20]In its software business, HP produces enterprise management software, software-as-a-service, and cloud computing services and, as shown in Table 3.1, is ranked sixth in worldwide software revenues.

There are also a number of prominent non-U.S. companies in the top 30 software suppliers, such as SAP. These companies will be profiled in Chapter 4 where the global aspects of the software industry are covered.

The services segment is a significant part of the software industry. Custom programming services are a primary alternative to the use of packaged software. Some companies provide custom programming to modify a software package to better fit a customer's need. Other companies provide custom programming of entire applications. Software development is only one of many IT services offered by firms in the services segment of the software industry. The broader IT services industry has been evolving toward a one-stop model, in which a single company provides a comprehensive set of services to its clients. For this reason, the companies may not report custom software programming services separately from other IT service revenue. As noted in Chapter 1, Forrester Research has projected that in 2013, custom-built software by contractors and consultants will generate over $130 billion in worldwide revenues (about 25 percent of the total revenues in the global software industry in 2013). Global revenues for IT consulting and systems integration services are projected at $389 billion.

Industry leaders in the software services segment include IBM and HP, as well as Oracle, Computer Sciences Corporation (CSC), and Accenture. Although the United States is a leader in programming services, because it is difficult for companies to find sufficient high-tech workers, the industry has become more dependent on skilled contract workers overseas. In many cases, the major companies in this segment have opened up offshore software development facilities in countries like India, Ireland, Israel, and Brazil to tap into the global IT workforce. In recent years, foreign companies have emerged to provide custom programming and other IT services and have become major competitors to their U.S. counterparts. Chapter 4 will discuss the globalization of the software industry and the emergence of these companies overseas.

## Software Value Chain

A *value chain* is the set of processes or activities by which a company adds value to something it produces. Primary activities include production, marketing, sales, and after-sales support. Supporting activities include procurement, human resources, research and development, and firm infrastructure.[21]

The software industry has its own unique value chain, which is quite different from one in, for example, industries that manufacture physical products. The main product in the software industry is software and its ancillary services. Software is not physical and does not need to be stored or transported through physical channels (especially today with the Internet as a major distribution channel). Software products can be distributed on digital media in retail outlets, as well as downloaded from the Internet.

**Figure 3.4 *Software value chain***

*Source*: Adapted by permission from Porter (1985).

Figure 3.4 shows a visual depiction of a value chain in the software industry. As can be seen in Figure 3.4, the basic product is software, which is documented, packaged, marketed and sold, distributed, integrated with the customer's other software, supported, and maintained.

A key feature of the software industry concerns the nature and length of product development life cycles. Product development life cycles vary considerably by type of software and domain of its application. For example, consider the product development life cycle of video game software. A video game can take two to four years to develop. But, once it is released to the market, its shelf life (life cycle) is usually about six weeks to six months![22] On the other hand, large systems in the public sector are used for decades.[23] For example, the state of New Jersey's payroll system dates back to1969, and states' benefits systems are 22 years old on average with some systems more than 40 years old.[24]

However, continued enhancements are required to keep the systems useful and relevant. Given the nature of software product life cycles and the need for innovation and enhancement of software features, R&D investments are essential for continued new product development and existing product enhancement. Software firms often invest in high levels of R&D spending: In fact, companies in the software industry spend as much as 20 percent or more of their revenues on R&D—considerably higher than for most other industries.[25] For example, a study of the software industry found that software companies spent on average of 28.7 percent of their sales on R&D, whereas computer hardware companies averaged 11.0 percent and pharmaceutical firms averaged 18.7 percent of their sales on R&D during the same timeframe.[26]

Software products need to be documented and packaged (if sold on physical media). Marketing, sales, and advertising can be extremely important activities in the software industry, given the need to promote a new product. In fact, sales and advertising expenses are one of the software industry's largest budget items.[27] Software products also need to be integrated within an existing suite or system and may require training, support, and maintenance.

The distribution of software products differs by segment. In the high-end or mainframe market, software firms may have a direct sales force to market large, complex, and difficult-to-understand products directly to customers with mainframe computers. Some software firms may bundle their software products with another firms' hardware and sell the whole package as an integrated system to a customer.

In the low-end or personal computer market, software firms may develop relationships with hardware manufacturers to preload their products on PCs or other devices. Firms can also sell their products directly via the Internet and via more traditional distribution channels such as mail-order catalogs, retail stores, and specialty retailers such as Best Buy or mass merchandisers such as Wal-Mart Stores.

Of the supporting activities in the software value chain, R&D and human resources are critical, given the need for talented developers to create new products and enhance existing products, and the difficulty of hiring and retaining these developers. Chapter 5 describes the occupations and workforce issues and trends in the software industry.

The software value chain depicts the software production process. In terms of revenues, the traditional revenue streams of software companies include license revenues, maintenance revenues, and service revenues. Recently, some companies have bundled license and maintenance services, selling them on a subscription basis.

License revenue derives from sales of individual copies of software. It is considered a key indicator of demand for a firm's core software products.[28] Traditionally, the licenses are perpetual because a customer acquires rights to the product for its entire life when purchasing the software. However, in recent years, other innovative licensing schemes have emerged. Chapter 7 will discuss some of the new business models for selling or renting software to customers. For example, subscription revenues are gaining in importance in the software industry. Under a subscription business model, rather than selling software products individually, a software company sells periodic (monthly or yearly or seasonal) use or access to the product. The subscription business model was pioneered by magazines and newspapers. It is an attractive model for software companies because a one-time sale of a software product can be transformed to a recurring sale and can build brand loyalty. For customers, subscriptions can be attractive because they provide more flexibility by offering pricing that varies based on usage—such as number of users or over a certain time period of use.

Maintenance revenues are typically sold via contract and provide the customer with upgrades and enhancements for the relevant software products.

Service revenue derives from the various services that a company provides to software customers, such as consulting, training, support, and integration. Like maintenance, such services are typically provided via a contract. As described in Chapter 4 on the globalization of the software industry, services have become increasingly important to software companies. As software becomes more complex and sophisticated and critical to global operations, there is a greater demand for services. Service revenues are thus becoming a larger percentage of total revenues in the software industry. As noted in Chapter 1, Forrester Research has projected that in 2013, custom software development services will account for six percent of the total revenues in the information technology industry. In addition to software-related services, IT facilities outsourcing, maintenance, consulting, and integration services are projected to account for 40 percent of the total revenues in the IT industry in 2013.[29]

In terms of profitability, the software industry is highly profitable when compared to other industries, with gross margins as much as 80 percent.[30] This is because, although the cost to develop a product is significant, the variable cost of reproducing, documenting, packaging, and distributing a software product is relatively small.[31] The highest margins are on licenses for new software; gross margins for maintenance and especially for software services are considerably lower, as training, consulting, implementation, support, and other services are quite labor intensive and require highly skilled individuals to perform them.

# The Economics of Software

There are a number of unique aspects of the economics of the software industry that directly affect its structure and competitive dynamics.

First, it is important to understand pricing dynamics of software products and services. The size of the computer system for which a software application is designed is a critical factor affecting price. Software applications for high-end or mainframe computer systems typically have a greater degree of customization, low unit volume, long product life cycles, and very high maintenance costs; these applications tend to be quite expensive, ranging in price from the thousands to millions of dollars (such as for enterprise software). Such software is often licensed or leased rather than sold. In contrast, software applications intended for low-end personal computer systems and mobile devices typically have less customization, high unit volume, short product cycles, and low maintenance costs; these applications tend to be inexpensive, ranging in price from free to hundreds of dollars.

Second, it is important to understand the cost dynamics of producing software products and services. As just noted, in the software business, there are very high fixed costs of R&D and marketing, but very low costs to replicate, document, package, and distribute a particular software product. For example, N2 Research estimates the average price of creating a new video game at close to $28 million, with some video games such as Gran Turismo and Modern Warfare costing twice as much to develop.[32] However, once the original software code for these games has been written, it may cost only a few dollars each to make copies or close to nothing to distribute the video games over the Internet.

Such cost dynamics can be characterized in terms of economies of scale. *Economies of scale* is an economic term describing a business model in which it costs a company less to produce each product the more it produces and sells. Technically, it refers to a situation in which the long-run average cost curve for producing something declines as production increases as there are low marginal costs to replicate and distribute the product relative to average costs to produce the first copy. Economies of scale are certainly present and are very powerful in the software industry,[33] and these economies affect the structure of the industry. One consequence is that the cost dynamics can lead to market concentration as it is most efficient for one or a few large firms to dominate the industry. Naturally, this can raise questions of monopoly. Chapter 6 discusses legal actions taken by the United States and European governments to restrain the monopolistic power of large software firms like Microsoft.

A second important cost aspect of the software industry has to do with *compatibility*, standards, and network effects. When two products can communicate with each other or can be used with the same complementary components, they are compatible. In the world of software, compatibility exists when software products—such as a spreadsheet program and a word processing program—can exchange or share files in a common format. It also exists when a particular software application can run on a particular operating system.

Compatibility may be achieved through standardization or by developing adapters or converters that can translate between incompatible parts.[34] *Standardization* means that there is an explicit or an implicit agreement to do certain things in a certain way. In software, standards for file formats, user interface designs, or other interfaces are critical for ensuring compatibility between products. Application programming interfaces specify how software components should interact with each other. *POSIX* is an example of an international standard for maintaining compatibility between operating systems.[35]

Compatibility and network effects (or externalities) are critical dimensions of software industry structure and conduct. *Network effects* refer to the effects that one consumer of a good or service has on the value of that product to other people. A product that has network effects is more valuable to consumers when more consumers purchase it. A classic example is the telephone: Having a telephone is more valuable to a consumer when there are more consumers with a compatible telephone whom the consumer wishes to call.

In the world of software, network effects or externalities can occur because a single piece of software is usually not valuable by itself—it typically must be used with other software, hardware, and services. For example, a spreadsheet application requires an operating system to work. Network effects can also arise when different software products are compatible such that the users can share information and files. For example, a file created by one user's spreadsheet application can be shared with another user's compatible application.[36]

The *installed base* is the set of consumers who have installed and use a particular product. Consumers who have adopted a particular product may be reluctant to switch to another product, due to costs of learning. This behavior favors the incumbent product. Because a community or network of users values the ability to share and exchange files and documents, new users also tend to adopt the software with the largest community of users—this again favors the incumbent or most popular product to the detriment of its competitors. Switching costs and network externalities can cause the market to tip to a single dominant vendor or technology for a particular software genre.[37] The tendency for a single product to dominate a software genre is a notable feature of the software industry.

These dynamics have a number of implications for the industry. For example, in the spreadsheet software market, findings from a study of this market reveal that:

1. Positive externality effects deriving from a software product's large installed base and compatibility with a dominant standard are as important as the product's intrinsic features.[38]
2. Compatibility decisions are critical and impact the success of a new product in the software industry.
3. It is valuable for a software company to build up its installed base quickly to increase the benefits of externalities and to leverage on the inertial effects of switching costs.
4. The value of complementary goods can increase positive network externalities for a software product—for example, the ability to exchange files between Windows-compatible word processing and spreadsheet software is valuable to consumers and may tie them to the supporting platform.

The economic aspects of software thus directly impact the competitive dynamics and strategies of companies in the industry.

## Competitive Forces and Strategies in the Software Industry

In the final section of this chapter, the competitive dynamics in the software industry are analyzed. Michael Porter's Five Forces Model is used to

**Threat of new entry**

- Economies of scale
- Proprietary product differences
- Brand identity
- Switching costs
- Capital requirements
- Access to distribution
- Absolute cost advantages
- Government policy
- Expected retaliation

**Bargaining Power of suppliers**

- Differentiation of inputs
- Switching costs
- Presence of substitute inputs
- Supplier concentration
- Importance of volume to supplier
- Cost relative to total purchases
- Impact of inputs on cost or differentiation
- Threat of forward integration

**Rivalry among existing competitors**

- Industry growth
- Fixed costs/value added
- Overcapacity
- Product differences
- Brand identity
- Switching costs
- Concentration and balance
- Informational complexity
- Diversity of competitors
- Corporate stakes
- Exit barriers

**Bargaining power of customers**

- Buyer concentration
- Buyer volume
- Buyer switching costs
- Buyer information
- Ability to integrate backward
- Substitute products
- Price/total purchases
- Product differences
- Brand identity
- Impact of quality/ performance
- Buyer profits

**Threat of substitutes**

- Relative price performance of substitutes
- Switching costs
- Buyer propensity to substitute

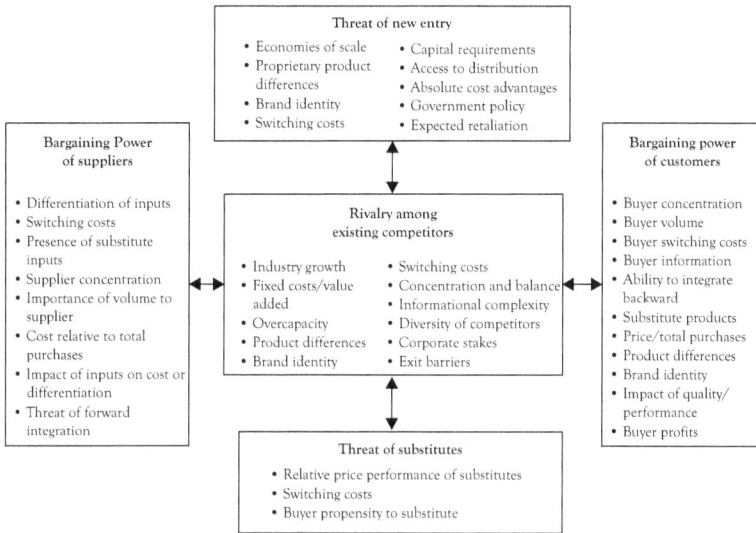

*Figure 3.5 Porter's Five Forces Model*

Source: Adapted with permission from Porter (1985)

understand the competitive forces in the software industry.[39] According to Porter's model, the nature and intensity of competition in an industry is influenced by five important forces: threat of new entry, threat of substitutes, rivalry among existing competitors, bargaining power of customers, and bargaining power of suppliers.

Figure 3.5 shows a graphical depiction of these forces. Examining the software industry from the perspective of the Five Forces Model suggests the following about the nature of the industry.

## Threat of New Entry

One important force that determines competition in an industry is the threat of new entry. Industries that are dynamic have many new entrants. New companies entering an industry bring new products, resources, and capacity and can bid down prices or inflate costs affecting profitability in the industry. The ease of entry into an industry is determined by the nature of incumbent firms (e.g., whether the firms are large and well established with well-known brands) and whether there are barriers to entry such as the need to invest large financial resources in order to compete, the presence of economies of scale, and switching costs. Switching costs are one-time costs of switching from one firm's product to another's. If switching costs are high, a new entrant must offer a substantial improvement in product quality or cost to induce customers to switch. Proprietary technologies that are kept proprietary through patents can also erect a high barrier to entry.

Essentially, if it costs little in time or money to enter an industry and compete, if there are few scale economies, low switching costs or little protection for intellectual property, it is easy for a new company to enter an industry.

In the software industry, the nature of entry barriers is mixed. On the one hand, there are limited financial resources required to create a new software product—as noted earlier in the chapter, almost any talented individual with a computer can create a popular software application. For example, an eighth grader created a physics-based puzzle game Bubble Ball for the iPhone, in one month. Bubble Ball became so popular that it knocked Angry Birds from the top spot on Apple's free app chart after being released; the game has over two million downloads.[40]

However, creating a software product and making money from it are two different things! As also noted earlier, firms in the software industry spend considerable resources on R&D and advertising and marketing their products. There are quite significant economies of scale, favoring large producers, and switching costs can be high as customers can be reluctant to switch from one firm's products to another's.

Software firms producing mature products like basic desktop applications (such as word processing, spreadsheets, and databases) or enterprise software (such as customer relationship management systems or enterprise resource planning systems) usually form an oligopoly market where there are a few well-established software firms such as Microsoft, SAP, and Oracle that dominate the market. As noted earlier, Microsoft is by far the largest software company in the world, accounting for more than 17 percent of global software revenues. Firms such as Microsoft are entrenched in the desktop application segment and have large installed bases of customers who may be reluctant to switch to a competing product.

Even if a new firm's product is superior, the established firm can upgrade and enhance its product to match the features. In addition, customers may believe that an established firm is likely to remain in business, whereas a software start-up might fail, leaving customers with product enhancement and support problems. For all of these reasons, it can be challenging for new entrants to compete with established firms in the more mature segments of the software industry. However, new software firms can thrive in new segments.

In addition, established software firms are increasingly relying on software patents to protect important intellectual property and are using patents to prevent competitors from entering or competing in a market segment. Chapter 6 discusses the nature and role of software patents in the software industry.

## Rivalry Between Existing Competitors

An industry in which there is intense rivalry among competing firms experiences significant price competition, advertising battles, frequent product introductions, and increased customer service offerings or warranties. Competitors feel pressure or see opportunities to improve their position. When one firm makes a competitive move, it may incite corresponding moves by other firms to retaliate. Industries with many competitors have high degrees of rivalry. In contrast, industries with a few dominant firms may be more stable as power is concentrated in a few leaders. Certain characteristics of an industry increase rivalry: slow growth, high fixed costs, commodity products, foreign competitors, and high exit barriers.

Essentially, rivalry in an industry is determined by the number and capability of the competing firms. If there are many competitors who offer equally attractive products and services, then firms have little power, because suppliers and buyers will go elsewhere if they don't get a good bargain.

In the software industry, rivalry increases or decreases with the maturity of particular market segments. When a market segment is new—such as the market for personal computer software in the 1970s and 1980s, there are many competing firms and there is intense jockeying for position. However, the nature of software economics (which favors large firms who can benefit from economies of scale) eventually leads to dominance of one or a few firms in a segment for a mature software product.

### Threat of Substitutes

Substitutes refer to the ability of customers to find a different alternative for a firm's product or service. For example, high-fructose corn syrup is a substitute for sugar. Substitutes place a limit on the prices that firms in an industry can charge and thus limit the profit potential of the industry. If substitution is easy and viable, then the competitive power of firms in the industry is weakened.

In the software industry, the threat of substitutes, per se, may be less salient than in other industries. As noted, switching costs are relatively high, as customers are reluctant to switch from one firm's product to another's due to the high costs of implementation, training, and learning a new software system.

There is also no easy substitute product for software. Computer hardware is largely a commodity, and customers may use various different types of products (e.g., mobile phone, tablet, laptop) to accomplish the same tasks. A mobile phone, for example, may be a substitute product for a laptop computer. For software, an alternative may be to accomplish a task manually—but this may not be a realistic substitute for many customers! Therefore, one may argue that the threat of substitute products is relatively low in the software industry.

### Bargaining Power of Buyers

Customers can be a powerful competitive force because they can bid down prices, demand higher quality or better services, or play off competing firms against one another. This comes at the expense of industry profitability. Generally, when the number of buyers is large, as a group, buyers will have more power. In addition, buyers who purchase large volumes or a significant fraction of total purchases will have higher power. On the other hand, switching costs can mitigate buyer power. When a product is customized to a buyer's needs or deeply integrated into the buyer's industry, the buyer is locked in, and it is more difficult for the buyer to switch to another firm's products.

In sum, buyer power reflects the ease with which buyers can drive down prices. This is driven by the number of buyers, the importance of each individual buyer to the business, the cost to switch from one firm's products and services to those of another. If firms in the industry deal with a few, powerful buyers, then the buyers are often able to dictate terms.

In the software industry, the bargaining power of buyers is mixed. In some segments of the industry (such as enterprise software) there are significant switching costs and also relatively high customization of products to end users, but large companies purchase this type of software and that may give them some leverage in negotiating pricing. In other segments of the industry (such as mobile phone apps or personal computer software) there are many small customers who can easily download alternative apps that are compatible with their particular device, so the software firms producing such apps often make them freely available, and tie the apps to a particular platform.

Many consumers, firms, and industries buy software products. Most customers, except for gaming software, are business, finance, and production companies. Gaming, enterprise, and security software products are also purchased by end users for personal use or for business use. Financial institutions (banks and investment services firms) are the largest customer segment for the software industry, accounting for an estimated 30 percent of software revenues. Figure 3.6 shows the top industries that are customers of the software industry.[41]

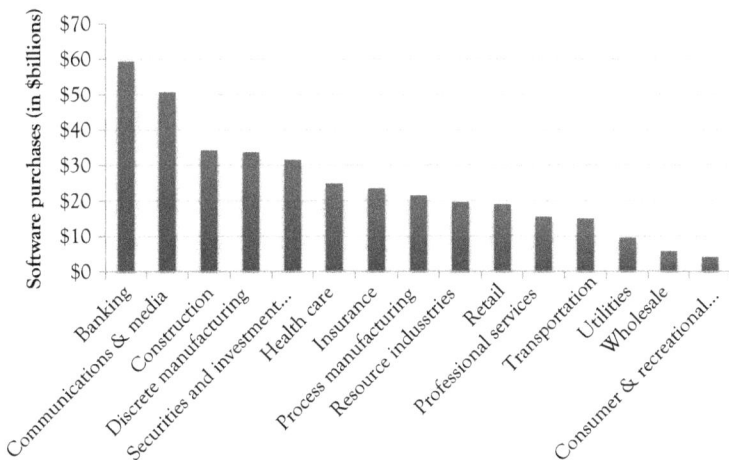

*Figure 3.6  Top customers of the software industry*

Source: Based on data from the Business Software Alliance (2009).

## Bargaining Power of Suppliers

Suppliers can be a powerful force in an industry. They can raise prices or reduce the quality of the goods or services they sell to the producing firms. Such actions can reduce profitability from an industry. Generally, suppliers are more powerful when the supplier group is dominated by a few companies and is more concentrated than the industry to which it sells. In addition, if there is product differentiation and high switching costs, buyers cannot play one supplier against another, and supplier power is higher. On the other hand, if there are substitute products, then supplier power is lower.

In essence, supplier power is a function of how easy it is for suppliers to drive up prices. This is influenced by the number of suppliers of each key input, the uniqueness of their product or service, their strength and control over the producing firms, and the cost of switching from one to another. The fewer supplier choices there are, and the more dependence on suppliers, the more powerful they are.

To assess the power of suppliers in the software industry, it is helpful to review the software value chain presented earlier in the chapter. As illustrated in the value chain, software firms can provide software applications and/or one or more of the supporting activities in the value chain. Thus, in some cases, one supplier could be providing a particular software application, another supplier could provide documentation and yet another could provide marketing, sales, and distribution services. The primary firm could act as a system integrator to integrate these different products and services into one offering for a customer. Many of the major software firms provide all of the products and services in the value chain; however, smaller firms may provide only one piece.

In addition to partnerships and mergers, strategic alliances are a way that suppliers can work together to provide an integrated set of products and services. A strategic alliance is "an agreement between firms to do business together in ways that go beyond normal company-to-company dealings but fall short of a merger or a full partnership."[42] Alliances can range from informal agreements to formal contractual arrangements or joint ventures. In the software industry, strategic alliances can be formed to produce software, software services, or both. For example, a strategic alliance was formed between Apple, Sony, Motorola, Philips, AT&T, and Matsushita to develop Telescript communications software.[43] In the software services area, an example is Cisco's Collaboration Alliance and Partnering Ecosystem program in which Cisco partners with companies such as IBM, Microsoft, and Accenture to provide a range of consulting, resale, outsourcing, services, and technology integration that offer customers a comprehensive collaboration strategy.[44] To the extent that such partnerships, mergers and alliances are successful, supplier power in the software industry is strengthened.

A significant transformation of the value chain that has affected supplier power in the software industry stems from the Internet. The Internet has emerged as a major computing and communications platform in the software industry. The Internet is becoming the primary distribution channel for software as it is relatively easy for customers to download the products from the producing firms or from online retailers. This has significantly reduced the power of brick and mortar suppliers such as Best Buy who have traditionally provided outlets for physical distribution of software products. According to Standard and Poor's, online distribution will increasingly dominate software sales, suggesting that the power of physical distributors will continue to weaken.[45] Examples of software firms who rely on online distribution for their products include McAfee and Symantec.

Based on this discussion, Figure 3.7 summarizes the competitive forces for the software industry.

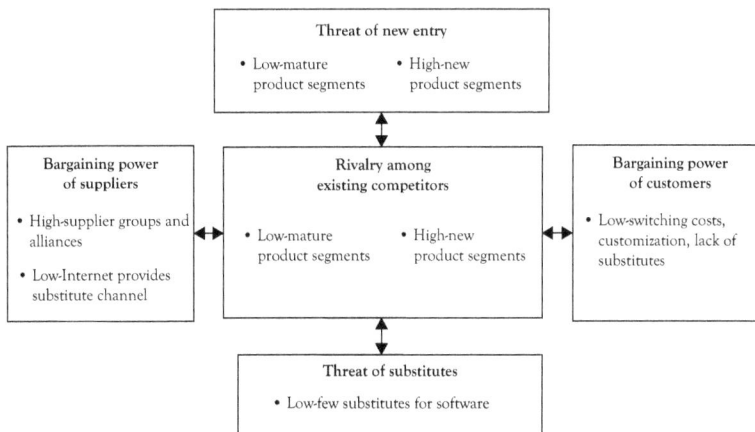

*Figure 3.7 Competitive forces in the software industry*

Source: Adapted with permission from Porter (1985).

## Key Takeaways

The software industry is highly dynamic and fluid with many entries and exits. Partnering, strategic alliances, and mergers and acquisitions are popular. Software firms produce applications software and systems software and provide software services. There are different subsegments in these markets that are more or less mature. In newer technology segments, competition can be intense with fierce jockeying for position. However, in more mature technology segments, one or a few firms dominate and it is very difficult for new firms to compete.

The software industry has some unique economics that affect its structure. The costs to develop and market new products are quite significant, and software firms spend large amounts on R&D, advertising, and marketing. But, once the products are developed, the costs to reproduce and distribute them are negligible, particularly with the Internet as a growing distribution channel. In addition, software markets are characterized by switching costs, network effects, and economies of scale. All of these factors lead to the tendency for a single product and firm to dominate a software market segment.

Competitive forces in the software industry are varied—although it is relatively easy to create a new product, it can be very difficult for a new firm to compete with that product in a software market that is mature with an entrenched incumbent. Most opportunities for new firms are in new segments for new technologies. Buyers span many industries and vary considerably in size from major institutions that purchase large enterprise systems to individual consumers who download apps. Suppliers are increasingly forming partnerships and alliances to offer an integrated solution (software and services) to customers. The Internet is transforming the software industry, sparking the creation of new types of applications and new processes for software development, and is changing the nature of software product and service distribution as online distribution of software is displacing physical distribution outlets.

In sum, the software industry is innovative, dynamic, competitive, and quickly evolving and may naturally tend to monopoly or oligopoly in mature market segments given its unique economics. The next chapter explores the globalization of the software industry.

# CHAPTER 4

# Globalization of the Software Industry

Historically, the United States has dominated the software industry. Government support for the computer hardware and software industries and programs from the U.S. Department of Defense and NASA as well as the SAGE project in the 1950s and 1960s were critical in creating a domestic market for software on a large scale.[1] The United States had a first mover advantage as the diffusion of computers in the United States was years ahead of that in Europe and in other parts of the world. In addition, the size of the U.S. domestic market for packaged software was more than 20 times larger than that of any other country.[2] This gave U.S. firms an edge in producing software products that could be sold on a mass scale. Finally, U.S. firms benefited from widespread use of the English language. Firms in smaller countries, such as Japan, may have been at a disadvantage as Japanese was not widely spoken and the firms did not have an abundance of skilled personnel versed in foreign languages and practices to develop software for export.[3] In the 1970s and 1980s, major U.S. packaged software firms not only sold their products in the United States but also developed marketing operations in Europe or sold under license in Japan. U.S.-based firms produced more than 80 percent of the world's software products, and almost all of the top 20 software suppliers were based in the United States.[4]

However, in the 1990s and 2000s, the phenomenon of outsourcing emerged, and it has been changing the global dynamics of the software industry. Outsourcing is the process of contracting out some or all of the information technology function (i.e., software development and management of the IT infrastructure of computer hardware, systems, data, and telecommunications). Prior to the 1990s, many U.S. firms had developed their own customized computer systems internally. However, this

approach grew increasingly costly as skilled IT labor became more difficult to find. Therefore, firms moved more and more to packaged software
applications. In addition, the demand for skilled programmers increased
dramatically with the emergence of the Internet and the demand for
ecommerce applications in the 1990s as well as the need to address the
Y2K problem, and the demand exceeded the capacity of the IT labor
market in the United States.

As a result, outsourcing took on a global dimension and became
offshoring—the outsourcing of software development and other services
to countries outside the United States, often to software services firms
in emerging economies such as India, Ireland, and Russia. Improved
data communications and the number and quality of software professionals in these countries, combined with their relatively low labor rates
(i.e., salaries at 1/5 to 1/10 of those of U.S. developers)[5] made these countries attractive destinations for software development. As described in the
next section, major IT service providers emerged in these countries to
meet this demand.

Today, the software industry has become truly global. As shown in the
list of top firms in the software industry in Table 3.1, most large software
firms are headquartered in the United States, but non-U.S. software firms
are on the rise. SAP (which is among the top five largest software firms
in the world) is a German firm. Major software and computing firms are
in France and Japan. The outsourcing and offshoring of software development has also led to the rise of software services industries in emerging
economies such as in India, Ireland, Brazil, Mexico, China, Israel, and
Russia. Given the lower labor costs and availability of skilled software
developers in these emerging economies, it is not surprising that significant growth in the software industry has occurred outside the United
States. India, for example, has numerous large software development
and services companies (such as Infosys, Wipro, and Tata Consulting
Services).

It is also increasingly common for U.S.-based software firms to create offshore software development centers or overseas software Research
and Development (R&D) centers. For example, Microsoft has set up
offshore software development centers in India, China, Israel, and the
United Kingdom[6] and Adobe performs its software development R&D

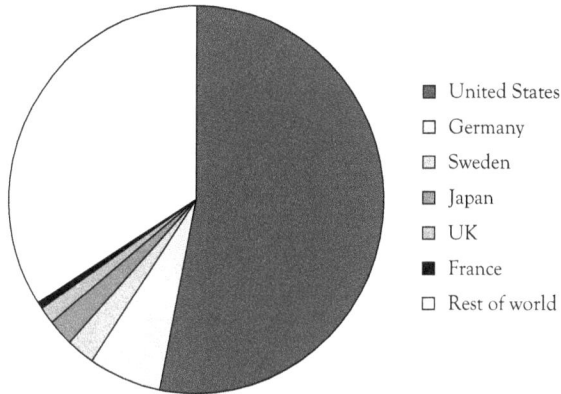

*Figure 4.1  Percentage of global sales of packaged software by country*

Sources: PwC (2013) and Gale Group (2013a).

in the United States, Canada, Germany, Japan, and India.[7] IT services firms such as IBM and Hewlett-Packard have long had a global presence.

Figure 4.1 shows the global revenues from sales of software products by the top countries.[8] As can be seen in this figure, the United States accounted for just over half (53 percent) of the global revenues from software products (considerably smaller than its historical percentage), followed by Germany at six percent, Sweden at three percent,[9] Japan at two percent, the United Kingdom and France each at one percent, and the rest of the world at 32 percent.

## The Software Industry in Key Countries in Europe, Africa and the Middle East, Australasia, and Latin America

Figure 4.2 shows the location of a number of significant countries in the global software industry. Specific countries were sampled because they currently have (or are growing to have) significant market share in the global software industry. In an effort to be globally representative, several countries were selected from each major region in the world (except Antarctica which currently does not have a software industry!). The next sections present profiles of the software industries in countries organized by major region, in the following sequence: Europe—Germany, France,

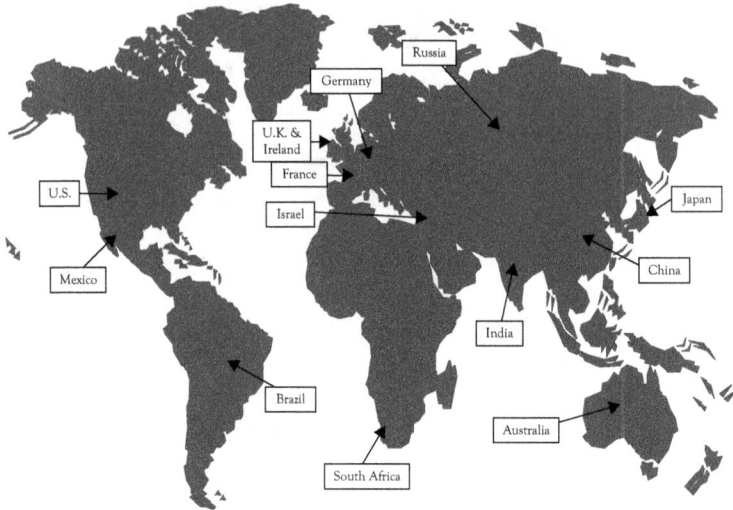

*Figure 4.2  Selected countries in the global software industry*

United Kingdom, and Ireland; Africa and the Middle East—Israel and South Africa; Australasia—Russia, China, Japan, India, and Australia; and Latin America—Brazil and Mexico.

A few software firms in each country are also profiled. The specific software firms were selected for a variety of reasons: 1) they are significant in terms of contribution to software products or software services revenues; 2) they are significant for the history of the software industry in the country, or 3) they represent an important or growing segment of the software industry in the country.

### Europe

There are a number of countries in Europe that are included in the top echelon in the world in terms of software revenues.[10] Of these, Germany, France, United Kingdom, and Ireland are profiled below.

### Germany

German companies dominate the European software market and accounted for 48 percent of the European software revenues in 2012.[11] Four of the top 10 software firms in Europe are based in Germany, and the German software firm SAP (profiled below) accounts for more than one-third of all software revenues in the European continent.[12]

As in the United States, the German software industry got its start after IBM's unbundling decision, although it did not go into effect in Germany until 1972.[13] There were relatively few software firms at first in the German industry, although the 1970s saw the emergence of key firms, notably SAP in 1972. Most software firms in the German industry were national. Microsoft and Oracle started to have more influence in the German market in the 1980s. Auditing and consulting firms, such as Arthur Andersen, also became more prevalent in Germany. In the 1990s, U.S. firms acquired major German software firms. For example, EDS acquired the oldest German software company (MBP) in 1993, and CSC acquired a German firm called The EDVStudio Plönzke, in 1994.[14]

By 2003, Germany was the second leading software market world-wide and was valued at U.S. $18.75 billion.[15] The German software industry grew about four percent in 2004 with an increased demand for security software. The industry remained highly fragmented in the early 2000s, with the top 25 companies controlling about 40 percent of the software market, although the industry was consolidating. Many software products were still imported from the United States and sold through German-based subsidiaries. Of the total German software market, net-working software sales were about U.S. $1.6 billion in 2003, PC business software sales were U.S. $2.2 billion, and multimedia software sales were about U.S. $1.6 billion.[16] Products such as Internet browsers and e-mail software were the primary areas of growth in the PC business software sector, whereas software for commercial use dominated sales in the mul-timedia sector.[17]

The rise of the Internet and e-commerce has inspired a more dynamic German software industry today with many German start-up firms entering the industry. Federal German states, such as Bavaria, Frankfurt, Hamburg, and Berlin provide special subsidies for IT companies, and universities support current and former students who create start-up firms.[18] The Technical University at Munich, for example provides an incubator for new software start-ups.[19] In contrast to founders of the U.S. software start-ups, founders of Germany's software start-ups not only have advanced degrees but also have worked on average for more than

17 years, 11 of which they have spent in the industry in which they go on to start their firm.[20] The average age of a German start-up founder is 38 years—considerably older than in the United States. Perhaps as a result, German start-ups have a high success rate: 60 percent are still in the market, 5 years after their founding.[21]

German firms SAP and Siemens are among the top 30 firms in the world producing software today, and a brief profile of each company follows.

## SAP

SAP was founded in 1972 by five former employees of IBM Germany and is headquartered in Walldorf, Germany. The employees were working on developing an enterprise-wide system when IBM canceled the project, and they decided to leave IBM and start their own company—SAP. SAP in German is Systeme, Anwendungen, Produkte (Systems, Applications, Products).[22] SAP's primary products are enterprise resource planning (ERP) applications and enterprise data warehouse software products. The products provide software applications for business areas, such as accounting, manufacturing, and Human Resources (HR) that are highly integrated with each other. The unique value of SAP's enterprise products is to provide a single solution to integrating business operations. In contrast to IBM systems, the SAP applications store data locally. For this reason, the applications were called real-time software, designated with an "R" in the name (i.e., SAP R/1).

The firms' founders started the company without loans or venture capital and built it up from cash flow from German customers. The product evolved from a mainframe-based (SAP R/2) to client–server architecture (SAP R/3) in the 1980s and 1990s. The firm was publicly traded in Germany in the late 1980s and in the United States in 2003. By 2005, SAP was the world's third largest independent software supplier and the largest provider of enterprise software products. In 2010, SAP reported 52,921 employees and over 105,000 customers in more than 120 countries.[23] As shown in Table 3.1, SAP is fourth in rank among the top 30 global software producers with revenues of almost U.S. $17 billion in 2012.

One other interesting aspect of SAP concerns its lawsuit with Oracle. In November 2010, SAP lost a $1.3 billion intellectual property lawsuit (deriving from actions of the SAP subsidiary TomorrowNow) to Oracle. This verdict was one of the largest software intellectual property judgments in history. However, SAP filed post-trial motions to lower the damage awarded to Oracle, and in September 2011, the verdict was overturned.[24]

Battles over intellectual property are numerous and intense in the software industry, and Chapter 6 discusses intellectual property issues.

### Siemens

Siemens is an engineering and electronics conglomerate headquartered in Munich and Berlin, Germany. It is the largest Europe-based electronics and electrical engineering firm and produces a wide range of products including buildings-related products; drives, automation, and industrial plant-related products; energy-related products; lighting; medical products; and transportation and logistics-related products. Siemens employs 370,000 people across 190 countries and reported global revenues of U.S. $102 billion for the year of 2012.[25] The firm has a venerable history: It was founded by Werner von Siemens in 1847 who invented a technology based on the telegraph.[26] However, over the years the firm has become involved in a number of controversies, such as reports that it provided electrical parts and forced labor to concentration camps in World War II and more recent claims of bribery and illegal financing.[27]

Although Siemens is primarily an electronics and automation firm, it does produce software for manufacturing automation. Its former subsidiary—Siemens Business Services (SBS)—produces software and software services (such as a major outsourcing deal with the BBC in the UK)[28] on a global scale. Today, SBS is part of a joint venture with a firm called Atos Origin. Siemens IT Solutions and Services (SIS) was formed in 2007 from the merger of SBS (Germany), Program and System Engineering (Austria), Siemens Information Ltd (India), Business Innovation Center (Switzerland), and Development Innovations and Projects (Greece). In December 2010, it was announced that Atos Origin would form a strategic partnership with Siemens AG. The deal concluded in July 2011, where Siemens contributed its SIS to Atos Origin in order to create a European IT branch. Siemens is a shareholder of Atos Origin with a 15 percent stake.[29]

As shown in Table 3.1, Siemens is 16th in rank among the top 30 global software producers with $2.5 billion in software sales in 2012.

## France

Like in other countries in Europe, most firms in the French software industry are national. However, although the packaged software industry in France is dominated by exports from the United States (as much as 70 percent of the packaged software used in France is imported from the United States), there are several notable French software products and services firms. By and large, the software developed in France is created primarily for the domestic aeronautics, finance, defense, and manufacturing industries.[30]

According to Truffle Capital (a venture capital firm that rates the top software firms in Europe), in 2012, 17 of the top 100 European software firms were headquartered in France, and software product sales from these firms generated more than U.S. $5.3 billion.[31] Despite the uncertain economic climate in Europe, the European software industry as a whole has been growing. In France, the software industry grew at a rate of about five percent in the 2000s and more than 30,000 people were employed in the industry in 2005.[32] However, in 2008, several leading French national software firms were acquired by foreign companies, and as a result, revenues of the top 100 software firms in France fell some 13.2 percent.[33] There is concern in France about the ability of French software firms to remain viable in light of strong competition from the United States and emerging economies. According to Laurent Calot, CEO of CXP Group, the French software industry is facing significant challenges such as a new tax on capital gains and a complex and uncertain business climate.[34]

Two of the top French firms in the global software industry—Cap Gemini (a software services firm) and Dassault Systèmes (a software products firm) are profiled below.

*Cap Gemini*

Cap Gemini S.A. is a French multinational corporation headquartered in Paris, France. The company provides information technology services, including programming, software design, data processing, management, and outsourcing services.

The firm was founded by Serge Kampf in 1967 to provide enterprise management and data processing services.[35] The firm's original name was Sogeti, which was an acronym for "Société de Gestion des Entrepriseset de Traitement de l'Information" or "Society of Business Administration and Information Processing." In 1973 and 1974, the firm acquired CAP (its major European competitor) and a U.S. company by the name of Gemini Computer Systems, and in 1975, renamed itself CAP Gemini Sogeti.[36] In 1996 the firm dropped Sogeti from its name (Sogeti is today a wholly owned subsidiary). The firm made numerous acquisitions over the years, acquiring companies in Europe and in the United States, such as Ernst & Young Consulting in 2000.[37] It has also acquired computing and IT consulting companies in Brazil, China, and India.

Today, Cap Gemini is one of the world's largest IT and professional services companies with U.S. $13.1 billion in revenues, and 120,000 employees in 40 countries.[38] Its main business is technology services, including custom application development and systems integration for its customers. Its other primary business line includes management of IT systems and their associated business processes for applications and infra-structures of customers. These two lines of business together generated more than 80 percent of the firm's revenues in 2012.[39]

*Dassault Systèmes*

Dassault Systèmes is a French software company, headquartered in the suburbs of Paris and is a subsidiary of a large conglomerate (Dassault Group).The firm produces three-dimensional design and product line management software that supports industrial processes by providing a 3D perspective of product lifecycles from inception to maintenance.[40] Its customers range across diverse industries such as aerospace, life sci-ences, engineering, energy, transportation, consumer goods, and financial services.

The firm and its primary software product have an interesting history. The firm's origins can be traced to the avionics industry and an aircraft manufacturing company created by Marcell Dassault in the first part of the 20th century. Marcell Dassault (born Marcell Bloch) invented an aircraft propeller that was used by the French army during World War I. In World War II, after refusing to collaborate with the German aviation industry, and of Jewish heritage, Dassault was deported to the Buchenwald concentration camp. He survived the camp and changed his name in 1949 to Dassault (meaning battle tank—a code name used by his brother who was a general in the French resistance). After the war, Dassault went on to build the aircraft manufacturing company, Avions Marcell Dassault. The firm is now the *Groupe Industriel Marcel Dassault* (or Dassault Group), and its CEO is Serge Dassault, Marcel's son.[41]

In 1977, 15 engineers from Avions Marcel Dassault developed a 3D computer-aided design software—called Computer Aided Three-dimensional Interactive Application (CATIA)—for the aircraft building process.[42] CATIA was revolutionary in that it enabled the full integration of design, analysis and simulation, and manufacturing based on a single database, leading to dramatic improvements in cost, cycle time, and quality in aircraft manufacturing.[43] The company quickly realized the potential of the software for other industries, and in 1981, created a new company, called Dassault Systèmes. Initially, the firm struck a deal with IBM to market and sell CATIA and to split the revenues. As the software's popularity grew, IBM eventually became a customer of CATIA. CATIA was first used in aircraft manufacturing but was then deployed in other sectors, such as automotive. The software was renamed PLM (Product Lifecycle Management) in 2002.

Today the firm employs 11,000 and has 34 global R&D labs; it has 170,000 enterprise customers in 140 countries with revenues of U.S. $2.3 billion in 2012.[44] As shown in Table 3.1, the firm is ranked 16th overall among global software producers.

United Kingdom

Although many important innovations in the computing industry came from the United Kingdom (for example, see Chapter 2 for a description of the computing industry's origins in Charles Babbage's Analytical Machine, Ada Lovelace as the first programmer, and Alan Turing and the Turing Machine), the U.K.'s participation in the software industry has lagged that of the United States.

As in other European countries, most of the software companies in the United Kingdom are national. According to Truffle Capital, the United Kingdom ranked second in software revenues in Europe in 2011, with 22 of the top 100 European software firms headquartered in the United Kingdom, and software product sales of more than U.S. $7.2 billion.[45] The U.K. software industry is strong in digital media, Web 2.0, and video game development, and in 2008, had the largest share of venture capital investment in Europe in software firms.[46] However, British software firms have frequently been a target for acquisition by U.S. firms, and the United Kingdom does not have significant initiatives to foster software start-ups, as does, for example, Germany.

The largest British software firm and third largest software firm in Europe—Sage—is profiled below.

### Sage

The Sage Group plc (known as Sage) is a multinational enterprise software firm and is headquartered in Newcastle upon Tyne in the United Kingdom. The firm is the third largest producer of ERP software in the world (behind SAP and Oracle).

The firm was created in 1981 in a local printing works on Newcastle's Quayside. Entrepreneur David Goldman wanted to automate the print estimating process in his business. He worked with a team of Newcastle University students who developed software to manage both print estimating and basic accounting for small businesses.[47] The firm's first product (accounting software called Sage Accounts) was developed by one of the Newcastle University students—Graham Wylie. Sales of the firm's products grew rapidly in the 1980s, and the firm was listed on the London Stock Exchange in 1989. The firm continued to expand in the 1990s, acquiring a British software firm called Tetra, and launched an Irish division in Dublin. Graham Wylie retired in 2003 at age 43, with shares in the firm worth U.S. $228 million.[48]

Today, Sage has over 6 million customers and more than 13,600 employees in 24 countries in Europe, North America, South Africa, Australia, Asia, and Brazil.[49] It provides enterprise software to small and medium-sized firms in a variety of industries such as healthcare, construction, transportation, manufacturing, retailing, and automotive. In 2012, the firm earned U.S. $1.8 billion in revenues and is ranked 24th among the top 30 global software producers.[50]

## Ireland

The software industry in Ireland was born in the 1970s and 1980s and grew substantially in the 1990s due to foreign direct investment from major multinational IT firms and support from the Irish government. The Irish Industrial Development Agency (IDA Ireland) played a major role in the creation of the software industry. The IDA is an Irish government agency that secures new overseas investment in manufacturing and services sectors and that encourages investors to develop and expand their businesses.[51] In the 1980s, the IDA instituted policies to recruit major computer companies from the United States and other countries (such as Apple, Fujitsu, IBM, Microsoft, and Oracle) and convinced them to locate operations in Ireland, by offering the lowest tax rate on manufacturing in Europe (10 percent).[52] Ireland was attractive to multinationals because it was a convenient, low-cost, English-speaking country, and Ireland soon became an offshore platform for access to the rest of Europe.

In 1990, there were 305 software firms registered with the IDA of which only nine had more than 50 employees (and five of those firms were foreign-owned); almost three-fourths of the software firms in Ireland at that time were small, indigenous companies.[53] Most of these firms were located around Dublin.

From 1990 to 2008, the software industry boomed in Ireland. The software sector was one of the most rapidly expanding sectors in Ireland over that time period, and by 2000, Ireland accounted for more than 40 percent of all packaged software and 60 percent of all business software sold in Europe.[54] Ireland was ranked first worldwide in terms of software service exports in 2002.[55] By 2005, there were an estimated 900 software firms (of which 140 were foreign owned), and the Irish software industry was estimated to export more than U.S. $20 billion.[56] Most of the software exports (more than 90 percent) went to Europe, followed by Asia and were in the digital media, systems software, banking and finance, and telecommunications application areas.

Employment in the software sector in Ireland peaked in 2001 at more than 30,000, and today the sector employs just under that number (the IT sector as a whole employs eight percent of the Irish workforce).[57] As the software and IT industry grew, the ability of Ireland to produce the skilled graduates at the rate needed was limited. Labor costs have inevitably risen, and many of the multinationals have relocated to lower cost labor markets. Multinationals that remain in Ireland have moved up the value chain, and recent foreign direct investments (such as by Google and Yahoo) are more strategic than aimed at low cost.

Today, the United States is by far the largest investor in the Irish software industry, as almost half of all U.S. software investment is in Ireland and more than 60 percent of all R&D centers in Ireland are from U.S. companies; 75 percent of all customer help centers in Ireland are for U.S. firms.[58] Of the 250 top exporters from Ireland, Microsoft Ireland ranks first, with more than U.S. $18 billion in software exports from Ireland.[59]

A distinct challenge for Irish-owned software firms is the ability to create the scale needed to be competitive in the global market. Given the small size of the Irish market, indigenous software firms must target entering foreign markets almost from their very beginning. The Irish Software Association currently lists 160 member software firms (of a total 730 indigenous software firms that all together employ over 10,000 people and account for more than U.S. $2.5 billion in annual sales).[60] As in other countries in Europe, indigenous software firms are often acquired by multinationals.

To give a flavor of Irish-owned software firms, two Irish software product firms and one Irish software and business services firm are briefly profiled.[61]

### CR2 Limited

Founded in 1997 and headquartered in Dublin, Ireland, CR2 is the leading global provider of self-service banking software solutions. CR2's primary software product BankWorld enables financial institutions to deliver retail banking services via a variety of channels including ATM, Internet, Mobile, and Kiosk from a single self-service platform. Bank-World provides a consolidated view of a customer's accounts and services across all channels. CR2's software is deployed in 110 financial institutions in 60 countries and four continents, and serves millions of Internet and mobile banking customers.[62]

### CelTech

Headquartered in Dublin, Ireland, CelTech Software International Ltd (or CelTech) was founded in 1992 by a team of IT specialists who were working in the retail industry. The firm's primary software product—called ab initio—is a real-time store, warehouse, and head-office operations management system for high-volume retail and wholesale chain stores, and has processed more than 300 million transactions in the retail industry since 2003.[63] The firm also produces a software product called One for smaller retail chains and independents. Its clients are retailers—such as Blockbuster and Kwik Save—in the United States, Australia, the United Kingdom, and Ireland.

### Conduit

Conduit is one of the largest indigenous Irish companies in the software services industry and provides call center services and solutions.[64] The company designs, develops, and delivers customer contact management systems for different stages of the customer lifecycle. It was founded in 1996 in Dublin and has 1,500 staff in the United Kingdom and Ireland. Its call center handles more than 30,000 transactions per day and serves clients in 15 countries.[65] Some of the company's notable products include the development of an e-mail automation system for Aer Lingus and the introduction of a directory assistance service called 118.com. Conduit operates a directory assistance and information service not only for its own retail brands (11850/118118) but also for some of the world's largest telecommunications companies, such as Orange and Vodafone.[66]

In 2006, Conduit was acquired by a company called INFONXX, now named kgb—a privately held, New York-based company that provides directory assistance and enhanced information services across Europe and North America.

### Africa and Middle East

Although none of the countries in Africa and the Middle East are among the top revenue generators for the global software industry, two countries—Israel and South Africa—are interesting to highlight due to the nature of their software industries and their prominence within the region. These countries are profiled below.

### Israel

The Israeli software industry is unique and differs in important ways from that in many other countries, especially in emerging economies. Like in the United States, the Israeli software industry (and the computing industry in general) benefited from military and government investment. In the 1960s the Israeli government, under critical security threats, decided to focus on science and technology as a basis for Israel's economy. The government supported defense-based R&D activities in the information technology sector, in conjunction with major universities. Like in the United States, the Israeli computer hardware industry developed first. The software industry followed in the late 1970s and 1980s, and yielded prominent software producers such as OptiSystems Solutions (founded in 1982), Magic Software Enterprises (founded in 1983), which created a tool for database applications, and Cimatron (founded in 1982), which created Computer-Aided Design/Computer-Aided Manufacturing (CAD/CAM) software for the tool industry.[67]

The Israeli government provided funding for R&D as well as demand for the products created by the software industry. For example, Magic Software Enterprises was created by a team of former officers of the Israeli military's central computer unit, and the company's first software product was sold to the military.[68]

The Israeli government strongly influenced the development of the software industry and its products. The Office of Chief Scientist (OCS) in the Ministry of Trade and Industry focused on supporting industrial R&D, and its support increased the emphasis on R&D in the Israeli software industry.[69] One other government unit with a strong influence on the software industry was the Bi-national Industrial Research and Development Foundation (BIRD) that was established in 1975 to create development and financing cooperation between Israeli and U.S.-based firms. BIRD was responsible for encouraging U.S. multinationals to establish R&D units in Israel.

Supported by government units like OCS and BIRD, in the 1980s and 1990s, the Israeli software industry grew extensively. Many of the Israeli software firms produced software tools and technologies for the telecommunications industry. In the early 1990s the first Israeli software firms had Initial Public Offering (IPOs) on the National Association of Securities Dealers Automated Quotations (NASDAQ). The number of Israeli software startup firms accelerated in the 1990s peaking at 3,000 per year from 1999 to 2001.[70] Software firms were often founded by new graduates of the military's technological and intelligence units. An example is Checkpoint, founded by three graduates of the military's technology and intelligence units. Checkpoint is a leading firm in creating security software and is profiled below.

The Israeli software industry is closely linked to the U.S. software industry. The expansion of the Israeli software industry required significant venture capital. Government organizations like OCS provided support to create a venture capital industry for software startups. Israeli software entrepreneurs also become successful at attracting funding from venture capitalists in Silicon Valley in the United States, and Israeli software firms created products that were popular in the U.S. market. Organizations such as BIRD were successful in attracting U.S. multinationals like IBM to establish software R&D centers in Israel.

Today, the Israeli software industry is highly successful. Software exports rose more than 400 percent from $1.5 billion in 1998 to $6.2 billion in 2009.[71] Almost 40 years since its start, the industry still reflects its origins with a high level of R&D intensity and a focus on software product innovation, substantial numbers of software startups (many of which launch successful IPOs on NASDAQ) and the ability of Israeli startups to attract venture capital from around the globe. The industry remains closely connected with that in the United States and continues to attract multinationals with Israeli R&D operations such as SAP and Microsoft, who export more than $3 billion annually.[72]

Of the many interesting and successful Israeli software firms, several are profiled here: Amdocs, Checkpoint, and Comverse.

*Amdocs*

Founded in Israel in 1982 as Aurec Information and Directory Systems and currently headquartered in Chesterfield, Missouri, Amdocs provides software and services for communications, media, and entertainment firms. Amdocs had its origins in a team that worked for the Israeli Postal and Telecommunications Ministry. Its first product was a system developed as a joint venture with the company that had the license to organize and sell the telephone directory of Israel.[73] In 1984, the company was acquired by Southwestern Bell.

A key event in the history of the company was the realization by one of its founders—Avinoam Naor—that there was a large market for software products to serve the telecommunications industry. The firm developed a full-service billing and customer care software system, called Ensemble, released to the market in 1995.[74] The introduction of Ensemble was a turning point in transforming the company from a small-sized niche market player to an industry powerhouse ranked among the world's top software companies. As part of its transformation, Aurec Information was restructured into a new holding company, called Amdocs Ltd. Amdocs had its IPO on the New York Stock Exchange in 1998 and has continued innovation of its core products and growth in its markets.

Today, the company's portfolio of software products includes billing systems, customer relationship management (CRM) systems, and operations support systems (OSS), and it is a market leader in the provision of telecommunication billing services to such companies as AT&T, Sprint, BT Telecom, T Mobile, and Comcast.[75] In 2013, Amdocs earned a revenue of $3.3 billion. The firm has a workforce of over 20,000 and serves customers in more than 70 countries worldwide. It retains the bulk of its R&D activity and almost half of its employees in Ra'anana, Israel, where it was founded.

*Checkpoint*

Check Point was established in Ramat-Gan, Israel in 1993, by Gil Shwed, Marius Nacht, and Shlomo Kramer—the three were graduates of the Israeli military's intelligence and technology units. The company's first products were firewalls and virtual private networks. The ideas for these products originated in one of the founders' experiences while serving in the Israel Defense Forces, where he worked on securing classified networks. The firm signed distribution agreements with Sun Microsystems and HP, and by 1996 was the world leader in firewall products with a market share of 40 percent and had its initial IPO on the NASDAQ.[76]

The company has continued to innovate and develop its software product suite. In early 2009, Check Point introduced a novel security innovation product with its Software Blade architecture: an architecture that delivers secure, flexible, and simple solutions that can be fully customized to meet the exact security needs of any organization or environment. The company continues to develop new products today that are based on this architecture. It offers a suite of security products for networks, data, mobile devices, and endpoint applications as well as for security management. The firm also provides ZoneAlarm solutions that protect consumers from hackers, spyware, and identity theft.

The company is currently headquartered in Tel Aviv, Israel, and employs more than 2,700. Its 2012 revenues were $1.3 billion, and it serves more than 100,000 businesses and individual users worldwide.[77]

*Comverse, Inc.*

Comverse, Inc., has an interesting history with numerous ups and downs. The firm was originally founded by investment banker Jacob Alexander, engineer Boaz Misholi, and computer science professor, Yechiam Yemini, in Israel in 1982.[78] In 1984, the team founded Comverse in the United States, calling it Comverse as a fusion of the words communication and versatility. The firm had its IPO on NASDAQ in 1986 and raised $20 million, but soon afterward the founders had major disagreements and split up.[79] By 1987 the company's fortunes went downhill, leaving it a penny stock. However, Alexander remained and eventually turned the company around.

The firm originally specialized in centralized hardware systems for voice and fax messaging and sold the systems to firms in the telecommunications industry. It received significant funding from Israeli government subsidies and tax credits for R&D from the OCS. By 1995, the firm developed one of its most successful products—AudioDisk—which allowed legal authorities and intelligence agencies to record and store data collected from intercepted communications.[80]

By the late 1990s, Comverse's voice messaging software became its main product. The surge in mobile phone use accelerated the sales and growth of the company, and it earned more than $1 billion in revenues by 2000.[81]

Although considered a success story of the Israeli software industry, the firm suffered a significant setback in 2006 when it was involved in an options backdating scandal. Alexander and other top executives of the company were charged in the United States with multiple counts of conspiracy, fraud, money laundering, and making false filings.[82] Alexander fled the country to Namibia where he has since fought extradition and in 2011, he settled the civil charges with the Securities and Exchange Commission (SEC) paying out $53.6 million.[83] The company was delisted from NASDAQ and removed from the S&P 500. Instead of developing new software products, the firm had to spend the next few years restating its financial reports. The firm experienced several rounds of large-scale layoffs and sold off parts of its business.

In 2012, Comverse Technology (its parent company) divested itself of all its holdings and Comverse Network Systems was called just Comverse. The firm earned $680 million in revenues in 2012, and its software products and services are sold to more than 450 telecommunications providers in more than 125 countries. Verizon is its top customer and accounts for about 15 percent of its sales.[84] Comverse has offices in 40 countries and generates most of its revenues in Europe, the Middle East, and Africa.[85] The firm is headquartered in the United States (in Wakefield, Massachusetts), but most of its manufacturing and R&D is performed in Israel. The firm is one of Israel's largest employers of software engineers.

## South Africa

The leading software industry in Africa is located in South Africa. Revenues from sales of software and software-related services by South African firms are projected to reach $2.5 billion by 2014, and the industry is growing at a fast pace—between six to eight percent.[86] South Africa's IT industry is, in fact, the largest in the Africa Middle East region.[87] South Africa is also seen as the gateway to Africa, and its software industry provides services to the rest of Africa.

The software industry in South Africa got its start in the mid-1990s with the first democratic elections in the country and with the liberalization of the telecommunications monopoly. In 1994, the country became a signatory of the General Agreement on Tariffs and Trade (GATT) and has been liberalizing trade and reducing tariffs ever since. These actions, and particularly the breakup of the telecommunications monopoly coupled with government incentives to foster innovation, have helped to stimulate the growth of the software industry. The country has the most developed telecommunications network in Africa (almost 100 percent digital) and its economy is highly Internet-enabled.

The South African government has been subsidizing investments in the software industry in hopes of growing the industry. For example, the government amended the Income Tax Act to stimulate local innovation and create jobs by allowing software development firms to claim back 150 percent of their R&D expenses against tax. As a result, the software industry has grown rapidly, and there are around 1,000 software development firms in South Africa.[88]

Given the availability of skilled and relatively low cost labor, South Africa has also become a popular software offshore destination, especially for business process outsourcing. For example, Microsoft, IBM, Unisys, and other large companies operate subsidiaries in South Africa. In 2010/11, Gartner ranked South Africa among the global top 30 software development outsourcing destinations.[89]

In terms of the structure of its software industry, in 2011, packaged software applications accounted for 41.8 percent of the South African software market, application development and deployment represented 24.8 percent and systems infrastructure software was 33.4 percent of the market.[90] South African firms are world leaders in mobile software and electronic banking services, as well as prepayment, revenue management, and fraud prevention systems and embedded software design. South Africa is known for developing niche applications for specific vertical industries, for example, the mining sector, the financial sector, the government sector, and the mobile communications industry.

Since 2006, the country has fostered the adoption of the Capability Maturity Model Integration (CMMI®) process improvement product suite in its software industry. The Joburg Centre for Software Engineering (JCSE) at Wits University launched a program to bring CMMI® into the South Africa. The JCSE began by training local resources to be able to offer CMMI® consulting and launched a CMMI® pilot with half dozen companies.[91] The South African government has provided funding for training. A number of software companies in the country—especially those offering software and IT services—are in the process of adopting the CMMI®.

Among others, two prominent South African software companies include Dimension Data and Online Innovations.

## Dimension Data

Founded in 1983, Dimension Data is headquartered in South Africa with divisions and operations in 50 countries around the world. The company provides software and IT-related services to over 6,000 clients, including its latest cloud services unit to support its enterprise customers.[92] The company is also a leader in green or sustainable IT services, security services, Microsoft solutions, and other IT-related services. It employs 15,000, and in 2012, earned almost $6 billion in revenues.[93]

The company was acquired in 2010 by Nippon Telephone and Telegraph for more than $3 billion.

## Online Innovations

Online Innovations was founded in 2000 and is based in Port Elizabeth, South Africa.[94] The company provides website solutions including web applications design and development. The company also offers services for eCommerce, Internet Marketing, Social Media, and Search Engine optimization.

The company is small and privately held but is included as one of the top Information and Communications Technology (ICT) companies in South Africa. It serves clients in South Africa, the United Kingdom, the United States, and Europe. One of its prominent projects includes the Nelson Mandela Bay Tourism site.

## Australasia

The Australasia region has many countries with growing software industries. Some of the largest and most prominent software industries in the region—in Russia, China, Japan, India, and Australia—are profiled below.

### Russia

Like the United States, after World War II, Russia possessed relatively sophisticated computer technology. However, in contrast to the United States, Russia did not have the incentives or market structure to deploy and diffuse computing technology into the economy. Thus, there was little commercial development of the military's computing technology.

In the 1960s and 1970s, Russia copied Western designs for computer hardware. Software was custom developed in Russia for the military, but there was still little involvement of commercial firms. In the 1980s PCs began to diffuse, but very slowly. Software development was done for custom military and government applications.[95]

However, the situation changed in the 1990s, and the Russian software industry grew more rapidly. After the end of the Cold War and the dissolution of the former USSR, many trained Russian engineers and technicians were displaced from their employment in military research, and these technically skilled workers provided a ready workforce for the IT industry. PCs began to diffuse more extensively in the domestic economy, software cooperatives, and nongovernment enterprises as well as joint ventures with Western firms took hold and an R&D offshoring model was initiated.[96] By 2000, there was a critical mass of firms providing software outsourcing services to Western companies.

Today, despite having advantages in an abundant, skilled IT workforce whose wages are significantly lower than in Western countries, the IT industry in Russia is still relatively small, compared to for example, India or China. In 2012, the International Data Corporation (IDC) and the Russian Software Developers Association (RUSSSOFT) estimate that the Russian software industry generated U.S. $4 to 5 billion in revenues, of which software development services accounted for U.S. $2.1 billion and software product sales for $1.6 billion.[97]

The Russian software industry consists of three types of firms: firms providing outsourcing services, independent software vendors, and subsidiaries of foreign companies. The following sections profile several of these different types of firms: offshore outsourcing service providers including Auriga, Artezio, and EPAM, and software product firms Kaspersky Labs and Devexperts.

*Auriga*

Auriga is a software R&D and outsourcing services provider that was founded in Moscow, Russia, and has been operating development centers in Russia since 1990.[98] Although software development is done in Russia, the company is incorporated in Wilton, New Hampshire in the United States. The firm provides custom software development and a range of software services for companies in the technology, telecommunications, media, healthcare, and finance industries, among others. The firm has special expertise in embedded systems, real-time applications, and operating systems (such as Linux). It has won numerous awards and recognition, such as being named by Ernst & Young as one of the leading Russian software offshore outsourcing providers.

The company employs over 320 software engineers, operates software development centers in Russia and Lithuania, and earned over U.S. $10 million in revenues in 2012.[99]

*Artezio*

Artezio was established in 2000 in Moscow, Russia, by four software engineers[100]. It is an ISO 9001 certified software development and consulting company that develops software for the telecommunications, financial services, and healthcare sectors. The company provides services ranging from custom software development to software integration and testing services for clients in the United States, United Kingdom, Germany, Switzerland, Japan, Austria, and Russia. In 2012, the firm earned U.S. $10.5 million and employed about 500 people in development centers in Russia, Belarus, and Ukraine.

## Effective Programming for America

Effective Programming for America (EPAM) is one of the largest software services providers in Russia. According to the company history, EPAM was founded in 1993 as a software engineering services company, with its headquarters in a bedroom in New Jersey in the United States (today incorporated in Newtown, Pennsylvania) and its software development center in a bedroom in downtown Minsk, Belarus.[101] The firm targeted emerging software product companies that could not afford anybody else.[102]

The company specializes in complex software product engineering for major software and technology vendors, as well as development, testing, maintenance, and support of mission critical business applications and vertically oriented IT consulting services.

From its humble beginnings, the firm has grown considerably, today employing over 10,000 employees, with 2012 revenues of U.S. $434 million.[103] The firm has development centers in North America and throughout Europe and serves clients around the globe. In 2012, EPAM Systems had its IPO and was listed on the New York Stock Exchange as EPAM. The firm occupies the sixth position on Forbes' list of fastest growing technology companies.[104]

## Devexperts

Devexperts is a Russian software products firm. The company provides financial trading software for on-line brokerage, exchange, and financial activities on stock, options, and foreign exchange markets. The company was founded in 2002 and is headquartered in St. Petersburg, Russia.[105] Devexperts specializes in development, implementation, and

24 × 7 support of its financial software. The firm also provides consulting services to financial institutions and individual brokers in the United States, United Kingdom, Russia, China, and Japan.

The firm's most well-known products include a software platform (DealBook 360) for foreign exchange international online trading and a software trading platform (thinkorswim) for future options and stock online trading. The thinkorswim platform is used by TD Ameritrade for online trading of individual futures, options, and stocks by private traders. In 2012, the firm earned U.S. $20 million in revenues, and employed about 350 software and design engineers.[106]

*Kaspersky Lab*

Kaspersky Lab is the largest Russian software products firm. The company was founded in 1997 by then husband and wife, Eugene and Natalia Kaspersky and is headquartered in Moscow, Russia.

Kaspersky Lab develops computer security software such as antivirus, mobile security, and Internet security software. It is one of the leading vendors of antivirus software today and operates in 200 countries and territories around the globe. Its more than 250,000 corporate clients include both large and small-to-medium-sized businesses worldwide, and the company also serves more than 300 million individual users.[107]

The firm may perhaps be most recognized generally for its identification of the software virus it called Flame. In 2012, the firm was asked by the United Nations International Telecommunications Union to investigate reports of a virus affecting Iranian Oil Ministry computers.[108] Researchers at Kaspersky Lab found information that appeared only on computers from Middle Eastern nations. According to Kaspersky, the virus was designed primarily to spy on the users of infected computers and steal data from them, including documents, recorded conversations, and keystrokes; it also opened a backdoor to infected computers, allowing attackers to update the software.[109] Embedded in the code of the malware was a module named Flame, leading Kaspersky to refer to the virus as the Flame Virus. Kaspersky estimated that more than 1,000 computers were infected with the virus in countries such as Iran, Israel, and Lebanon.[110]

Kaspersky Lab is currently fourth in the ranking of world manufacturers of software security solutions for end users by the IDC,[111] and its 2012 revenues were $628 million.[112]

## China

The Chinese software industry has developed quickly from only a handful of firms in the 1980s and 1990s to thousands of firms today. According to the Chinese Software Industry Association, sales of software products by Chinese firms were valued at about U.S. $7.2 billion in 2000, but by 2003 had reached about U.S. $19.3 billion software, with a compound annual growth rate averaging 39 percent to 2007 and 22 percent from 2008 to today.[113] By 2000, China was home to over 8,000 software firms that marketed approximately 18,000 products; and of those firms, the top four (IBM, Microsoft, Oracle, and Sybase) received only 19 percent of total industry sales.[114] Thus, the domestic software market and firms are quite important in China (in contrast to other countries whose software market is dominated by multinationals).

Like in many other countries, the computer hardware industry in China started before the software industry and both industries were heavily supported by the government and government institutions. Institutes of the Chinese Academy of Science (CAS) provided incubators that spun off software firms in the 1980s and 1990s.[115] These startup firms were funded by the government or private capital. A number of other firms were spin offs from major universities such as Beijing University, Tsinghua University, and Fudan University. The early software firms produced operating systems or systems software. For example, two CAS spin-off companies—CASS and Red Flag Linux—produced operating systems.[116] A computer hardware manufacturing firm called Legend, also a CAS spin off (today known as Lenovo) has become the world's second leading supplier of personal computers.

In addition to the substantial support provided by the Chinese government, the software industry in China has benefited from the significant growth of the Chinese economy, and its transformation from agrarian to manufacturing with growing service sectors. The growth of the domestic economy created demand for software products, especially in government and manufacturing sectors. Industries such as finance, telecommunications, and retailing also have significant software demand. For example, in 2000, the banking and telecommunications industries accounted for over 30 percent of total software demand in China.[117] Consumers with growing incomes have also increased their purchases of computing devices, increasing demand for software. The PC business market for software grew an estimated 215 percent between 2003 and 2008; the business software portion of the market was valued at U.S. $2.4 billion in 2003.[118] Applications software was the largest segment of this sector, accounting for more than 50 percent of market value.[119] All of these factors contributed to the development of a significant domestic software market in China.

There are two primary types of firms in the Chinese software industry—large systems integrators that are diverse in capability and scope, and small software products firms.[120] As noted earlier, major multinationals compete in the Chinese software industry but do not dominate it. Most of the multinationals sell enterprise software (SAP), middleware and software tools (IBM), or desktop software (Microsoft). However, multinationals have generally not created strong local operations for customizing their software, so there is a demand for domestic software firms to provide customization of software for multinationals. Much of the software industry is concentrated in large cities, such as Beijing and Shanghai, primarily in the eastern part of the country, although there are major software firms in other parts of the country.

The Chinese software industry is complex and dynamic. Although there are many opportunities for local firms and high growth sectors of the industry, competition is intense, and the market is fragmented. It can be difficult for domestic firms to achieve economies of scale. In addition, IT professionals in China have historically tended to lack skills in project and process management and in complex programming, when compared to India, although this situation appears to be rapidly changing. For example, most of the software firms appraised at the highest level of software process capability (Level 5 in the Software Engineering Institute's CMMI®) are in India, but more and more Chinese software firms are adopting the CMMI® and being appraised at high levels of software process capability. In the latest report on CMMI® appraisals, of the over

4,000 companies reporting appraisals in the CMMI® from 2007 to 2012, only six percent attained Level 5 appraisals, and of that percentage, India accounted for more than half (144 Level 5 firms), followed by the United States (71), and China (68).[121] However, China overtook the United States in 2009 in terms of sheer numbers of appraisals, and, over the period 2007 to 2012, Chinese firms have attained the highest number of appraisals (2,545), followed by the United States (1,519) and India (662). Clearly, the software industry in China is evolving and maturing rapidly.

Given the thousands of software firms in China, entire books could be written about the Chinese software industry. This book will focus on three of the largest and most significant Chinese software firms: Neusoft, Shanda, and Yonyou. Firms in the Chinese computer hardware industry are also quite important from the perspective of understanding the complete IT industry in China, but a full coverage of their history is beyond the scope of this book.

*Neusoft*

Neusoft is the largest China-based software company (based on 2012 revenues of more than U.S. $1 billion).[122] Incorporated in 1991, it is headquartered in Shenyang, China. The firm was started in 1998 by a Chinese professor by the name of Liu Jiren, and his students in a research laboratory at Northeastern University in Shenyang, China, with a capital equivalent to U.S. $500.[123] The professor and his students developed software solutions for a Japanese company called Alpine Electronics, Inc. In 1991, Neusoft (an acronym of Northeastern University Software) was incorporated. Since 1991, Neusoft has rapidly expanded its scope from software and services, and IT education and training, to medical systems, and in 1996, the firm became the first listed software company on the Shanghai Stock Exchange in China.[124]

The company provides a broad range of software products and services, from engineering and embedded software for the manufacturing, automotive, telecommunications, and transportation industries to business software applications (such as CRM systems, HR management, and financial systems) to telemedicine and health systems and business process outsourcing services. In 2004, Neusoft was the first Chinese software firm to attain a Level 5 appraisal in the CMMI® and has won numerous awards for its performance as a top outsourcing firm.[125]

Today, the firm employs more than 20,000, and has set up six software operations units, eight regional headquarters, and a marketing and service network in over 40 cities across China, and it has subsidiaries in North America, Asia, Europe, and the Middle East.[126]

*Shanda*

Shanda Interactive Entertainment, Ltd. (now Shanda Games after its reorganization in 2008), is a Chinese software video game producer. It is one of China's leading online game companies in terms of the size and diversity of its game portfolio, game revenues, and game player base. The company got its start in 1999 and is based in Shanghai. Shanda develops a particular type of software video game called an MMORPG.

A massively multiplayer online role-playing game (MMORPG) is a genre of role-playing video games or web-browser-based games in which a very large number of players interact with one another within a virtual game world.[127] In an MMORPG, players assume the role of a character (often in a fantasy world or science-fiction world) and take control over the character's actions. MMORPGs differ from single-player or small multiplayer online video games as they have a very large number of players, and a persistent world hosted by the game's publisher that continues to exist and evolve while the player is offline and away from the game.[128]

In November 2001, Shanda launched its first MMORPG, Mir II, which it had licensed from a South Korean firm called Actoz. In October 2003, Shanda launched Woool, its first in-house developed online game. Some of Shanda's MMORPGs include: AION, MapleStory, The World of Legend, The Sign, The Age, Magical Land, Ragnarok Online, D.O., Dungeons & Dragons Online, Bomb and Bubble, Shanda Rich Man, Warlord of the Three Kingdoms, and GetAmped.[129]

Shanda's game player base is one of the largest in China, and consisted of 18.6 million average monthly active users and 3.4 million average monthly paying users in 2012.[130]

Shanda develops and sources a broad array of games via in-house development, licensing, investment, acquisition, joint development, and joint operation. In 2013, the firm operated 52 online games and mobile games, created by 1,600 game development personnel and using the firm's proprietary game development platform. The firm also licenses games from international and domestic developers. In 2012, the firm received 55 percent of its net revenues from online games that were licensed from third parties, including Mir II and its sequels, from which the firm derived 1/3 of its net revenues in 2012. The firm earned over U.S. $750 million in revenues in 2012.[131] It is listed on the NASDAQ.

## Yonyou

Yonyou, or Yonyou Software Company Ltd., is the largest Chinese enterprise software firm. The company was founded in 1988 and is headquartered in Beijing. It offers a range of management software products including Enterprise Resource Planning (ERP), Supply Chain Management (SCM), CRM, HR, Business Intelligence (BI), and Office Automation (OA) products. It also develops software solutions for e-Government, finance, and asset management and provides software outsourcing services. The company has been appraised at Level 5 in the CMMI®.

In 2012, the firm earned almost U.S. $700 million in revenues.[132] It has over 1.5 million enterprise customers in China and Asian countries; more than 60 percent of the China Top 500 enterprises use Yonyou software.[133] The company leads with 23 percent of the market share for enterprise software in China, followed by SAP with 10 percent.[134] The firm has 41 branches in mainland China and overseas branches in Japan, Hong Kong, Thailand, and Singapore.

## Japan

Although the software industry in Japan originated soon after that in the United States, the Japanese software industry is substantially different in structure, products, and services. Except for a few products such as video games, Japanese software firms primarily develop custom software for other firms in the Japanese market. Customized software development for corporate firms accounts for over half of the sales in the software industry in Japan.[135] Few Japanese companies produce packaged software products: of the more than 3,300 firms in the Japanese industry, only 261 produce packaged software.[136] For those firms that do develop software packages, the market is almost exclusively domestic, and the entire industry, with the exception of video game software, exports very little.[137]

The Japanese software industry has its origins in the 1950s. Unlike the United States, there was no strong military influence on the industry. Instead, three large telecommunications companies—Fujitsu, Nippon Electric Company Ltd. (NEC), and Hitachi—who were suppliers to National Telephone and Telegraph (NTT), the telephone monopoly in Japan, became involved in the computing industry. The Japanese government took a number of steps to help foster the success of its new computer industry. Japan's Ministry of Economy, Trade and Industry (METI) put up trade barriers. Japan also sponsored the development of new computers via NTT, which created a guaranteed market for Japanese-made computers. The Japanese computing firms developed custom software for Japanese firms rather than mass market software products. It was common for the computing firms' software developers to reside at the customer site, and sometimes these dedicated developers would be spun off into captive software firms of the major computer firms.[138] NEC and Fujitsu organized their software developers in internal divisions, whereas Hitachi created captive subsidiaries. The target customers were the parent firms, customers, and suppliers. These arrangements led to the formation of a vertically structured software industry (not unlike the U.S. software industry of the 1970s discussed in Chapter 2). The vendor firms developed proprietary systems for their customers, remaining in long-term, stable contractual relationships.

In contrast to the software industry in the United States, which tended to favor product innovation and time to market for the mass market, the Japanese industry was focused on ensuring that software met the specific needs of particular user firms. This focus led to a quality mentality and the application of a software factory approach in the 1970s and 1980s. The software factory is an approach to impose discipline and rigor in software development by using standardized tools and methods, inspired by concepts and practices from manufacturing.[139] The software factory approach was attempted in the United States by firms such as IBM and Software Development Corporation (SDC) in the late 1970s, and largely abandoned,[140] although the capability model for software (CMM-SW®) discussed in Chapter 2 resulted from the efforts in the U.S. software industry to apply software factory discipline.

The Japanese software firms were much more successful in implementing the software factory approach and emphasized incremental innovation in product design, standardized components and methods, software reuse, computer-aided support tools, and quality control. Stability, quality, and performance were key objectives of the Japanese software firms in delivering customized software applications for user firms. As a result, the Japanese software industry had much more of a focus on software as a service than as a mass produced product.[141] By the mid-1990s, Japan held 13 percent of the worldwide software market.[142]

The movement of the global software industry to open client–server architectures and open standards in the 1990s and 2000s posed challenges for the Japanese software industry. Open standards allowed more producers to participate in the industry and enabled users to mix and match software products. This openness was in direct conflict with the vertical stovepipe structure of the Japanese software industry. Eventually, users desired more best of breed solutions, and competition in the Japanese software market became more intense, reducing costs. The Japanese software industry today has moved to a system integrator model, with user firms relying on a single large system integrator to integrate components and services that may be sourced from other vendors.[143]

Japanese firms Fujitsu, Hitachi, and NEC are among the top 30 firms in the world producing software today, and a brief profile of each company follows.

*Fujitsu Ltd.*

Fujitsu was created in 1935 by Fuji Electric Company to make telephone equipment. In 1954, the firm entered the computing industry with the development of Japan's first computer—the FACOM 100.[144] In the 1960s, METI helped fund and direct Fujitsu's development of mainframe systems. In 1972, Fujitsu invested in Amdahl Corporation (which was owned by the primary creator of IBM's System 360 computers) to get the technological knowledge it needed and to put the company on par with

IBM. Today, Fujitsu is the leading Japanese information and communication technology firm and offers a full range of technology products, solutions, and services to customers in over 100 countries. The firm reported consolidated revenues of 4.4 trillion yen (U.S. $47 billion) for the fiscal year ending March 31, 2013.[145] As shown in Table 3.1, Fujitsu is 11th in rank among the top 30 global software producers, with $3.1 billion in software sales in 2012.

*Hitachi Ltd.*

Hitachi is a Japanese multinational engineering and electronics conglomerate firm headquartered in Tokyo, Japan. Its name means sun rise.[146] It was founded in 1910 by an electrical engineer—Namihei Odaira—who was employed by Kuhara Mining, and its first product—an electric induction motor—was used in the Kuhara copper mines.[147] Today, the firm produces a variety of products ranging from information systems to electrical products and railway systems. It is often called the General Electric of Japan and is one of the world's 30 largest conglomerates.[148] As of March 2013, Hitachi's 326,000 employees supported consolidated revenues of more than 9 trillion yen (U.S. $100 billion).[149] As shown in Table 3.1, Hitachi is 22nd in rank among the top 30 global software producers with $2 billion in software sales in 2012.

*NEC*

NEC provides IT and network solutions to business enterprises, communications services providers, and government agencies. The firm has an interesting history. Its founders—KunihikoIwadare and Takeshiro Maeda—established the firm in 1898 using facilities that they had bought from Miyoshi Electrical Manufacturing Company. A U.S. firm—Western Electric, which had an interest in the Japanese phone market, became a partner and helped renovate the Miyoshi facilities. On July 17, 1899, a revised treaty between Japan and the United States went into effect, and Nippon Electric Company, Limited was organized with Western Electric Company to become the first Japanese joint venture with foreign capital.[150] The firm initially produced telephones and switches. In World War II, the shares of Western Electronic Company in the firm were seized, and the firm's production was severely compromised when its factories were bombed. After the War, computer R&D started in 1954, and NEC built its first computer in 1958.[151] More recently, NEC has entered into a number of joint ventures in the IT industry, such as its 2011 joint venture with *Lenovo*, the Chinese PC manufacturer.[152] NEC produces IT and communications products ranging from mobile phones to PCs to supercomputers. In terms of software, as shown in Table 3.1 in Chapter 3, NEC is 23rd in rank among the top 30 global software producers with $1.9 billion in software sales in 2012.

## India

The Indian software industry got its start in the 1980s. Prior to that, industries in India were constrained by excessive government regulations, prevention of domestic firms' entry into various sectors, high levels of tariff protection and restrictions against foreign competition. However, in the 1980s and 1990s the Indian government enacted a variety of policies related to the software industry that had the effect of opening it up to foreign competition, encouraging software exports, reducing taxes on software exports and imports, and simplifying procedures for software exports and imports.[153] The government also introduced initiatives to build telecommunications infrastructure and decrease Internet access costs for software exporters.

Perhaps as a result of the new incentives and liberalized policies combined with increased global demand for software from the Y2K problem and the rise of the Internet, the Indian software industry grew very rapidly, with software firms in the industry earning just over U.S. $500 million in revenues in 1993 and growing revenues to almost U.S. $90 billion in 2012.[154] Software revenues constitute the vast majority of revenues (87 percent) in the Indian IT industry as a whole, far more than hardware revenues.[155] Unsurprisingly, given the Indian government's incentives for exporting, most of the revenues in the software industry (averaging around 70 percent over the past two decades) are due to exports.[156] Of the total software revenues, software services accounts for 59 percent, followed by business process outsourcing and engineering services at 22 percent and software products at 19 percent.[157] In terms of total export and domestic revenues, application development and maintenance were originally and still are the bread and butter for Indian software companies, contributing to roughly 60 percent of Indian software firms' total revenues.[158] Most of the software and business processing outsourcing services performed by Indian software companies are for firms in the United States (60 percent) and Europe (29 percent).[159]

One other interesting aspect that distinguishes firms in the Indian software industry is the rate at which the firms have obtained CMMI® appraisals. After China and the United States, India has the third high-est total number of CMMI® appraisals. Further, Indian software firms account for more than one-third of the highest level of CMMI® appraisals (level 5).[160] An interesting study suggests that firms in the Indian soft-ware industry that are export oriented are more likely to obtain CMMI® appraisals. Once appraised, these firms experience significant improve-ments in exports, but do not appear to become more cost efficient. The researchers concluded that CMMI® appraisals help to demonstrate Indian software firms' capabilities to potential customers, rather than helping them to achieve cost savings, per se.[161]

As is clear from these numbers, the Indian software industry is similar in some respects but differs in a number of important ways from that in other countries. In contrast to the software industries of Brazil, China, and Japan, the Indian software industry is primarily export focused. Unlike the software industry in Israel but similar to that in Ireland, the Indian software industry has focused on custom-ized software services, rather than software products. To date, most software services performed in India have tended to be of lower value (i.e., software maintenance), although a number of firms are interested to move up the food chain to higher value services. Unlike the Irish software industry, but similar to the industries in Brazil and China, the Indian software industry is led by domestic software firms, not by large multinationals.

The three largest firms in India's software industry are domestic firms and are profiled below. They include Tata Consultancy Services, Wipro Technologies, and Infosys Technologies Limited.

## Tata Consultancy Services

Tata Consultancy Services (TCS), headquartered in Mumbai, India, is part of the Tata group, one of India's largest industrial conglomerates. TCS was established in 1968 as a division of Tata Sons Limited and was incorporated as a separate entity in 1995.

TCS provides IT and software services, consulting services, and business process outsourcing services to firms in a variety of industries, including banking and financial services, construction, telecommunications, retail, transportation, media, manufacturing, healthcare, and others. One of TCS' first contracts was to provide punched card processing services for the Central Bank of India. TCS went on to provide software and IT services for the financial industry in the 1970s and 1980s such as automating the financial securities market in Switzerland.[162]

TCS was the world's first organization to be appraised enterprise-wide at level 5 in the CMMI®.

Today, TCS is the largest IT services firm in India and among the top IT services firms in the world, generating U.S. $11.5 billion in revenues in the 2013 fiscal year and employing 276,000.[163] TCS operates in 44 countries and has 199 branches around the world.[164]

## Wipro Technologies

Wipro Technologies is a global software and IT services, consulting, and business process outsourcing company, headquartered in Bangalore, India. The firm has a long, varied, and interesting history. It was actually established in 1945 as Western India Vegetable Products Limited (abbreviated to Wipro) and manufactured vegetable oils under the trade names of Kisan, Sunflower, and Camel.[165] The company's logo still contains a sunflower to reflect the products of its original business. When the company's founder died in 1966, his son—Azim Premji—returned to India from Stanford University and took over the company at the age of 21. He still serves as Wipro's Chairman.

In 1981 Wipro first entered the fledgling IT industry in India, and it established a software products and exports subsidiary, Wipro Systems Ltd. in 1983.[166] At the same time, Wipro continued to make consumer products such as Wipro Jasmine soap and Wipro Baby Soft baby toiletries.

The company also marketed Indian-designed and manufactured PCs in the 1980s. Later in the decade, the firm entered into a joint venture with the large U.S. firm—General Electric—for the manufacture, sales, and service of diagnostic and imaging products.

In the 1990s Wipro entered into the software and IT services industry and was one of the first companies to develop the concept of an offshore development center—Odyssey 21—that undertook projects and product development in advanced technologies for overseas clients. Wipro achieved a variety of quality certifications in the 1990s such as ISO and appraisal at level 5 in the CMMI®.[167]

The company was listed on the New York Stock Exchange in 2000. Wipro entered the business process outsourcing sector in 2002 and the eco-energy business in 2008. In 2013, the company demerged its consumer products, engineering, and medical diagnostic businesses into a separate company called Wipro Enterprises.

Today, Wipro employs 145,000 who serve over 900 clients in 57 countries; the firm posted revenues of more than U.S. $6 billion for the financial year ending in March 2013.[168] Placing a value on innovation, the company has more than 50 dedicated emerging technology "Centers of Excellence" that explore the latest technologies for service delivery to its clients. Its software and IT services include Systems Integration, Consulting, Information Systems outsourcing, IT-enabled services, and R&D services. The company also is a value-added reseller of computer hardware products such as desktop computers, servers, and other devices.

### Infosys Technologies Limited

Infosys Technologies Limited (or Infosys) is a global software and IT services company, headquartered in Bangalore, India. The company was started in 1981 by N. R. Narayana Murthy and six engineers in Pune, India, with an initial capital of U.S. $250. In 1983 the firm signed up its first client: Data Basics Corporation in New York.[169] In the 1990s Infosys provided software application development and maintenance services such as updates to legacy systems to address the Y2K problem for large companies based in the United States. The firm grew quickly and opened up offices throughout North America and Europe to service its large corporate clients. In 1999, Infosys became the first Indian IT company to be listed on the NASDAQ.

From its small beginnings, the firm has grown to a global powerhouse, employing 155,000 and earning over U.S. $7.4 billion in revenues in 2012.[170] Infosys has 800 clients across 30 countries and earns the majority of its revenues from North America (62 percent) and Europe (23 percent).[171] Infosys also has the world's largest corporate university in Mysore, India, with a 270-acre campus that has 500 instructors and 200 classrooms and has the capacity to train 12,000 software engineers per year.[172]

Over the years, the company has received numerous awards and has achieved ISO certification as well as appraisal at level 5 in the CMMI®.[173]

Recently, Infosys has been shifting its operations outside of India to the United States and other countries to be closer to its clients. More than half of the firm's 87 global software development centers and almost all of its sales offices are located outside of India. For example, in 2012, Infosys announced a new delivery center in Milwaukee, Wisconsin, to better serve its clients in the Midwestern United States, including the Harley-Davidson motorcycle manufacturer.[174]

## Australia

As a whole, the IT industry in Australia is large—with an estimated size of more than $100 billion.[175] It is among the top five IT industries in the Asia-Pacific region and has been growing at double-digit rates since the 2000s. The industry employs almost half million workers and has more than 30,000 firms.

However, although the IT industry in Australia is large, the software products segment is small—just over two percent of the industry.[176] In contrast to other countries in which the government provides support or protection for the software industry, in Australia, there has been relatively little government involvement in the software segment of the IT industry.[177]

Most of the software industry in Australia is services oriented. The industry has benefited from comparatively low development costs and a highly skilled workforce, and as a result, is a popular destination for offshore software development and R&D. Companies such as IBM, HP (EDS), Google, and NEC have built major software development facilities in Australia. Logica CMG, Reuters, and Infosys have made Australia central to their global risk reduction strategies. Avaya, Canon, Computer Associates, Citrix, IBM, NEC, SAP Research, and Unisys all have global R&D labs in Australia.

Australia, does, however, have a vibrant and growing software video game segment of its industry. The digital game development sector alone generated over $120 million in revenues in 2007, and 93 percent of the revenues were derived from exports.[178] Australian software companies have also partnered with the film industry to produce animated features: for example, in 2006, the Australian firm Animal Logic partnered with Warner Bros. to produce the widely successful film *Happy Feet*.[179]

Two Australian software firms are profiled below—one is a large and growing software firm in the country—Atlassian—and the other is among the largest software video game producers in Australia—RedTribe.

### Atlassian

Atlassian is an enterprise software company that was founded in 2002 and is headquartered in Sydney, Australia, with offices in San Francisco and Amsterdam. Its founders—Mike Cannon-Brookes and Scott Farquhar—met while studying at the University of New South Wales and financed the company with $10,000 in credit card debt (in 2010, the company received $60 million from a venture capital firm).[180]

The company has an interesting business model. As described in Chapter 3, a number of software firms are leveraging the Internet as their primary sales and distribution mechanism (rather than using traditional sales and support personnel). This company is one of those firms. The company posts its products and prices on the Internet and uses the Internet for sales, support, and training of its products. In 2011, Atlassian announced sales of $102 million, up 35 percent from the year before.[181]

The company produces enterprise software tools for developers; its most popular software tools include its issue tracking application—JIRA, and its team collaboration product—Confluence. The company's products are used by over 25,000 customers worldwide and include clients such as Audi, NASA, and Twitter.[182]

The company has received numerous best places to work awards. It uses an innovative motivational approach called ShipIt days in which employees have 24 hours every quarter to work on a problem of their own choosing.[183]

### RedTribe

RedTribe is an Australian video game development firm that was founded in 2003 and is headquartered in Melbourne, Australia. RedTribe was the first Australian game developer to release a game on the XBox 360 and Wii—*Looney Tunes: Acme Arsenal* in 2007 (although the game was critically panned).[184]

Although the company has yet to release a video game that has received at least mediocre reviews from the critics, it has released a number of popular games including: *Space Chimps*—2008; *Jumper: Griffin's Story*—2008; and *Hairy Balls* for the iPhone and iPad—2012.

In 2007, RedTribe won the prestigious Business3000 "Export Business of the Year" and the overall "Business of the Year" awards.[185]

## Latin America

The Latin America region has a number of countries with growing software industries. Of these, Brazil and Mexico are the largest in the region and are profiled below.

### Brazil

The Brazilian software industry got its start in the 1990s. Prior to that, most software development in the country occurred in-house. The Brazilian government enacted a number of protectionist policies in the computing industry; for example, the Brazilian Informatics policy protected domestic computer hardware manufacturers from imports. In 1991, the Brazilian software market was $1.1 billion in size.[186]

In the early 1990s the informatics policy was replaced by a market competitiveness policy to support domestic firms for global competition. The government provided incentives for computing companies to invest a portion of their revenues in R&D activities, in partnership with research centers or universities. It also created a program called SOFTEX, which had a goal to introduce an entrepreneurial culture in universities and promoted the development of businesses in the software industry.[187]

After the Brazilian economy was liberalized and the various policies and initiatives described above were implemented, domestic demand for software grew rapidly along with outsourcing and increased deployment of computer hardware.[188] By 2001, the Brazilian software industry became the seventh largest in the world, comparable in size to India and China.[189] The software industry also grew to represent almost half of the entire IT market in Brazil (more than hardware and services), and the number of software firms increased significantly. In 1994 there were 4,300 software firms, but today there are nearly 10,300 firms that develop, produce, and distribute software and services.[190] The vast majority of these firms (93 percent) are small- and medium-sized enterprises.[191]

In contrast to India, Ireland, and Israel (whose software industries are export oriented), but similar to China, the domestic market was critical for the expansion of the software industry in Brazil. Most Brazilian software firms were involved in systems integration activities in the early 2000s, but today both software product firms and software outsourcing services firms are on the rise. There are continued efforts to foster an entrepreneurial culture in Brazil in the technology sector. An example is "Brazilian Innovators" launched by Bedy Yang, a Chinese-Brazilian entrepreneur, which has created a network of over 3000 entrepreneurs and investors to help young entrepreneurs launch their own businesses in the technology sector.[192] The software industry has also expanded from its original geographic focus in such large cities as Rio de Janeiro and São Paulo to many other regions in the country.

The size of the software industry today in Brazil is estimated at U.S. $7.6 billion, of which $148 million are exports; the computer services sector is U.S. $18.3 billion, of which $2.2 billion are exports.[193] Brazil's IT industry ranks among the top 10 worldwide and is forecasted to grow at more than 10 percent for the next few years. The 2016 Olympic Games in Brazil are also expected to increase demand for software. Most users of software products in Brazil are in the services and financial sectors (50 percent), followed by industry, trade, government, oil and gas, and agricultural sector. Forty-five percent of the software products developed are enterprise applications and one-third are systems software. As computers and mobile devices continue to diffuse throughout the Brazilian society with a growing middle class, there will be increasing demand for software applications. The Brazilian Association of Software Companies provides an organization and source of support and information for software firms in Brazil.[194]

As noted earlier, most software firms in Brazil are small or medium sized. The largest software firms (by revenues) are multinationals—Microsoft, Oracle, and SAP. One of the largest domestic software firms in Brazil is a company by the name of Microsiga. It is profiled below. Two other examples of software products firms—Consinco and Syhunt—are also profiled. Finally, the largest IT and software services firm—CPM Braxis—is profiled.

*Microsiga*

Microsiga Software creates enterprise software applications for corporate customers, most of which are small- or medium-sized businesses. One of its main products is an application called ERP Protheus. The firm was founded in 1983 and is headquartered in Nova Vicosa, Brazil.

Microsiga continued to grow rapidly via mergers and acquisitions, and in 2006, it was the first Latin American company in the IT sector to do an IPO in the New Market of the Stock Exchange of São Paulo in 2006 and become consolidated in the company TOTVS (the name based on the Latin for everything, everyone).[195] Today the company employs over 10,000 and has more than 40 locations in Brazil as well as in Argentina, Chile, Mexico, Paraguay, Puerto Rico, and Uruguay. It is the market leader in Brazil with more than 55 percent of market share and 35 percent of market share in Latin America, and in 2012, it generated more than U.S. $460 million in revenues (of which $150 million was for software product licenses, $200 million for services, and the remainder for maintenance).[196]

*Consinco*

Consinco is an example of how Brazilian companies are diversifying into software. Founded in 1990, Consinco sold cars for several years before a group of IT professionals turned it into a software producer.[197] Founded in 1990 and headquartered in Ribeirão Preto (in the state of São Paulo), Consinco is a provider of enterprise management and supply chain systems for wholesalers, distributors, and retailers. The company's software products are used by supermarkets and wholesale and distributors to increase efficiency of distribution and compliance with government regulatory standards.

The company has a presence in 25 states of Brazil, in more than 1,300 firms with more than 22,000 customers.[198] It employs 250 and has been ranked as one of the fastest growing companies in Brazil.[199] Consinco has now gained a strong foothold in the Brazilian IT market.[200]

*Syhunt*

Syhunt is an example of a systems software firm. It was founded in 2003 and is headquartered in Rio de Janeiro, Brazil. Its primary products are security software for web applications, specifically a web application security assessment software product known as Sandcat.[201] The company also produces security software for the open-source software language Apache/PHP.

Syhunt has operations worldwide and more than half its sales are outside of Brazil. Some of the firm's major customers include BearingPoint, Deloitte & Touche, Ernst & Young, KPMG, PricewaterhouseCoopers, Hewlett-Packard, IBM, Siemens, and Sun Microsystems.[202] The firm is currently privately held.

*CPM Braxis*

CPM Braxis, founded in 1982 and headquartered in Sao Paulo, Brazil, is the largest Brazilian IT services and outsourcing company. The firm provides IT consulting, software application development and maintenance, software integration, remote infrastructure support and business process outsourcing services to global companies in the financial services, telecommunications, consumer goods, manufacturing, and retail industries.[203]

In 2010, the company was acquired by CapGemini and operates today as a subsidiary of Cap Gemini, S.A. The firm has 12 software and service delivery centers and employs over 5,400. It was the first Brazilian IT services company to achieve CMMI® level 5 certification.[204]

## Mexico

Mexico's software industry, in contrast to Brazil's, is export oriented and is focused on services. Mexico is the world's main exporter of IT services after India, China, and the Philippines. Mexico has a relatively large outsourcing industry, with outsourcing services earning $13 billion in revenues in 2012 (60 percent of which are IT services outsourcing).[205] The outsourcing sector is growing rapidly at a 10 to 15 percent rate. Mexico's software and IT services industry includes over 600,000 IT professionals (of which 400,000 are focused on software)[206] and 2,500 IT companies ranging from small startups to large multinationals like IBM.[207] More than 100 Mexican universities and technical schools graduate 65,000 new IT professionals each year.[208]

The Mexican government has instituted strong incentives to stimulate the IT and software industry. Companies that wish to establish IT service operations in Mexico can get tax credits for R&D (up to 30 percent of the total R&D expense), a reduction of corporate taxes, and no value-added tax for exported services as well as cash grants of up to 50 percent of the total cost of their project.[209] Another program is called PROSOFT—the Software Industry and Information Technology Services Development Program. Introduced in 2004 by the Ministry of Economy, PROSOFT provides financial assistance for project investment and development, with funding contributed by state governments and industrial associations.[210] More than 500 companies and 121 universities across Mexico are currently participating in the program. PROSOFT has the goal of growing the software sector to $5 billion in 2013, which would make Mexico Latin America's leading developer of software and digital content in Spanish.

The Mexican government is also building technology parks across the country. One example is Guadalajara. Guadalajara (six hours north of

Mexico City) is rapidly becoming the Silicon Valley of Mexico due to a partnership between government, business, and universities. A key project is the Centro del Software—an incubator for small software startups. Established in 2006, there are now 34 companies and 700 people working in the Centro del Software.[211] The government subsidizes rent for the startups and provides technical and business advisory services. Each startup company works with the Instituto Jalisciense de Tecnologías de la Información, whose mission is to promote Guadalajara's IT and business process outsourcing (BPO) sectors.[212] The startups can also pool resources and collaborate to handle projects for large, global clients.

Although there are concerns about security, Mexico is an attractive near-shore IT outsourcing destination for U.S. firms as it is geographically close, culturally similar and aligned in the time zones. Given the North American Free Trade Agreement (NAFTA), trade between Mexico and the United States is streamlined and there are legal and intellectual property protections defined in the agreement. Near shoring is especially attractive for U.S. firms that wish to outsource work that requires close interaction and collaboration such as R&D, agile development (see Chapter 1 for details on agile development) and software testing. Mexican software firms have a high level of software development capability: the country is in the top 10 in the world in CMMI® certifications.[213]

There are many interesting software firms in Mexico. Two prominent firms—Softtek and Quarksoft—are profiled below.

### Softtek

Softtek was founded in 1982 in Monterrey, Mexico, and is headquartered there.[214] The company is a global provider of software, IT services, and business process outsourcing services with more than 8,000 employees in 30 offices in North America, Latin America, Europe, and Asia. In 1998, the company was the first in Latin America to open a Global Delivery Center. The company currently has 10 Global Delivery Centers (four in Mexico, one in Brazil, one in Argentina, one in the United States, one in India, one in China, and one in Spain) that offer software application development, IT infrastructure support, and BPO services to clients in more than 20 countries.

Softtek is the largest private IT service provider in Latin America. The company pioneered the Near Shore® service delivery model in 1997. Softtek created the Near Shore® concept as an alternative to traditional offshore outsourcing. The idea is to leverage Mexico's proximity, cost structure, and international trade agreements to provide U.S.-based companies with a more convenient alternative, minimal security issues, fewer language and cultural barriers, no time-zone differences, and low turnover rates. The delivery model is focused on lowering costs and risks associated with offshore engagements. The company is appraised at CMMI® level 5 and has won numerous awards for excellence in service delivery.

### QuarkSoft

Quarksoft was founded in 2001 by graduates from Carnegie Mellon University's Master of Software Engineering program and is head-quartered in Mexico City.[215] It is a CMMI® Level 5 certified software development company that designs and develops enterprise software solutions. The company provides a range of software development services including customized enterprise and desktop software development, hardware and software integration, SAP consulting and implementation services, software process improvement, assessment, training and implementation services, services-oriented architecture (SOA) design, consulting and implementation; software quality assurance (SQA), and testing.

The company serves major clients in the Financial Trading, Finance, Insurance, Banking, Retail, Government, Health Care, Manufacturing, and Mobile communications sectors in Mexico and the United States. Among the company's clients are the Mexican Stock Exchange and Banamex.

The company has more than 200 employees. Leveraging its strategic partnership with the Software Engineering Institute at Carnegie Mellon University, the company has collected and analyzed empirical data on its performance, showing savings for its customers ranging from 50 to 150 percent.

# Key Takeaways

For many years, the United States has dominated the software industry, with 80 percent of the market share for software products. Firms such as Microsoft and Oracle are world leaders in producing software products. The United States has also dominated the software services segment with firms like IBM and HP.

However, in recent years, with globalization, outsourcing and offshoring, significant software products and services industries have emerged in a number of countries around the world. Table 4.1 summarizes and compares the nature of the software industries in the key countries profiled and described in this chapter.

As shown in Table 4.1, the United States, South Africa, and Israel have a similar structure and orientation of their respective software industries, with a strong focus on software products and services, and with significant domestic and export markets (although the United States clearly has orders of magnitude greater share of the global market). Japan and Russia are currently more internally focused, with provision of custom software development and services for their domestic markets, and relatively little exports.

Ireland, Mexico, and India have a relatively low focus on software products but are very intensive in software services provision and are externally focused on exports. The countries have relatively weak domestic markets, although Mexico aims to produce software for Spanish-speaking Latin America. China and Brazil have large domestic markets for both software products and services, but have not to date been as export oriented as India, Mexico, and Ireland.

Finally, the European countries—Germany, United Kingdom, and France—and Australia—have significant domestic markets and are more service than product oriented. However all three European countries have major companies (e.g., SAP, SAGE, Cap Gemini) that are world leaders in segments of the software industry. Australia serves as an offshore destination for software services for firms in the United States, Europe, and Asia, and is an important R&D hub for multinational software firms.

In sum, the software industry is truly global today, and the growth of the industry outside of the United States will likely continue to increase.

*Table 4.1 Comparison of software industry in selected countries*

| Country | Software products intensity | Software services intensity | Domestic orientation | Export orientation | Example firms |
|---|---|---|---|---|---|
| United States | High | High | High | High | Microsoft, Oracle, IBM, Symantec, HP |
| South Africa | High | High | High | High | Dimension Data, Online Innovations |
| Israel | High | High | High | High | Checkpoint, Amdocs |
| Japan | Low | High | High | Low | Fujitsu, Hitachi, NEC |
| Russia | Low | High | High | Low | Kaspersky Labs, EPAM |
| Ireland | Low | High | Low | High | Conduit, CR2 |
| Mexico | Low | High | Low | High | Softtek, Quarksoft |
| India | Low | High | Low | High | TCS, Wipro, Infosys |
| China | Medium | High | High | Low | Neusoft, Yanyou |
| Brazil | Medium | High | High | Low | Microsiga, CPM Braxis |
| Germany | Medium | High | High | Medium | SAP, Siemens |
| UK | Medium | High | High | Medium | SAGE |
| Australia | Medium | High | High | Medium | Atlassian, Redtribe |
| France | Medium | High | High | Medium | Dassault Systemes, Cap Gemini |

# CHAPTER 5

# Occupations and Workforce Issues and Trends in the Software Industry

In a podcast entitled "Talent Matters: Why Application Development Cannot be Industrialized," Forrester analysts Mike Gualtieri and Jeffrey Hammond argue that it is critical for software companies to have exceptional software talent.[1] The best software developers, they argue, are rock stars—creative, passionate, and disciplined. They also assert that only highly talented individuals are able to successfully architect, design, build, and test software products and platforms that are tied to revenue and that require high levels of performance, scalability, and reliability.

Certainly, the behaviors of major high-tech companies bear this out.

In 2010, Hewlett-Packard sued Oracle for hiring its former CEO—Mark Hurd, claiming that Hurd's knowledge and experience would give Oracle (a competitor of HP's) an unfair advantage.[2] HP asked the courts to prevent Hurd from working at Oracle. HP also asked for a special monitor who would regularly check in on Hurd to make sure he wasn't using his knowledge and experience in ways that would disadvantage HP when working at Oracle.

Facebook CEO Mark Zuckerberg stated recently that: "We have not once bought a company for the company. We buy companies to get excellent people... In order to have a really entrepreneurial culture one of the key things is to make sure we're recruiting the best people. One of the ways to do this is to focus on acquiring great companies with great founders."[3]

In 2012, Google paid $15 million to acquire a company called Milk which created mobile apps. Google reportedly fired all Milk employees except for the product design team, which it re-deployed to work on

Google+. According to the report: "Google, Facebook, and Twitter have all been on acquisition sprees, scooping up startups to hire the entrepreneurs behind them. The actual products those entrepreneurs created are often an afterthought."[4]

In a report on the global software industry, Mark McCaffery, Global Software Leader at PricewaterhouseCoopers remarked that:

> ...the competition for key skills and experience has become a global war for talent. Large vendors are expanding to regions beyond their typical recruitment grounds in search of top-flight engineers, programmers, and executives. Companies are using their checkbooks and stock market valuations to acquire companies for their technology as well as their talented people.[5]

The software industry depends critically on human talent. In contrast to industries that manufacture a physical product, the software industry is significantly less capital-intensive. Labor is the primary factor of production in the industry. The majority of costs to build and maintain software products are due to the costs of skilled labor in the form of software developers. The innovative ideas of the software developers are crucial to competitive success in the industry. Thus, workforce issues are especially important for this industry.

This chapter identifies the major occupations in the software industry. It then examines the economics and demographics of the software workforce. Given the global nature of the software industry, the chapter concludes by considering the globalization of the software workforce.

## Major Occupations in the Software Industry

As described in Chapter 3 and shown in Figure 3.4, the value chain of primary activities for software firms includes software development, testing, and integration; documentation, packaging, and distribution; marketing, advertising, and sales; installation and training; and maintenance and support. These primary activities are supported by R&D, human resources, legal, finance and accounting, procurement, and management.

Individuals in the occupations in the industry perform these activities. The following sections describe selected key occupations in the software industry.[6]

Table 5.1 identifies and organizes the key occupations by activity in the software value chain:

- Software marketing, advertising, and sales;
- Software R&D and product development;
- Software product integration and testing;
- Software product documentation, packaging, and distribution; and
- Software product maintenance and support.

The following sections discuss each occupation in detail.

### Software Marketing, Advertising, and Sales

Software marketing activities are extremely important to software firms. As noted in Chapter 3, the costs of marketing, advertising, and sales activities are one of the major expenses for software firms. Key occupations in this area include software product marketing and sales. Related occupations for software services firms are client managers.

### Software Product Marketer

Software product marketers act as the interface between the market and the software firm.[7] They help the firm understand what the market needs and help customers understand how the firm's products can help them solve their problems or do their jobs better. Product marketing is the function within a software firm that focuses on marketing strategies and tactics such as market segmentation, product strategy, positioning, sales strategy, creating awareness of the product, competitive positioning, and interacting with customers. Software product marketers define and position software products in the market, provide the content for the website, write the white papers, speak at trade shows, and do product demonstrations for analysts. Software product marketers also develop the pricing

Table 5.1 Key occupations in the software industry—by activity in the software value chain

| Software value chain activity | Occupation | Brief description | Qualifications | Typical salary |
|---|---|---|---|---|
| *Software marketing, advertising, and sales* | Software product marketer | Develops product marketing, sales, and pricing strategies | MBA; marketing expertise; technical expertise | $148,530 |
| | Software product sales representative | Sell software products to customers | Bachelor's in Computer Science or Business; sales experience; technical knowledge | $78,860/$116,500 for complex products |
| | Software client manager | Develop and sustain relationships with clients | Bachelor's in Business or MBA; sales and customer service expertise; technical knowledge | $148,530 |
| *Software product development* | Software R&D engineer | Conduct basic and applied research on computer science and translate to new product ideas | PhD in computer science; technical experience | $115,110 |
| | Software architect | Design software architecture and platforms, define technical standards | Master's in Computer Science; extensive technical experience | $144,660 |
| | Software product/project manager | Manage product life cycle | Bachelor's or Master's in Computer Science often with MBA; technical experience | $144,580 |
| | Software developer/ engineer | Write and implement software code for products | Bachelor's in Computer Science; programming experience | $99,140 |
| | Software designer or content engineer | Design user experience, provide content | Bachelor's in Computer Science; technical experience | $70,900 |
| | Graphic artist | Create graphic designs for a product or brand, design website for a product | Specialized degree or training in graphic design; Bachelor's in Computer Science for Website design; experience using graphic design tools | $56,200 |

| | | | | |
|---|---|---|---|---|
| *Software integration and testing* | Software tester/test engineer | Test software products to make sure they work properly and satisfy requirements | Bachelor's in Computer Science; testing experience | $81,140 |
| | Software quality assurance engineer | Assure that the software product conforms to company's quality standards; test software products for usability and functionality; develop quality standards | Bachelor's or Master's in Computer Science or Information Systems; technical experience, quantitative skills | $81,140 |
| | Software integration engineer | Manage integration of the software components for a product, ensure components work together | Bachelor's or Master's in Software Engineering, Systems Engineering, Computer Science or Information Systems; technical experience | $104,960 |
| *Software product documentation, packaging and distribution* | Technical writer/documentation specialist | Develop product documentation, help guides, manuals, white papers | Bachelor's in Journalism, English, Economics, Business or other field; specialized training in technical writing | $78,110 |
| | Software packaging engineer | Design and develop packages for software products that are physically distributed | Bachelor's or Master's in Materials Engineering | $92,030 |
| *Software maintenance and support* | Product/technical support specialist | Provide assistance and communicate technical solutions to customers | May not require a degree unless the product is very complex; technical knowledge; excellent interpersonal skills | $59,120 |
| | Product maintenance engineer | Debug and fix product problems, monitor and improve technical performance of the product | Bachelor's in Computer Science or Software Engineering | $99,140 |

*Sources:* Salary data obtained from U.S. Bureau of Labor Statistics (2013a) and from the occupational database of O*NET (2013).

and product launch plan. They develop training materials for the sales force, promotional materials for the product, and the social media strategy for promoting the product.

Software product marketers perform market research to determine customer needs. They identify requirements based on market needs and work with the product manager to prioritize the features that go into the product. The product manager then manages the process of converting the requirements into an actual product.

Product marketers typically have MBAs with specialization in marketing as well as technical training or experience.

## Software Product Sales Representative

Software product sales representatives are responsible for the merchandising, distribution, and selling of software products. They would typically be deployed by a firm to sell complex, specialized, or high-value software products such as enterprise software.

Software product sales representatives provide detailed information to the customer about the technical specifications of the software product offered by the company. They advise customers on technical matters and solicit information about customer needs. They also take orders from customers. Sales representatives create sales pitches and presentations, demonstrate product features, and help customers to maximize the use of software features. They must also keep current on market trends and changes to the software product. They may have to travel to the customer site.

Software product sales representatives typically hold a bachelor's degree in computer science or business and have relevant sales experience.

## Software Client Manager

Client managers develop and sustain a relationship between a company and its clients. Client manager is an important occupation that is especially relevant to software services firms. Related titles include Client Services Manager or Client Relationship Manager. Retaining the client for repeat business is a key goal of software services firms, and client managers play an important role in achieving that goal. Client managers build relationships with different members of the client team who make or influence purchasing decisions, including senior executives, purchasing managers, technical managers, and finance directors. They identify and organize software-related services that facilitate the client relationship, such as training or planned software maintenance. They also work with the client to identify opportunities for new or updated services that can help the client to make more productive use of computing resources.

As might be expected, communication and coordination skills in addition to planning and analytical skills are essential for client managers. They develop and present plans for client services to the senior management team to gain approval and commitment. They also work with product development and service delivery teams to explain the needs of the client for new products and services. By developing a deep understanding of the technical and business challenges their clients face, client managers identify opportunities to increase sales of the company's products and services that meet those needs.

Client managers, like other sales management professionals, must have a bachelor's or master's degree in business, management, or marketing. They must also have extensive experience in sales and customer service, along with technical knowledge relevant to the software industry.

### Software R&D and Product Development

Software product development is, of course, the primary activity in the software industry. There are a number of occupations included in software product development. An important supporting occupation that directly works with software product development is software research and development. Other key jobs include software architect, software product manager, software developer/engineer, and software designer or artist.[8] A brief description of each follows.

Software Research and Development Engineer

As noted in Chapter 3, software firms spend significant portions of their budgets on R&D—as much as 20 percent or more. Researchers at IBM, for example, have generated thousands of patents and have won numerous awards including Nobel prizes. Clearly, research and development is a critical function in software firms. Some software firms have a separate R&D department, whereas others may have one or more individuals who work on R&D in the software development function.

The primary responsibilities of a software R&D engineer include conducting basic and applied research on challenging computer science problems and helping to translate that research into new product ideas. An example of software R&D could include development of an efficient algorithm to verify computer password strength (see Figure 6.1).

Researchers typically have a PhD and the ability to develop original research agendas as demonstrated by journal publications and conference papers, as well as participation on program committees, editorial boards, and advisory panels. Software R&D engineers must also have excellent communication skills and an ability to collaborate effectively with other researchers, software product marketers and managers, and software product development teams.

## Software Architect

Software architects are critical occupations in the industry. They make high-level design choices. They can oversee and direct the use of technical standards, including coding standards, tools, and platforms. At times, software architects may also be engaged in the design of the architecture of the hardware environment.

There are different types of software architects in the industry.[9] These include enterprise architects, solutions architects, and applications architects. Enterprise architects are focused on the high level and think about software architecture issues that extend across the products and projects in the software firm. They think abstractly to integrate the firm's various products into a common architecture. Solutions architects are focused on particular solutions that require interactions between multiple applications. Applications architects work at the most detailed level and consider the design and architecture of a single application.

As an illustrative example, at a software firm like Microsoft, an applications architect would focus on the architecture of a particular application like MS Excel. A solutions architect may consider the architecture of file exchanges between MS Excel and MS Word. An enterprise architect would be responsible for the architecture of the entire MS Office suite of applications.

Clearly, a software architect is a senior-level position that requires individuals with a comprehensive grasp of software design and an understanding of industry trends. Software architects make key decisions about how to put together products and typically oversee a large array of products and staff. Usually, individuals in this occupation have an advanced degree in computer science and extensive technical experience.

## Product Manager or Project Manager

Product managers are also an important occupation in the software industry. They are often charged with managing the entire life cycle of one or more product lines, including ensuring the profitability of existing products as well as developing new products. They work with the product marketer to specify and prioritize market requirements for current and future products and lead a team to build new products. Typically, product managers are expected to spend time in the market to understand customer problems and are charged with finding innovative solutions for the broader market. Sometimes, product managers must also develop partnering relationships with other software firms who may produce components of the product. They must have a blend of management and technical skills and must be able to communicate with software engineers and architects, product marketing and sales representatives, as well as customers.

Product managers take the software application from conception through development to the finished product. They help define the features that the product will encompass and work with teams of designers, engineers, writers, and quality-assurance testers. Product managers typically hold Bachelor's or Master's in Computer Science or Software Engineering plus an MBA and have extensive experience in the software field.

## Software Developer or Engineer

Software developers and engineers write the code for software applications using programming specifications and high-level design documents. They implement the identified components based on client requirements. Software developers also ensure that the implemented components are tested and can be integrated into the product. Senior software engineers will make higher level design decisions. Individuals in this occupation typically have a bachelor's or master's degree in computer science or software engineering and equivalent programming experience.

## Software Designer or Content Engineer

Software designers and content engineers work with software developers to provide tools that publish content to software applications. They are responsible for the user experience and logic flow of the content—how all the text, graphics, sound, and other information fit together. Well-designed content is natural, inviting, and easily understandable and is a key element of the user's experience with the product. Typically, individuals with a bachelor's degree in computer science and significant technical experience are desired for this occupation.

## Graphic Artist

Graphic design is the art of communication, stylizing, and problem solving through the use of type and image. Graphic design is the process by which a message is created and designs are generated. Examples of commercial graphic design include the creation of company logos or brand designs, publications, and package design. In the software industry, graphic or visual design artists work on web design and software design, for products where end-user interactivity is an important design consideration of the layout or interface. Graphic artists work with software developers to create both the look and feel of a website or software application and enhance the interactive experience of the user or website visitor. Individuals with specialized training in graphic design and experience using graphic design tools are desired for this occupation. For individuals performing website design, a Bachelor's in Computer Science is needed.

### Software Product Integration and Testing

Individuals in software product integration and testing occupations are involved at various points in the product development life cycle.

### Software Tester or Software Test Engineer

A software tester or test engineer must test a product or system to make sure that it functions according to specifications and customer requirements and meets the business needs. Testing activities cover all aspects of the product including function, component, performance, system, regression, and service testing. Software testers must have knowledge of the domain they are responsible for testing. Their knowledge of the product target market and customer environment is important. For example, a software tester who tests a tax preparation software product should have knowledge of tax preparation in order to understand which features of the software should be tested.

Software test engineers set up test environments, design test plans, develop test cases and scenarios, and execute these cases. They investigate problems uncovered during analysis and design and execute test cases as appropriate. They also provide feedback on usability of the product. Software testing is an important role at a software firm as it helps to ensure the quality of the product. Software testers typically have a bachelor's degree in computer science and relevant technical experience.

### Software Quality Assurance Engineer

Software quality assurance (SQA) engineers perform some similar activities as software test engineers; however, they are also responsible for assuring that the product conforms to the firm's quality standards. They evaluate and test software applications for usability and functionality. Although software testers may focus on test cases, scenarios, and use cases, software quality assurance engineers participate in the design process to understand how the software will function. They design, revise, and verify quality standards for the software design. After implementing and designing quality standards, software quality assurance engineers develop test procedures to ensure the software product works effectively.

After the software product has been developed, a quality assurance engineer tests the software for validity of results, accuracy, reliability, and conformance to the firm's established quality standards. The engineers document their evaluation of the product's performance and may suggest enhancements to the product designer to further improve the product.

Software quality assurance engineers must have knowledge of quality assurance processes and techniques. Typically, they have a bachelor's or master's degree in computer science or information systems and relevant technical experience plus quantitative skills (as quality assurance requires knowledge of statistics).

## Software Integration Engineer

Software integration engineers focus on ensuring the components of a software product work well together. They determine system specifications, input and output processes, and working parameters for hardware and software compatibility. They coordinate the design of subsystems and component interfaces and manage the integration of the total product or system. They may also interact with the development team and customer to track issues and resolve them. The engineers may be responsible for systems-level development and testing. They also work with other vendors, if components are made by other companies. This typically involves interactions with the contracts organization in the firm to negotiate contracts with other vendors.

Software integration engineers troubleshoot and debug integration issues and maintain and improve the efficiency of the integration environment including automated build and test tools, development tools and utility scripts, and configuration management tools. They provide a review of and inputs to the designs and code of multiple other subsystems and participate as requested in prototypes and investigations of cross-cutting design and implementation issues.

Software integration engineers typically have a bachelor's or master's degree in Software Engineering or Systems Engineering or in Information Systems, as well as relevant experience.

### Software Product Documentation, Packaging, and Distribution

Once software products are built and tested, they need to be documented, packaged, and distributed. One of the primary occupations in this area is a technical writer or documentation specialist.

### Technical Writer or Documentation Specialist

Technical writers and documentation specialists engage in technical writing to produce materials that support the software products, such as product documentation and marketing white papers. They prepare information which helps the users who use the product. The documentation includes online help, user guides and manuals, white papers, design specifications, system manuals, project plans, test plans, and business correspondence.

Technical writers and documentation specialists must create, assimilate, and convey technical material in a concise and effective manner. They may specialize in a particular area, such as documentation on the user interface or for a certain type of software product, such as enterprise software.

Technical writers have a mix of technical and writing abilities. They typically have a degree or certification in a technical field, but may have one in journalism, business, economics, or other fields.

### Software Packaging Engineer

Software packaging engineers design and develop packages for software products that are distributed in physical stores. They must design a package that sells and protects the product, while maintaining an efficient, cost-effective process cycle. Packaging engineers must interact with different functions in the software firm such as research and development, marketing, graphic design, purchasing, and planning. Packaging engineers typically have degrees in materials or related engineering disciplines.

Today, many software products are delivered via the Internet; this reduces the need for product packaging and physical distribution.

### Software Product Maintenance and Support

Product support is an important occupation in the software industry, as the life of software products can extend for years. Support is also necessary to help facilitate adoption and use of products. Some software firms generate most or all of their revenues from support services. For example, as described in Chapter 7, in the open-source software market segment, Red Hat, Inc. provides a free version of the open-source Linux operating system software to customers, but charges for a wide array of support services including customization, integration, installation, operations, documentation, maintenance, training, and technical support. The company generates more than one billion in revenues from support services.

Key occupations in this area are for product or technical support and for product maintenance.


### Product or Technical Support Specialist

Product and technical support specialists respond to questions and issues raised by customers who have purchased the firm's software products. They may provide or communicate technical solutions to customers. For example, a product support specialist could help a customer uninstall or install a software application or troubleshoot an issue with using the software.

Product and technical support specialists deliver service and support to end-users using and operating automated call distribution phone software, via remote connection or over the Internet. They interact with customers to provide and process information in response to inquiries, concerns, and requests about products and services. They diagnose and resolve technical and software issues and may offer alternative solutions to retain the customer.

They need to be familiar with the software products that they support, staying current with system information, changes, and updates to the products. They may also develop and update customer service processes.

Some firms refer to this occupation as Help Desk. Firms may outsource staffing of this occupation to countries such as India to leverage the lower cost, technically savvy workforce in those countries.

Typically, this occupation is entry level and does not require a college degree in computer science. However, technical support for software products that are complex and high value may require individuals with a bachelor's degree in computer science, information systems, or business or other fields. The occupation does require excellent interpersonal skills and an understanding of technical issues.

## Software Product Maintenance Engineer

Adding new features to a product is usually accomplished by the software product development function. However, from time to time, software products may require fixes to correct defects and keep the product working. Software product maintenance and operations engineers debug problems with the software product. They monitor the technical performance of the software product to verify whether it is functioning properly. They provide and test technical upgrades to the software product to keep it operating effectively.

Software product maintenance and operations engineers work with the software development engineers to plan, perform, and maintain routine product modifications, enhancements, and upgrades. They also work with software development engineers to propose improvements to the software product.

Given the technical nature of the occupation, individuals must have a degree in computer science or software engineering. Some firms use this occupation as entry level to product development and may transition a software product maintenance engineer to software development.

## *Average Salaries for Occupations in the Software Industry*

Figure 5.1 shows the average salary (in 2012) of selected occupations in the U.S. software industry. The salary data originate from the U.S. Bureau of Labor Statistics (BLS) annual occupational employment

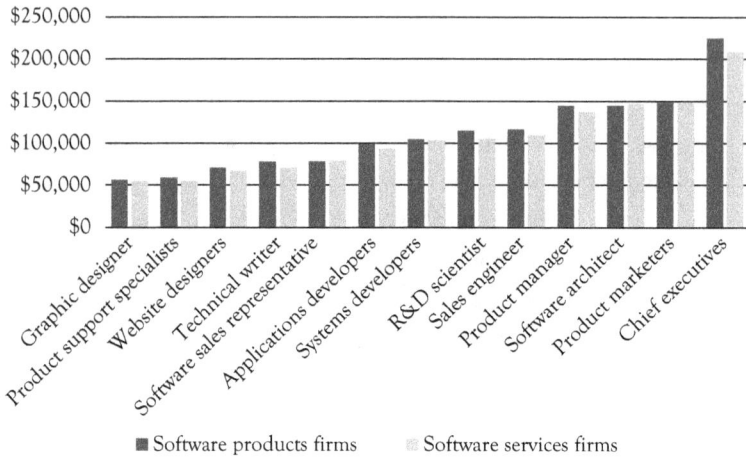

*Figure 5.1 Average salaries of key occupations in firms in the U.S. software industry*

Source: Based on Data from the U.S. Bureau of Labor Statistics (2013a).
Notes: The data for 2012 were downloaded from the U.S. Bureau of Labor Statistics Occupational Employment Survey Statistics website. The NAICS codes for which the data were obtained include: 511200 (Software Publishers) and 541500 (Computer Systems Design and Related Services).

statistics (OES) survey in which employers report the number of individuals in each occupation in their firms and the salaries for the individuals in those occupations. It is important to note that Figure 5.1 reports the salaries for these occupations *in the software industry* (not across all industries). Compensation studies suggest that individuals in software-related occupations in firms in the information technology industry earn higher salaries, on average, than those working in similar occupations outside of the industry.[10] Given the focus of this book on the software industry, it is thus relevant to report the salaries for workers in this industry.

As can be seen in Figure 5.1, salaries for almost all the reported occupations in the software industry tend to be somewhat higher in the software products firms than in the software services firms, although the differences are not substantial. As would be expected, key occupations such as executives, software architects, software product marketers, and software product managers are highly compensated.

# Economics and Demographics
# of the Software Workforce

## Supply and Demand for Software Workers

Imbalances in the supply and demand for workers have perennially posed a challenge for firms in the software industry. Generally, demand for qualified software professionals has outstripped supply. In the early days of the industry, there was no trained software workforce: Companies had to hire workers and train them to program. Each new innovation, problem, or opportunity in the software industry has further exacerbated the imbalance in labor supply and demand. For example, as described in Chapter 2, the introduction of the Internet and the dot.com boom in addition to the Y2K problem sharply increased the demand for software and software workers in the late 1990s. After the dot.com bust in the early 2000s, demand sharply decreased as software startups failed and workers were let go. Today, the industry is growing again. Demand for software is increasing as software is embedded into a growing number of goods and services in the global economy. Software-related occupations are now among the fastest growing occupations in the United States. The number of jobs in software-related occupations is expected to grow by 22 percent between 2010 and 2020.[11]

However, despite the promising environment today, the dot.com bust in the early 2000s had a negative effect on individuals' intentions to join the workforce. Many software companies went bankrupt in the dot.com bust, and their workers were out of a job. Attracting and retaining talented software professionals is still a challenge. In the United States, the number of software professionals entering the workforce decreased sharply after the dot.com bust. In 2004, the number of bachelor's degrees in computer science reached a peak of 60,000, but since then it has declined each year, and in 2009 the number dropped below 40,000.[12] In the United States computer science is the only scientific and engineering discipline with a downward trend in the number of undergraduate degrees during that time period. However, this downward trend may reverse as new jobs and opportunities open up in the industry. A later section of this chapter describes how U.S. software firms are also turning to the global software workforce to address labor supply and demand imbalances.

According to data from the BLS OES, there were over 1 million work-ers in computer-related occupations in the software industry in 2012.[13] Of this number, 145,000 were working in the software products firms and 910,000 were working in software services firms. Figure 5.2 graphs the number of workers in the software products industry and in the soft-ware services industry from 2003 to 2012. As can be seen in the figure, the software workforce has increased in size by almost 45 percent from 2003 to 2012, growing from 725,070 workers in 2003 to 1,055,520 in 2012. It is also clear that the majority of workers are employed by firms in the software services sector, not by software product firms. The growth rate of workers in the software services sector (an increase of 52 percent in the number of workers from 2003 to 2012) is also considerably greater than the growth rate in the software products sector (an increase in the number of workers of 15 percent from 2003 to 2012). These data suggest that much of the growth in the software industry is coming from the software services sector. Chapter 7 explores the implications of this trend for the software industry.

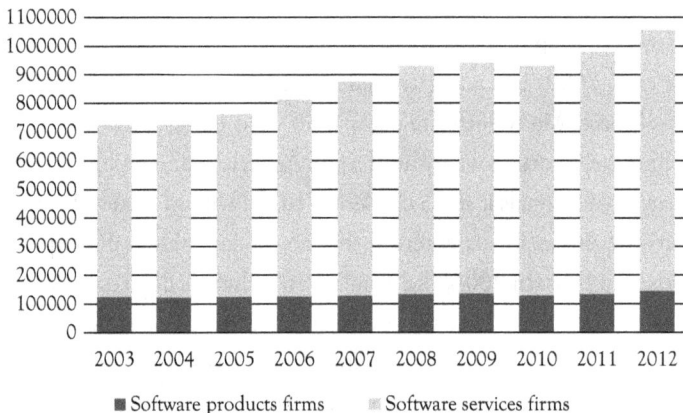

■ Software products firms    ▨ Software services firms

**Figure 5.2 Employment in the software industry workforce (2003 to 2012)**

Source: Based on data from the U.S. Bureau of Labor Statistics (2013a).
Notes: The data from 2003 to 2012 were downloaded from the U.S. Bureau of Labor Statistics Occupational Employment Survey Statistics website. The NAICS codes for which the data were obtained include 511200 (Software Publishers) and 541500 (Computer Systems Design and Related Services), occupation code of 15-0000 (Computer and Mathematical Occupations). Occupations do NOT include managers and executives within the software industry.

### Wages of Software Workers

Figure 5.3 shows the average annual salary of workers in computer-related occupations in the software industry from 2003 to 2012. The salary numbers are nominal (not deflated to a common year) and are separately reported for workers in software product firms and in software services firms.

As can be seen in Figure 5.3, workers employed by software product firms tend to earn more, on average, than those employed by software services firms, and the differences in salary have increased from 2003 to 2012. Studies of wages for information technology professionals suggest that workers' wages depend on their level and type of education, their work experience, the type of firm that employs them (e.g., large vs. small firm), and the type of industry in which the firm operates.[14] Generally, as noted earlier, workers in IT and information-intensive industries earn more, all else equal, than their counterparts who work in noninformation intensive industries.[15] Figure 5.3 also suggests a premium for workers in

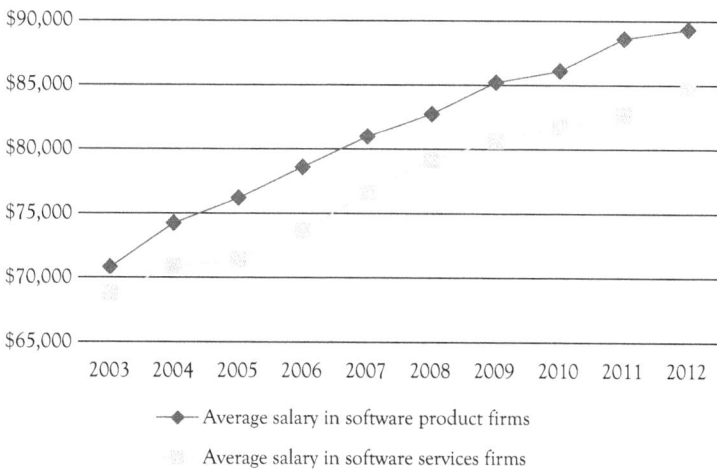

—◆— Average salary in software product firms

Average salary in software services firms

***Figure 5.3 Average annual salaries of workers in software industry (2003 to 2012)***

Source: Based on data from the U.S. Bureau of Labor Statistics (2013a).
Notes: The data from 2003 to 2012 were downloaded from the U.S. Bureau of Labor Statistics Occupational Employment Survey Statistics website. The NAICS codes for which the data were obtained include: 511200 (Software Publishers) and 541500 (Computer Systems Design and Related Services), occupation code of 15-0000 (Computer and Mathematical Occupations). Occupations do NOT include managers and executives within the software industry.

software product firms compared to software services firms, and the premium gap appears to be growing over time.

It is also interesting to consider the real average annual salary of workers in computer-related occupations in the software industry from 2003 to 2012, shown in Figure 5.4. The salary numbers are deflated to 2003 dollars using the Consumer Price Inflation tables[16] and are reported separately for workers in software product firms and in software services firms.

As can be seen in Figure 5.4, there is also a premium gap between salaries of workers in software product firms and software services firms, in real dollars. However, although employment in software services firms grew strongly from 2003 to 2012, salaries (in real terms) did not. In fact, a worker in a computer-related occupation in a software services firm earned about $1,000 *less* per year (in 2003 dollars) in 2012 ($67,872) than in 2003 ($68,780). In contrast, a worker in a computer-related occupation in a software products firm earned a bit more in 2012 ($71,574) than in 2003 ($70,830)—about $700 in 2003 dollars. Given the reported

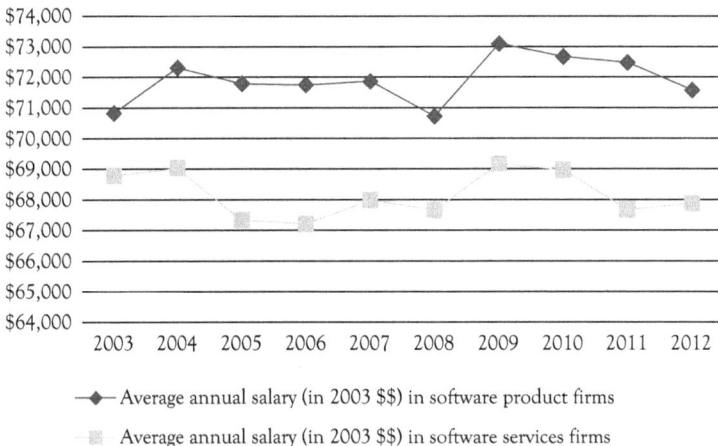

—◆— Average annual salary (in 2003 $$) in software product firms

▦    Average annual salary (in 2003 $$) in software services firms

*Figure 5.4 *Average annual salaries of workers in software industry (2003 to 2012). **Deflated to 2003 dollars using the CPI*

Source: *Based on data from the U.S. Bureau of Labor Statistics (2013a). The data from 2003 to 2012 were downloaded from the U.S. Bureau of Labor Statistics Occupational Employment Survey Statistics website. The NAICS codes for which the data were obtained include: 511200 (Software Publishers) and 541500 (Computer Systems Design and Related Services), occupation code of 15-0000 (Computer and Mathematical Occupations). Occupations do NOT include managers and executives within the software industry.
**U.S. Bureau of Labor Statistics (2013c). Notes: Numbers drawn from Consumer Price Inflation Tables.

shortage of workers in the computing industry in recent years (especially compared with 2003 which was right after the dot.com bust), it is surprising that wages are not substantially higher in real terms for workers in the software industry in 2012 than in 2003. A later section of this chapter on globalization of the software workforce explores potential explanations for this result.

### Demographics of the Software Workforce

In terms of demographics, compared to other industries, the software industry (at least in the United States) is not particularly diverse. Figure 5.5 shows the percentages of women, Black, Asian, and Hispanic workers in the software industry from 2003 to 2012.[17] As can be seen in the figure, the percentage of women has declined over the last decade (from 27.4 percent in 2003 to 24.8 percent in 2012). The percentages of Black and Hispanic workers in the software industry are low (about five percent for each) and have not changed much from 2003 to 2012 (for Blacks, 6.1 percent in 2003 to 5.8 percent in 2012; for Hispanics, four percent in 2003 to 5.1 percent in 2012). However, the percentage of

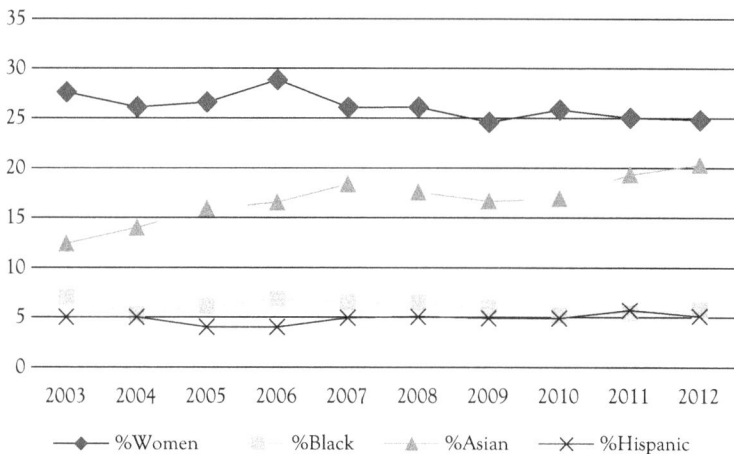

**Figure 5.5 Demographics of the software industry workforce**

Source: Based on data from the U.S. Bureau of Labor Statistics (2013b).
Notes: The data from 2003 to 2012 were downloaded from the U.S. Bureau of Labor Statistics Current Population Survey website. The NAICS codes for which the data were obtained include: 511200 (Software Publishers) and 541500 (Computer Systems Design and Related Services).

Asians in the software industry has increased, from 15.9 percent in 2003 to 20.3 percent in 2012).

In particular, the percentage of women in the software workforce has declined significantly from the early days of the industry. Although women made up 40 percent of the software workforce in the United States in 1989,[18] as shown in Figure 5.5, that proportion fell to 28 percent in 2003 and has continued its downward trend to below 25 percent in 2012. This percentage is significantly lower than the percentage employed in managerial and professional occupations in the United States (51.5 percent of workers in those occupations are female).[19]

The number of women enrolled in computer science undergraduate and graduate programs has also dropped to the lowest level in nearly a decade. There has been a 79 percent decline in the number of first-year undergraduate women interested in majoring in computer science in the United States.[20] Figure 5.6 shows the number of students graduating with a master's degree in computer science from 2000 to 2009.[21] As can be seen in the figure, in 2000, 34 percent of the graduate degrees in computer science were earned by women. By 2009, this percentage dropped to 27 percent. In contrast, in engineering, the percentage of women attaining graduate degrees increased from 20 percent in 2000 to 23 percent in 2009.[22]

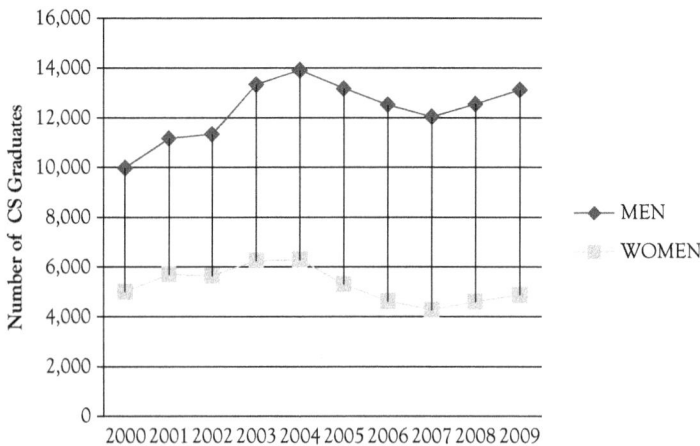

Figure 5.6 *Number of students graduating with a Master's degree in Computer Science*

Source: Based on data from the National Science Foundation (2012).

Studies suggest that some of the factors dissuading women from entering the computing profession include stereotyping of and hostility toward females, restricted career advancement opportunities, lack of informal networks to obtain information about alternative jobs and to gain access to them, limited training and development opportunities, work stress, and work-family conflict.[23] According to a study of women in the software workforce, about 75 percent of women reported liking their jobs, but 48 percent said there was an inequality that favored men; only 27 percent of women reported mentoring programs at their companies.[24] With respect to pay, studies suggest that women in computing jobs earn less than men, even if they have comparable education and experience.[25] Further, when faced with this relative pay gap, women tend to leave the computing profession (even taking a pay cut to do so), whereas men tend to take up another job in their company or leave their company for another computing job at higher pay.[26]

The lack of diversity in the software industry is of concern to policy-makers, educators, and proponents of the industry. Given the strong demand for software professionals and labor shortages in the industry, a critical success factor for software firms may be their ability to tap the talent of women and minorities.

## Globalization of the Software Workforce

### Offshore Software Development

As described in Chapter 4, the software industry has become global. Partly in response to the severe labor shortages in the software industry during the 1990s, major U.S. firms such as Microsoft, Adobe, and IBM set up offshore software delivery centers in countries like India and Ireland. An offshore delivery center works as a partner with the parent firm to provide products and services. These centers hire and train local workers to develop and maintain software applications and to provide software services such as technical support.

A number of the major firms in the software industry have set up a global delivery network as shown in Figure 5.7. In a global delivery network, different centers may specialize in different activities such as software design or software quality assurance or documentation. Different

*Figure 5.7 Example of a global delivery network for a firm in the software industry*

centers may also provide customization and tailoring of the firms' software products and services to the local country. IBM, for example, has set up global delivery centers in eight countries and four continents, with the largest in India (employing more than 60,000 workers;[27] by some accounts there are more than 100,000 workers in India working for IBM's software and services delivery centers).[28]

Offshore delivery centers offer a number of advantages to software firms. They can achieve greater cost efficiencies in software product, support and service delivery, leverage round the clock $24 \times 7$ development cycles, reduce risks involved in relying on a single market, provide better tailoring of the product software to the local market, and increase proximity to potential new markets for products and services.[29]

From a workforce perspective, establishing offshore delivery centers diversifies the software talent pool and allows firms increased access to a technically adept, larger, and more stable software workforce at a lower price.

For example, a software professional in India earns 1/6 to 1/10 as much as a software professional in the United States. The annual wages in India for a software engineer generally range from $8,000 to $10,000; for a senior software engineer, $12,000 to $15,000; and between $18,000 and $20,000 for a team lead.[30] A project manager in India may make as much as $31,000. Other countries may offer even cheaper sources of software labor (e.g., Philippines, Eastern European countries, or countries in Latin America).

As also described in Chapter 4, in addition to offshore development centers, local software firms and industries have emerged and flourished in countries outside of the United States. These industries have further contributed to the development of the software workforce and the supply of software workers in their respective countries.

## Software Immigrants

Globalization of the software workforce involves both outward and inward mobility. Offshoring and outsourcing represent *outward* flows of software jobs from the United States to other countries. There are also *inward* flows of foreign software workers into the United States to take up jobs with U.S.-based software firms. These are immigrants from countries like India who move to the United States with a work visa.

There are two primary ways that foreign software workers can enter into the U.S. workforce: permanent immigration and nonimmigrant or temporary work visa.[31] Permanent immigrants are sponsored by a family or an employer. If employer-sponsored (using an Employment-Based Immigrant Visa), the employer must show that admitting the immigrant will not adversely affect American workers. There is an annual cap on employer-sponsored permanent immigrants of 140,000, and there is a per-country limit that such visas (green cards) provided to immigrants from any country cannot exceed seven percent of the total.

Temporary work visa programs are used more frequently to bring in foreign software workers. H-1B is a temporary work visa that is issued to employers to hire workers in occupations requiring at least a bachelor's degree and highly specialized knowledge and skills. There is currently an annual cap of 65,000 for H-1B.[32] L1 is a visa that can be used by employers to transfer specialized knowledge workers within their company to the United States for temporary assignments up to seven years. There is no annual cap or prevailing wage requirement on an L1 visa. A TN visa permits workers in Canada or Mexico to work in the United States in qualifying occupations, per the terms of the North American Free Trade Agreement.

Of the various temporary work visas, it is the H-1B that is most relevant for software firms and that has been the most contentious. More than 60 percent of the H-1B visas are issued to the software industry.[33] Two important issues concern the cap (or limit) on the number of H-1B visas issued each year and the potential for an H-1B visa holder to become a legal permanent resident (H-1B visa holders can apply for legal permanent resident or green card status while holding the H-1B visa).

The maximum number of new H-1B visas permitted to be issued each year has varied, with an annual limit of 65,000 from 1991 to 1998; 115,000 from 1999 to 2000; 195,000 from 2001 to 2003; and back down to 65,000 from 2004 to today. Since 2005, the U.S. Congress has permitted an additional number of 20,000 H-1B visas per year for foreigners who graduate from U.S. universities with a master's or higher degree.

According to the U.S. Citizenship and Immigration Services (USCIS), the filing period for H-1B visas for fiscal year 2014 reached the statutory H-1B cap of 65,000 within the first week of the filing period, which ended on April 5, 2013. USCIS also received more than 20,000 H-1B petitions filed on behalf of persons exempt from the cap under the advanced degree exemption. USCIS received a total of 124,000 H-1B petitions during the filing period, including petitions filed for the advanced degree exemption, suggesting that 2/3 of applications for H-1B visas for 2014 were filled.

Software firms such as Microsoft and Oracle have intensely lobbied the U.S. Congress for permission to admit more immigrants under the H-1B visa program.

Not surprisingly, there is considerable debate about this program.

Advocates argue that employing foreign workers in the United States has many benefits for U.S. firms and the regional or national economy. Studies suggest that high-skill immigrants create new jobs in the United States and enhance ties to emerging economies, increasing the flow of trade and investment.[34] For example, skilled immigrants and international graduates from U.S. universities have made significant contributions to patent activity and innovation. A study of H-1B visas and patents found that admitting more H-1B visa holders was associated with an increased invention activity by Indians in software firms such as Microsoft and Oracle.[35]

On the other hand, there are significant concerns about abuse of the program and about adverse impacts on jobs and wages of U.S. software workers. For example, the Indian software company—Infosys—is the subject of a probe by the U.S. Justice Department over its visa practices and is reportedly facing a record immigration fine.[36] The Justice Department claims that Infosys improperly used business travel documents to place Indian employees in long-term positions in U.S. companies. The investigation fuels a debate over whether foreign workers, particularly in the software industry, are displacing qualified Americans because they are cheaper. Some further argue that lower wages may reduce student enrollments in computer science, software engineering, and information systems programs, creating a vicious cycle. In this negative cycle of events, importing foreign software workers into the United States depresses wages in the U.S. software industry, making it less attractive to U.S. workers. This reduces the attractiveness of software occupations, reducing enrollments in computer science, which further limits the supply of U.S. software workers and increases incentives of firms to import software workers.

Interestingly, the salary data drawn from the BLS suggest that average salaries in software-related occupations in the United States have been largely stagnant or even decreasing, in real terms, over the last decade (Figure 5.4). Data from the National Science Foundation's Science and Engineering Indicators on degrees attained in scientific, technology, and engineering fields also suggest that students in the United States have been favoring other disciplines over computer science as a major since the dot.com bust, to at least as recently as 2009. For example, there were 59,476 bachelor's degrees awarded in engineering fields in 2000 and this number increased to 70,600 degrees by 2009. In contrast, in computer science there were 37,519 bachelor's degrees awarded in 2000 and 38,495 in 2009 (the number of computer science degrees awarded peaked at 59,968 in 2004 and decreased thereafter with a slight increase in 2009).[37]

Whether immigration policies and offshoring of software work contribute to these trends, or whether these trends are determined by global macroeconomic, microeconomic, or other forces merits further study and is beyond the scope of this book.

# Key Takeaways

Human talent is critical to the success of software firms. The software industry is labor—not capital—intensive.

Primary occupations in the industry are in software product development, but there are a variety of occupations that support development activities, such as quality assurance, documentation, and graphic design.

Generally, software-related occupations are highly compensated and require advanced degrees, skills, and training.

In the United States, there has been a chronic imbalance in the supply and demand for software workers. Workers in the industry are most likely to be white males. Women have largely exited the industry, dropping to less than one-fourth of the workforce.

To become more cost efficient and ensure a more stable workforce, U.S. firms have created offshore delivery centers in countries with lower cost, technically skilled workers.

With the globalization of the software industry, there are also flows of software workers coming into the United States. The United States has adopted a number of visa policies to accommodate these workers, but the effects of these policies on U.S. workers are hotly debated.

# CHAPTER 6

# Regulation in the Software Industry

Given the economic dynamics of the software industry, there have long been concerns about monopolist behavior of firms. As described in Chapter 3, software markets tend to be natural monopolies due to certain features such as network effects that create a cycle in which the strong get stronger and the weak get weaker. As a result, it is not uncommon for a leading software product to become dominant and tip the market to a monopoly.

Both IBM and Microsoft have been accused of monopolistic behavior to pre-empt competition, and these firms have entered into consent decrees with the U.S. Department of Justice to settle antitrust charges. Although there are significant concerns about monopolization in the software industry, some feel that existing federal antitrust policy may not fit software markets as well as it does markets for more traditional products.

Given the nature of software, as an almost purely thought product, intellectual property is a central concern in the industry. In 1995, the U.S. Patent and Trade Office created guidelines for examining and issuing software patents. Although software patents have been criticized for many reasons, the number of new patents has increased dramatically over the past 20 years, such that a substantial proportion of the new patents granted today are for software.[1] In addition to patents, copyrights and trademarks are other ways to legally protect software innovations, and many countries do extend copyright protections to software. However, despite these protections, software piracy (the unauthorized copying of computer software) is widespread.

This chapter examines three critical aspects of regulation in the software industry, namely, antitrust issues, intellectual property, and software piracy. It then discusses the challenges and trends in the use of intellectual property protections in the software industry and draws out the implications for innovation and competition in the industry.

## Antitrust Regulation of the Software Industry

Antitrust policies are important to consumers and to markets. The ultimate objective of antitrust laws is to protect consumers. Antitrust laws influence industrial competition and cooperation among firms as well as firms' incentives to undertake R&D, improve productivity, grow, and bring new products to market.[2]

The major law governing antitrust issues in industry in the United States is the Sherman Antitrust Act passed by Congress in 1890.[3] The Act is a federal statute that prohibits business activities deemed anticompetitive by federal regulators and requires the federal government to investigate and pursue firms that may be in violation. It was the first federal statute to limit cartels and monopolies. It is still the basis for most antitrust litigation by the Federal government in the United States. The Sherman Act intends to prevent monopolistic behavior that raises prices by restricting trade or supply. However, the Act does not limit all monopolies: A monopoly gained by merit (e.g., by superior strategy, operations, and marketing) is considered in accord with the provisions of the Act.[4]

Antitrust regulation is very important in the software industry. In fact, if the U.S. Department of Justice (DOJ) had not intervened in the late 1960s, there might not be a software industry today.

It may be helpful to briefly review that critical event, since it foreshadows other similar events in the software industry. Recall that IBM was dominant in the computing industry in the 1960s. The extent of its dominance led to antitrust inquiries by the DOJ, and on January 17, 1969, the DOJ filed the case *U.S. vs. IBM* in the U.S. District Court of New York. The suit alleged that IBM violated Section 2 of the Sherman Act by monopolizing (or attempting to monopolize) the digital computer system market for business. The case lasted for over 13 years, until in 1982, the Justice Department finally dropped the case. However, the antitrust litigation prompted IBM to disaggregate its software and services from its hardware sales in 1969.[5]

Another key antitrust case that has important implications for the software industry is an antitrust case against AT&T. In 1949, the U.S. Department of Justice brought an antitrust case against AT&T, claiming that it was running a price-fixing conspiracy.[6] The case was settled by a Consent Decree in 1956, and AT&T agreed to limit its activities to those related to running the national telephone system and special projects for the federal government.[7] AT&T also agreed to license patents for its innovations to competitors upon request. A later antitrust case brought against AT&T in 1974 was settled in 1982 by AT&T's agreement to divest itself of its local telephone operations (leading to the creation of the Baby Bells in 1984). In return, the Justice department lifted the restrictions on AT&T activities contained in the 1956 Consent Decree.[8]

The antitrust cases are important to the software industry because their aftereffects may have helped to spark the open-source software movement via the development of the UNIX operating system.[9] After settling the antitrust cases, AT&T became more cautious about exploiting innovations from its R&D arm (Bell Labs) that were not directly related to the telephone. Bell Labs originally worked on a version of UNIX (called Multics) for a GE mainframe computer in the 1960s. When Bell Labs eventually pulled out of the Multics project in 1969, some of the Bell Labs researchers decided to persist with the effort but re-do it on a smaller scale. The result was UNIX, released in 1971.[10] However, in an effort to avoid further antitrust issues, AT&T offered patents for UNIX to any requestor. For a nominal license fee users could obtain the source code. AT&T was reportedly overwhelmed with requests for UNIX patents.[11] AT&T also did not provide support for UNIX. These events may have motivated individuals and organizations to share ideas, tinker, and improve the operating system in a way foreshadowing the open-source movement.[12]

The software industry has continued to be very prone to antitrust issues and concerns. Microsoft, in particular, has been a frequent target of antitrust litigation. In the 1990s, the DOJ launched numerous antitrust probes of Microsoft. In 1994, the U.S. Justice Department investigated Microsoft's licensing practices for MS-DOS, questioning Microsoft's policy of selling operating systems based on the number of processors.[13] As a result, Microsoft agreed to start selling its operating systems to personal computer makers based on the number of PCs purchased, rather than based on the number of processors sold. In 1995, Microsoft was again a target of antitrust concerns when three online services companies— CompuServe, America Online, and Prodigy—complained to Congress that Microsoft was introducing its own online service, and by bundling it with Windows 95 would have an unfair advantage in the market.[14] In 1998, Microsoft was yet again the target of antitrust litigation by the U.S. government and 20 states that accused Microsoft of extending its monopoly of the PC software market into the then new markets of Internet software and commerce by bundling its web browser, Internet Explorer, into its latest release of Windows.[15] The judge in that case, Judge Thomas Penfield Jackson, ruled to break up Microsoft into separate companies: an operating systems company and an applications company. Microsoft appealed, and in 2001, the government settled its case with Microsoft without requiring the firm to break up. However, in 2002, new lawsuits were filed against Microsoft by America Online (AOL) Time Warner and Netscape Communications Corporation that claimed Microsoft had used unfair trade practices to boost its Explorer browser.[16] In March 2002, Sun Microsystems pursued a $1 billion lawsuit against Microsoft, accusing the company of using anticompetitive practices against Sun's Java platform when Microsoft removed the Java program from Windows XP.[17] In 2003– 2004, the European Commission investigated the bundling of Windows Media Player into Windows and fined Microsoft a record fine of over $600 million for breaching EU competition law.[18] Microsoft appealed, but the appeal was denied, and in 2008, European antitrust regulators fined Microsoft $1.3 billion for failing to comply with the 2004 judgment.[19] These fines by the EU were the largest it had ever imposed on a single firm.

Not surprisingly, given the extent of litigation, entire books have been written on Microsoft antitrust activities![20] However, it is important to note that despite the efforts at antitrust litigation against Microsoft, its position as the number one firm in the global software industry and its dominance of the PC software market are still unshaken.

The software industry is challenging to regulate for a number of reasons.[21]

First and foremost, the software industry is characterized by network effects. As described in Chapter 3, in the software market, a software application's value increases with the number of others who run and use that same software application. This increased value is due to the greater number of other users with whom one can communicate and share data, and the larger number of complements (i.e., other hardware, software, etc.) for popular software applications. Thus, network effects can create a positive feedback loop in which increased demand for a software application will in turn stimulate even more demand for that application, reducing demand for competing products. As a result, the market can tip to a popular application. A spreadsheet application is a good example of this phenomenon. In the early 1980s, Visicorp was a popular spreadsheet, but then Lotus 1-2-3 was introduced and the market quickly moved away from Visicorp to Lotus. For the reasons listed above, network effects can be a good thing for consumers if everyone is using common software. However, given the dynamics of network effects, a company with a popular software product can soon corner the market leading to monopolistic pricing. Antitrust policies, therefore, need to take network effects into account when regulating the software market.

A second defining feature of software markets that contributes to the difficulty in regulating them is economies of scale. As described in Chapter 3, although a software application can require millions of dollars to create the first copy, other copies may be created and distributed at very low (approaching $0) cost. Thus, in software markets, the marginal cost (the incremental cost to make an additional copy) is orders of magnitude less than the average cost of production (the development costs amortized over the number of copies). This feature of software markets causes difficulties for regulators to determine what should be the fair or competitive price for a software application. Further, given the structure of costs, it is natural for a firm to exploit economies of scale by selling as many copies of the software as possible.

One other factor that poses interesting challenges for antitrust regulation in software markets is durability. A software application does not wear out like a physical product. It can only become obsolete if it ceases to function properly in its larger system. This can create a problem with compatibility across generations of a software product. A software firm can compete against its own installed base of users for the prior version of its product. This introduces incentives for the software firm to continually move its installed base to new versions of the software product via planned obsolescence. However, due to switching costs (the difficulty and effort of learning to use a new software application) users of the prior version may be reluctant to switch. In order to motivate the installed base of users to move to the new version, the software firm may try to lower prices on the new version of the software, below its own cost of production.

Because of network effects, switching costs, economies of scale and durability, compatibility and standards are also critical dimensions of competition and antitrust regulation in the software industry. If all software products were fully compatible (i.e., could communicate and be run with the same system components), there would be no monopolies. But, if software products were not compatible at all, then markets could tip and create monopolies. These dynamics could motivate software firms to create products that may not be compatible with others; it also motivates software firms to try to set the standard for a product early so that the product can become dominant.

As noted in Chapter 3, in the world of software, a standard is a characteristic of the software product or its interface. Interface standards allow two or more components to work together, although a product design standard emerges when a product beats out competing products to become the dominant design. Standards can also be open (published and freely available), closed (not freely available), or proprietary (owned by an entity, and neither open nor closed).[22] Standards offer many benefits such as promoting market efficiency, lowering barriers to entry, and enabling interoperability of products.

Problems, from the perspective of antitrust, occur when a product standard can pre-empt competition and thereby disadvantage consumers. Standards (especially closed or proprietary standards) may prevent firms with complementary products or systems from access to an essential product, and antitrust proceedings may be brought by competitors requesting reasonable access to these technological standards. Standards may also be set by consortia of firms in an effort to limit competition by creating a dominant technology platform. For example, an antitrust case in the mid-1990s challenged a cooperative effort to establish compatibility standards by an industry consortium that was formed to develop a platform-independent version of the UNIX computer operating system

(*Addamax Corporation vs. Open Software Foundation, Inc.*).[23] Although the case was unsuccessful, in 2000, the DOJ and the Federal Trade Commission issued antitrust guidelines for establishing and operating legal alliances and joint ventures, including standards setting.

One other area in which antitrust plays an important role in the software industry is in mergers and acquisitions of firms within the industry. Although individual firms such as Microsoft and IBM have often been the focus of antitrust litigation, the majority of antitrust enforcement actions in the software industry actually involve mergers and acquisitions.[24] When assessing whether a specific merger or acquisition will have antitrust implications, regulators consider unilateral competitive effects (i.e., whether the firm could raise prices after the merger), whether a cartel could form, and the nature of merger synergies. Regulators also consider whether a merger could make entry into the market more difficult.

Examples of mergers investigated by the U.S. Department of Justice include: Borland and Ashton-Tate (1991), Adobe and Aldus (1994), Microsoft and Intuit (1995), Autodesk and SoftDesk (1997), SunGard and Comdisco (2001), Oracle and PeopleSoft (2004), H&R Block and 2SS Holdings, Inc. (2011), and ITA Software, Inc. and Google (2011). Some of these mergers were allowed to go through without constraints; for example SunGard and Comdisco, Oracle and PeopleSoft. Other mergers were allowed, conditional on special licensing arrangements to ensure that consumers had an alternative outside the merged company; for example Borland and Ashton-Tate, Adobe and Aldus. Others were rejected; for example, Microsoft and Intuit, H&R Block and 2SS Holdings, Inc.

When evaluating whether a merger or acquisition would lead to antitrust issues, federal regulators evaluate the proposed merger or acquisition by: (1) defining the relevant product market; (2) identifying market participants and measuring market shares before and after the merger; (3) and assessing the impact of the merger on market entry conditions.[25]

As examples of how antitrust concerns can influence the software industry, consider an unsuccessful acquisition—H&R Block and 2SS Holdings—(rejected by the DOJ) and a successful acquisition—ITA Software and Google—(approved by the DOJ, but with conditions).

In October, 2010, H&R Block offered $288 million (cash) to acquire 2SS (2nd Story Software) Holdings, Inc., developer of the TaxACT digital tax preparation software, to enhance its tax preparation digital offerings. At the time, H&R Block's At Home software competed with Intuit's TurboTax software, which was gaining market share from H&R Block and with Jackson Hewitt Tax Service Inc.'s software as more and more people moved to do-it-yourself tax preparation. H&R planned to combine its At Home digital business and the acquired TaxACT business into a single unit led by the TaxACT management team, but proposed to continue to offer both brands in the market.[26]

In evaluating the proposed acquisition for possible antitrust issues, the DOJ began by defining the product market relevant to the acquisition— that is, the market for digital do-it-yourself (DDIY) tax preparation software products.[27] The DOJ rejected H&R Block's proposed definition of the market (which included pen and paper, hiring a tax professional, and using DDIY software).[28] The DOJ argued that H&R Block's definition included tax preparation methods that were fundamentally different from using DDIY software, that the company ran the DDIY software as a separate business unit, and that DDIY software was a distinct method, technology, and user experience.

Once the DOJ defined the product market, it considered the market share of the three leading DDIY tax preparation software products, including Intuit's TurboTax, H&R Block's At Home, and TaxACT. According to IRS data, those three products accounted for almost 90 percent of the DDIY-prepared federal tax returns in 2010. Intuit accounted for 62 percent of DDIY software product sales, and the proposed H&R Block/TaxACT market share was 28 percent. The DOJ showed that, after the proposed merger, its measure of market concentration—the Herfindahl-Hirschmann Index or HHI[29]—would increase by 400 points to 4,691, well over the threshold of 2,500 for highly concentrated markets.[30] The Court agreed with the DOJ's assessment that the proposed acquisition would substantially lessen competition in the DDIY tax preparation software market and rejected the proposed merger.

In contrast, consider the merger of ITA Software and Google— successful, albeit with conditions. In 2010, Google Inc., offered $700 million to acquire a company called ITA Software. ITA Software produces a key software product called QPX, which is used by many airlines, online travel agents, and online travel search sites to provide complex, customized flight services.[31] Google handles most Internet searches in the United States but is not dominant in online travel searches. The proposed merger encountered fierce opposition from FairSearch—a group of online travel companies including Expedia, Kayak, and Travelocity—which argued that if Google acquired ITA Software, it would control the online travel market. The DOJ considered this argument and initially agreed, filing a suit to block the merger, saying that the proposed merger would have substantially lessened competition among providers of comparative flight search software and would have hurt consumers. However the DOJ also proposed a settlement to which both sides agreed. According to the terms of the settlement, Google must continue to sell QPX software (at fair and reasonable prices) to customers into 2016 and must fund R&D of the product at similar levels as ITA. Google must also develop and offer ITA's next-generation software product—InstaSearch—to travel website companies. Finally, Google is required to implement a firewall to prevent unauthorized use of sensitive data gathered from ITA's customers.[32]

## Software Intellectual Property

Intellectual property protection is another critical factor that influences innovation and competition in an industry and given the nature of software products and services, it is particularly important for firms in the software industry.

There are three primary ways in which software firms protect their intellectual property: trademarks, copyrights, and patents.

### Trademarks

According to the U.S. Patent and Trademark Office (USPTO), a trademark is a word, name, symbol, or device that is used to indicate the source of a product and to distinguish it from the products of others. A servicemark is the same as a trademark except that it identifies and distinguishes the source of a service rather than a product. The terms trademark and mark are commonly used to refer to both trademarks and servicemarks.[33]

Although trademarks and service marks can be used to prevent other companies from using a similar mark, they cannot prevent other companies from producing and selling the same products or services under a different mark.

Examples of trademarks in the software industry include: the Capability Maturity Model for Integration (CMMI®)—which is a registered service mark of Carnegie Mellon University, Adobe AIR® which is a registered trademark of Adobe Systems and Oracle® which is a registered trademark of Oracle, Inc.; Apache™ which is a trademark of the Apache Software Foundation; and Quicken Health℠ which is a service mark of Intuit, Inc.

Although a trademark can be extremely valuable to the firm producing the trademarked product or service, the ultimate purpose of a trademark is to protect consumers. Trademarks inform the consumer where the products or services originate. The consumer, knowing the origin of the products or services can make better purchasing decisions based on prior knowledge, reputation, or marketing.

### Copyrights

According to the USPTO, a copyright protects the authors of original works of authorship including literary, dramatic, musical, artistic, and certain other intellectual works, both published and unpublished. Copyrights are registered by the Copyright Office of the Library of Congress. The U.S. 1976 Copyright Act generally gives the owner of copyright the exclusive right to reproduce the copyrighted work, to prepare derivative works, to distribute copies or recordings of the copyrighted work, to perform the copyrighted work publicly, or to display the copyrighted work publicly.[34]

It is important to note that a copyright protects the *form of expression* of an idea rather than the idea itself. For example, a description of a machine could be copyrighted, but this would only prevent others from copying the description; it would not prevent others from writing a description of their own or from making and using the machine.

In terms of its copyright protection, computer software is considered a literary work, that is, a work expressed in words, numbers, or other verbal or numerical symbols, regardless of the particular media (e.g., tape, disk, card) in which it is expressed.

Historically, computer software programs were not effectively protected by copyrights. There was much disagreement as to whether a computer software program was entitled to copyright protection, especially when the program existed only in magnetic or electronic form or on a silicon chip. The Copyright Act of 1976[35] did state that a copyrighted work could be fixed in any medium, although there was still much confusion as to whether that provision applied to software. The Computer Software Copyright Act of 1980[36] provided more clarity by defining software (a set of statements or instructions to be used directly or indirectly in a computer in order to bring about a certain result), specifying that the 1976 Copyright Act did extend to software and also allowing the owner of a software program to copy or adapt that program if that was required to use it.

This legislation, plus subsequent court decisions clarified that the 1976 Copyright Act gave computer programs the copyright status of literary works. In response, software firms began to claim that they licensed rather than sold their products, in order to avoid the transfer of intellectual property rights to the end-user; these software license agreements are often referred to as end-user license agreements.

There have been numerous court cases involving claims of copyright infringement. Not surprisingly, given the fungible nature of software and the almost infinite number of ways in which software features and functions can be designed and implemented, there has been much fuzziness as to what constitutes copyright infringement.

One of the important cases that helped to define the extent of software copyright protection involved Lotus Development Corporation versus Borland International.[37] This case went all the way to the U.S. Supreme Court. The case involved two spreadsheet products: Quattro Pro (made by Borland) and Lotus 1-2-3 (made by Lotus). Although none of the source or machine code in these spreadsheets was similar, there were features of Quattro Pro that essentially copied those of Lotus 1-2-3 (namely, the Menu hierarchy and command structure). Lotus initially filed a copyright infringement suit in the U.S. District Court in Massachusetts in 1990, and the district court ruled that Borland infringed Lotus' copyright. Borland removed the Lotus-based menu system but retained other features relating to the menu hierarchy, and Lotus again filed a copyright infringement claim against these features. The district court in Massachusetts again ruled that this infringed on Lotus' copyright. However, Borland appealed the decision, arguing that a menu hierarchy is a method of operation which cannot be copyrighted. The U.S. Court of Appeals reversed the district court's decision saying that menu hierarchies should not be copyrightable or users would have to learn how to perform the same command in a different way for every computer program. Lotus then petitioned the U.S. Supreme Court in 1995, but the Supreme Court affirmed the Circuit Court's opinion and Lotus' petition was denied.

Ironically, by the time the lawsuit ended, Borland had sold Quattro Pro to Novell, and Lotus was facing stiff competition from Microsoft's Excel (which is today the dominant spreadsheet product).

The Lotus versus Borland case is important for copyrights in the software industry as it distinguished between an interface of a software product (of which the available operations and mechanics of their activation cannot be copyrighted) and the actual implementation (code) of a software product (which can be copyrighted).

The case also illustrates a key lesson that innovation in the software industry moves quickly: by the time that legal cases relating to software copyrights are resolved, the issues at hand may be moot.

In 1998, The United States Congress passed the Digital Millennium Copyright Act (DMCA).[38] The DMCA criminalizes the evasion of copyright protection and the destruction or mismanagement of copyright management information, and those convicted can pay fines of up to $250,000 and spend up to 5 years in prison. In addition, the DMCA allows users to copy a program for maintenance, repair, or backup as long as these copies are destroyed in the event that continued possession of the computer program should cease to be rightful. Since 1998, a number of laws have been proposed to broaden the definition of what constitutes software copyright infringement.

Today, software copyright has become an extremely important tool in the software industry to combat software piracy. Software is copyrightable in countries outside of the United States. There are several international copyright treaties (including the Berne Convention and the General

Agreement on Tariffs and Trade [GATT]). Under these treaties, member countries (over 150), including virtually all industrialized nations, must offer copyright protection to nationals of any member country.[39] Together, the Berne Copyright Convention and the GATT allow U.S. software firms to enforce their copyrights in most industrialized nations and allow the software firms in those nations to enforce their copyrights in the United States.

Finally, it should also be noted that free software licenses for open-source software rely on existing copyright law. A copyleft is a type of copyright license used extensively for open-source software products that allows redistributing the software (with or without changes) on the condition that recipients are also granted these rights. Copyleft uses existing copyright law to ensure the software remains freely available. The GNU General Public License, originally written by Richard Stallman, was the first copyleft license and continues to dominate the licensing of copylefted software.[40] GNU is a recursive acronym and means "GNU is Not Unix."

## Patents

Patents are a third way for software firms to protect their intellectual property. According to the USPTO, a patent for an invention is the grant of a property right to the inventor, issued by the United States Patent and Trademark Office.[41] Generally, the term of a new patent is 20 years from the date on which the application for the patent was filed in the United States or, in special cases, from the date an earlier related application was filed, subject to the payment of maintenance fees. U.S. patent grants are effective only within the United States, U.S. territories, and U.S. possessions. Under certain circumstances, patent term extensions or adjustments may be available.

The right conferred by the patent grant is, in the language of the statute and of the grant itself, "the right to exclude others from making, using, offering for sale, or selling" the invention in the United States or importing the invention into the United States. What is granted is not the right to make, use, offer for sale, sell or import, but the right to *exclude others* from making, using, offering for sale, selling, or importing the invention. Once a patent is issued, the patentee must enforce the patent without aid of the USPTO.[42]

There are several types of patents relevant to the software industry[43]:

1. Utility patents may be granted to anyone who invents or discovers any new and useful process, machine, article of manufacture, or composition of matter, or any new and useful improvement of it.
2. Design patents may be granted to anyone who invents a new, original, and ornamental design for an article of manufacture.

To receive a patent, an invention must be novel, not obvious, and useful.

An example of a software patent is shown in Figure 6.1. This is patent number 8,108,932, filed June 12, 2008, and granted almost 4 years later—January 31, 2012. It is assigned to IBM, and references seven other patents. The patent is for a software algorithm that automatically computes a score for computer password strength based on the layout positions of the password entered on an input device.

Historically, although computer hardware could be patented, the USPTO was reluctant to grant patents for software. As noted in Chapter 2, one of the first software patents granted in the United States was in 1965 to Martin Goetz.[44] Goetz, a programmer working for a company called Applied Digital Research (ADR), invented a sorting algorithm to help mainframe computers sort data more quickly. On April 8, 1965, he filed for a software patent and received it 3 years later on April 28, 1968—as U.S. Patent No. 3,380,029 for Sorting System.[45] Another early software patent was filed in the United Kingdom on May 21, 1962, entitled "A Computer Arranged for the Automatic Solution of Linear Programming Problems" assigned to British Petroleum Company.[46] The invention was a software program that performed efficient memory management for the simplex algorithm. The patent was granted on August 17, 1966.

Although the USPTO granted Goetz' patent, it created formal guidelines in 1968 for computer-related inventions which stated that a software program, whether claimed as an apparatus or as a process, was not patentable. The USPTO tended to view software as an abstract idea or mental step that could not be patented—not as a process or machine

United States Patent          8,108,932

Himberger et al.      January 31, 2012

*Calculating a password strength score based upon character proximity and relative position upon an input device*

### Abstract

A solution for computing password strength based upon layout positions of input mechanisms of an input device that entered a password. A password including an ordered sequence of at least two characters can be identified. A position of each of the characters of the sequence can be determined relative to a layout of an input device used for password entry. Each position can correspond to an input region (key) of the input device (keyboard). A proximity algorithm can generate a proximately score for the determined positions based upon a pattern produced by the positions given the layout of the input device. A password strength score can be computed based at least in part upon the proximity score.

Inventors:     Himberger; Kevin D. (Durham, NC), Parees; Benjamin M. (Durham, NC)

Assignee:      International Business Machines Corporation (Armonk, NY)

Family ID:    41415995

Appl. No.:    12/137,645

Filed:        June 12, 2008

Current U.S. Class:        726/25; 713/183

Current International Class:  G06F 11/00 (20060101); G06F 12/14 (20060101); G06F 12/16 (20060101); G08B 23/00 (20060101)

Current CPC Class:        G06F 21/46 (20130101); G06F 2221/2117 (20130101)

Field of Search:        726/25 713/183,184

References Cited [Referenced By] U.S. Patent Documents

| 5430827 | July 1995 | Rissanen |
| 6839667 | January 2005 | Reich |
| 7367053 | April 2008 | Sanai et al. |
| 2008/0066167 | March 2008 | Andri |
| 2009/0150677 | June 2009 | Vedula et al. |
| 2010/0031343 | February 2010 | Childress et al. |
| 2010/0114560 | May 2010 | Spataro |

Primary Examiner: Zand; Kambiz;

Assistant Examiner: Harriman; DantShaifer;

Attorney, Agent or Firm: Patents on Demand P.A. Buchheit; Brian K. Garrett; Scott M.

## Figure 6.1  *Example of a software patent*

*Source*: U.S. Patent and Trademark Office (2013a) and (2013c).

which can be patented. In the 1970s the U.S. Supreme Court reviewed several cases filed on software patents, but ruled negatively. It was not until 1981 that the U.S. Supreme Court ruled affirmatively to uphold a software patent claim (in the *Diamond vs. Diehr* case[47]). Still there was much confusion and dissent about whether software could be patented. In the 1990s the U.S. Federal Circuit Court tried to clarify when software could be patented—if the software were a mere abstract algorithm (such as to convert from one number system to another) then it could not be patented. However, if the software manipulated actual data (such as a program that recorded and sorted temperature readings), then it could be patented. In 1995, the USPTO created broad guidelines for examining and issuing software patents.

A watershed case for software patents was *State Street Bank & Trust vs. Signature Financial Group*, decided in 1998.[48] In this case, Signature Financial had obtained a patent on a method of handling mutual funds in which several mutual funds pooled their investment assets into a single investment portfolio. A computer software program then calculated the value of each fund based upon a percentage ownership of each of the assets in the portfolio. State Street Bank asked the court to declare this invention not patentable as an algorithm or business method. However, the Federal Circuit rejected the arguments of State Street Bank, and instead upheld the patent by explicitly stating that business methods can form patentable subject matter. The court emphasized that software or other processes that yield a useful, concrete, and tangible result should be considered patentable.

After that case, both the Federal Circuit and the U.S. Supreme Court weighed in on various cases. Among these cases, one with significant implications for software and business patents is *Bilski vs. Kappos*[49] and in Bilski which addressed the patentability of business methods. In 1997, applicants Bilski and Warsaw filed an application to patent a business method of hedging risks in commodities trading via a fixed bill system. Their patent application described a method for providing a fixed bill energy contract to consumers. The patent examiner rejected the patent, saying that it was an abstract idea and solved a purely mathematical problem without a practical application. The applicants appealed the decision to the Board of Patent Appeals and Interferences, but the Board rejected their appeal. They then appealed this decision to the Federal Circuit which upheld the rejection in 2008. In 2009, Bilski and Warsaw appealed this decision to the U.S. Supreme Court which rejected the Federal Circuit's reasoning for its judgment, but still ruled that the Bilski invention was not patent-eligible subject matter.

This case is an important one for the software industry because the decision narrowed the criteria by which a business method, including one implemented in a software program, could qualify as patent-eligible material.

Despite the equivocality and controversy surrounding the patentability of software, the number of software patents granted in the United States has grown significantly, both in sheer numbers and as a percentage of total patents. Figure 6.2 shows the total number of patents granted by the USPTO since 1971 and the number of software patents granted over that same time period. The data were created based on queries of the USPTO patent database,[50] and software patents were identified using the approach of Bessen and Hunt.[51] The number of software patents granted grew from a handful in 1971 to almost 100,000 in 2012. As a proportion

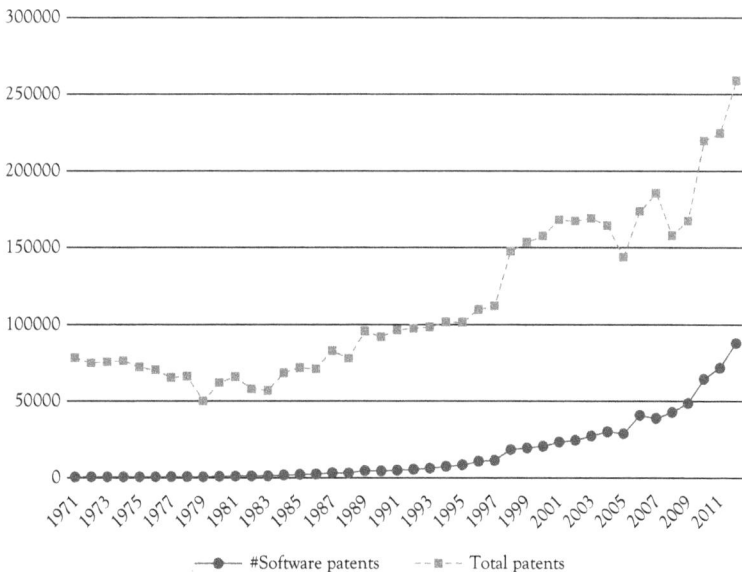

**Figure 6.2  Patents granted by the USPTO from 1971 to 2012**

Source: U.S. Patent and Trademark Office (2013c).

of total patents, software patents granted grew from less than 1 percent in 1971 to more than 34 percent in 2012.

It is important to emphasize that patents apply only in the country in which they are granted. Thus, a software company must file patent applications in each and every country in which it wants a patent. However, the European Patent Office has the power to grant patents which can then be brought into effect in its member states. There is also an international procedure for filing a single international application under the Patent Cooperation Treaty, which can then give rise to patent protection in most countries (currently 148 countries participate).[52] Different countries and regional offices have different standards for granting patents. This is particularly true of software or computer-implemented inventions, and especially where the software is implementing a business method.

Although there are numerous safeguards and protections for intellectual property, it can be difficult to enforce intellectual property protections in the software industry. This becomes obvious when one considers software piracy.

## Software Piracy

Software piracy is a form of copyright infringement. It includes a number of practices which involve the unauthorized copying of computer software: using works under copyright, infringing the copyright holder's rights to reproduce, distribute, display, or perform the copyrighted work, or making derivative works, without permission from the copyright holder.

Software piracy is a major issue in the software industry.

In 2012, Microsoft settled 3,265 software piracy cases worldwide, of which 35 cases were in the United States in 19 different states, and 3,230 were international cases that took place in 42 different countries.[53] Google removed 2,544,209 URLs for websites with pirated or counterfeit software from 2011 to 2012.[54]

In 2012, the Software and Information Industry Association (SIIA) removed 24,000 websites of firms and individuals who were involved in software piracy.[55] SIIA also reported bringing a record number of lawsuits against sellers of pirated software. For example, SIIA assisted the Federal government to prosecute a software pirate by the name of James Baxter.[56] Mr. Baxter of Wichita Falls, Texas, was especially prolific and sophisticated in pirating software. He owned and operated various websites that offered so-called backup copies of Adobe, Microsoft, and Autodesk software for sale at about one-fifth of their value. He also provided counterfeit product registration codes that were distributed with the software so that the customer could install the software. Between 2004 and 2007, he established at least 17 assumed business names with accompanying merchant bank accounts to process credit card payments for the software orders. Baxter pled guilty to copyright infringement for illegally reproducing copies of Adobe software and selling it over the Internet and was sentenced to 57 months in Federal prison and ordered to pay $402,417 in restitution.[57]

According to a study conducted by the Business Software Alliance (BSA) in 2011, over 57 percent of the 15,000 computer users surveyed in 33 countries admitted that they pirate software and more than 42 percent of software installed on PCs worldwide has been pirated.[58] The BSA estimated the global losses from software piracy in 2011 at more than $63 billion.[59] It should be noted that these estimates are based on the idea that every pirated copy of software would have otherwise earned full-price (which is unlikely to be true). Thus, the losses from piracy may be somewhat overstated. On the other hand, it should be further noted that although piracy may have some benefits for the producer such as an increase in network effects and in implicit advertising, a review of the research on digital media piracy effects suggests that, overall, illegal file sharing significantly harms product sales.[60] On balance, software firms are more likely to suffer than benefit from piracy.

According to the BSA, the profile of a typical software pirate is someone who is: young, male, living in an emerging economy, and acquiring software through channels that tend to be illegal, such as buying software from retail stores stocked with illegal name-brand software, installing a single copy of a software program on more computers than allowed or downloading illicit software programs from file sharing peer-to-peer sites such as Kazaa or Morpheus.[61] Interestingly, business users of computer software admit to pirating more than nonbusiness users; they tend to copy software onto more machines than allowed by the software license.

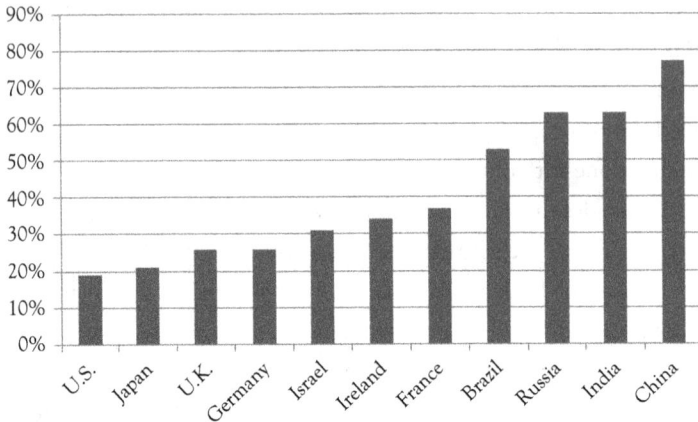

**Figure 6.3 Software piracy rates (percent) in key countries in the software industry**

Source: Business Software Alliance (2011, p. 6).
Note: Piracy rates computed as the ratio of pirated value divided by legal software sales value.

Generally, computer users in emerging economies pirate software at almost three times the rate of users in developed economies. For example, the United States has the world's lowest software piracy rate (19 percent), although the piracy rate in China is estimated at 77 percent.[62] Figure 6.3 shows software piracy rates in the various countries with significant software industries that were profiled in Chapter 4. Figure 6.4 shows the estimated pirated value (losses from piracy) for these countries. As can be seen in these figures, although the United States has the lowest software piracy rate, it also has the greatest losses due to piracy. China, Russia, India, Brazil, and France have both a high software piracy rate and a relatively high level of losses from piracy.

Regulatory agencies worldwide have been involved in addressing software piracy. In the United States the 1974 Trade Act (amended in 1988) authorized trade representatives to investigate infringements of intellectual property rights worldwide.[63] Countries with inadequate protection of intellectual property rights were placed on a priority list and faced possible trade sanctions and restrictions. In 1993, the European Union developed measures of its own to protect intellectual property rights, introducing the Directive on the Legal Protection of Computer Programs (amended in 2009) which protected computer programs as intellectual property.[64]

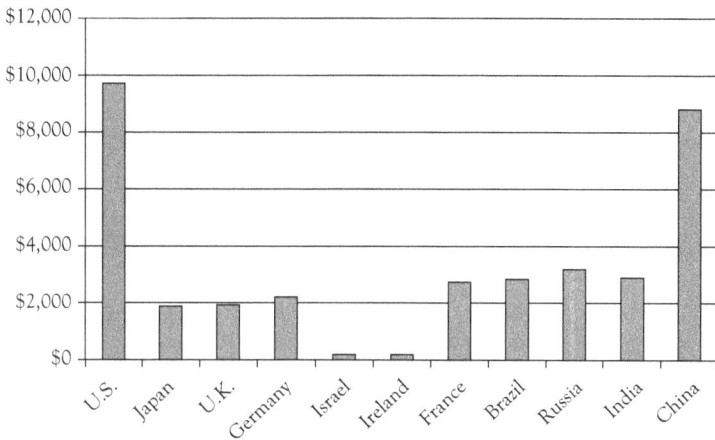

**Figure 6.4** *Software pirated value (in $M) in key countries in the software industry*

*Source*: Business Software Alliance (2011, p. 6).

In Asia, a number of countries have joined the Berne Convention, an international organization designed to protect the intellectual property rights of any of its members.[65] More than 90 countries have signed the World Intellectual Property Organization Copyright Treaty—a global antipiracy agreement.[66]

However, despite the efforts of regulators and industry associations and groups, software piracy has continued to thrive. According to David Finn, Microsoft's Associate General Counsel, Worldwide Anti-piracy and Anti-counterfeiting, sophisticated criminal syndicates and drug cartels are generating large sums of money from selling illegal software and are using these funds for drug trafficking, arms and weapons trafficking, kidnapping, extortion, and other violent crimes.[67] In Mexico, for example, drug cartels have sophisticated distribution networks for pirated software in stores, markets, and kiosks, earning more than $2.2 million dollars in revenue per day.[68]

In 2007, the largest software piracy bust in history, code-named Operation Summer Solstice, was conducted by a joint task force including the FBI and the Chinese Ministry of Public Security. The bust occurred in Guangdong, China, and yielded more than $500 million in Microsoft Windows software and 25 arrests.[69] Products from this operation were found in 36 different countries, but most of the software was sold over the Internet to customers in the United States and Europe.[70] The operation was very sophisticated and used expensive machines to manufacture high-quality counterfeit software that appeared almost identical to the real products.

## Challenges and Trends in Use of Software Intellectual Property Protections

Protecting software intellectual property is difficult. Software piracy is rising around the world and is significantly infringing on software copyrights. This chapter has discussed the importance of trademarks, copyrights, and patents for protecting firms' intellectual property in the software industry. For the most part, firms in the software industry have enthusiastically embraced these legal protections. However, some software firms are using these protections in unintended ways. Rather than being used to protect intellectual property, software patents are increasingly used as weapons to deter competition, innovation, and entry into the industry. There are also increasing doubts as to whether the protections are stifling or facilitating innovation and competition in the industry. The following sections identify challenges and trends in the use of intellectual property protections by firms in the software industry.

### Challenges in the use of Software Patents

Battles over software patents are escalating in the software industry as firms accumulate patents into competitive arsenals. In particular, the patent war is shifting from filing as many patents as possible for each innovation a firm creates to buying as many patents as possible. Recent multibillion dollar patent deals illustrate this trend.

Consider the acquisition of Motorola Mobility by Google. In 2012, Google paid $12.4 billion to acquire Motorola Mobility Holdings, Inc. In its filing with the U.S. Securities and Exchange Commission, Google attributed almost half of the total purchase price—$5.5 billion—to patents.[71] In essence, it appears that a primary reason for Google's acquisition was not to acquire Motorola's phones but rather to obtain ownership of Motorola's portfolio of 17,000 software patents.

There are firms in the software industry whose sole *raison d'être* is to buy patents and defend them. These companies are sometimes called patent trolls. Patent trolls are firms that buy up patents for products and services that they didn't invent and don't produce. The companies make money by litigating to enforce patent rights against accused infringers. Related names include: patent holding companies, patent assertion entities, patent monetization entities, and nonpracticing entities.

Patent trolls reportedly accounted for more than half of the patent infringement lawsuits filed in the United States in 2012.[72] However, interestingly, patent trolls are generally unsuccessful if their cases actually do go to court: In an analysis of litigated patents, researchers found that patent trolls (which they refer to as repeat patent plaintiffs) win only about 10 percent of the time when their lawsuits go to trial.[73]

Patent trolls are quite active in the software industry. The software industry may be especially vulnerable to these companies because of the lack of clarity on what constitutes patent-suitable material for software products.

Lodsys LLC is a company considered to be a software patent troll. Lodsys has one employee (its CEO) and is headquartered in Marshall, Texas (where most patent infringement lawsuits are filed).[74] The company has four patents for software that support customer help functions via the Internet (e.g., online help and tutorials), but the company does not, and has not ever produced a software product or service. Over the past few years, the company has been busily suing companies as varied as General Motors, Canon, Best Buy, Hewlett Packard, Supervalu, Adidas, Motorola, Novell, Kaspersky Lab and Apple iPhone, and Google Android developers for patent infringement.[75] Out of the 55 companies sued by Lodsys to date, Kaspersky Lab is the only one to be successful in defending against the Lodsys' lawsuits; other companies have settled with Lodsys out of court.[76]

Litigation from patent claims, not only from patent trolls, but from legitimate software firms in the industry has also increased significantly. Large companies such as Apple, Google, and Hewlett Packard have been aggressive in patenting their technologies and enforcing their software patents.

Apple in particular has been assertive in protecting its intellectual property. A specific and significant recent case involves the battle between Apple and Samsung over software patents for smartphones.[77]

In April of 2011 Apple accused Samsung of copying its iPhone and iPad. Samsung retaliated by countersuing Apple, accusing Apple of infringing on Samsung's software patents. A jury found for Apple, and fined Samsung over $1 billion in damages. This was later reduced, but both companies appealed the ruling. To quote Samsung: "it is unfortunate that patent law can be manipulated to give one company a monopoly over rectangles with rounded corners."[78]

In another skirmish, Samsung sued Apple in June 2011, claiming that the iPhone 4 and iPad 2 violated Samsung's software patents. This suit was judged by the International Trade Commission (ITC) who ruled in favor of Samsung in June 2013. The ITC ruled that Apple could not sell the iPhone 4 and iPad 2 in the United States. However, ITC's order was vetoed by Barack Obama (the ITC is required to present such orders to the President for a review).[79]

A week later, Apple filed a countersuit against Samsung, this time for patent infringements on the design of the iPhone. The ITC made a preliminary ruling for Apple, and President Obama declined to veto the ruling.[80] Therefore, there is a ban currently in effect that prohibits the import of older Samsung smartphones and tablets into the United States, as a penalty for violating Apple's patent portfolio on the iPhone design.

In February 2012, Apple filed another patent infringement lawsuit, alleging that Samsung violated Apple's utility patents. Samsung again retaliated by fining a countersuit claiming that all generations of the iPhone and iPad infringe on Samsung's patents. This case was scheduled for trial in March 2014.[81]

Apple reportedly spent more money in 2011 on patent litigation and acquisitions than it did on R&D.[82] Probably, so did Samsung.

The U.S. Government Accountability Office found that a disproportionate share of patent litigation concerns software patents, with the number of defendants in patent lawsuits more than doubling from 2007 through 2011.[83] Software patents accounted for almost 90 percent of the increase in litigation. A recent study reveals that software patents constitute 20.8 percent of the once-litigated patents but 74.1 percent of the most-litigated patents.[84] A new trend in patent litigation involves firms suing *users* (not producers) of software such as online retailers who use shopping software on their websites, coffee shops that use Wi-Fi technologies, or users of copy machines and fax machines that have scan-to-copy software.[85]

In addition to patent trolls, patent thickets can be used to inhibit competition and entry into the software industry. Patent thickets refer to overlapping sets of patent rights. These thickets require innovators to negotiate licensing deals for multiple patents from multiple sources.[86] Patent thickets are used to defend against competitors designing around a single patent. A hypothetical example of a software patent thicket could be in the Internet-based education software market. A number of firms could own patents that cover almost every aspect of the e-learning process such as virtual learning environments, discussion forums, delivering classes via webcast or podcast, retrieving and displaying educational material online, providing online testing materials, etc. If such a packet thicket exists, it could prevent or deter a new firm from entering and innovating in the e-learning business.

One other use of patents to influence competition, innovation, and entry into the software industry is a patent pool. A patent pool involves a consortium of at least two companies that agree to cross-license patents relating to a particular technology. An example of a patent pool in the software industry is for the MPEG-2 technology, formed in 1997. MPEG-2 is a system for video and audio data compression; it enables the storage and transmission of movies. The MPEG-2 patent pool included 27 patents from nine different companies and was eventually licensed to 1,518 firms.[87] A study of this patent pool found that after the pool formed, patent rates dropped for the technology for firms inside and outside the pool; however, firms shifted their R&D from inventing to implementing the technology in new products and reaped significant revenues.[88]

Some argue that patent pools decrease innovation, but others claim that patent pools can be useful to foster and protect innovation. For example, studies have found that patent pools can help firms enter the software industry. In the open-source software community, a recent study found that the introduction of a royalty-free patent pool—called "The Commons" (created by the Open Source Development Labs and IBM in 2005) boosted the rate of entry in the market by start-up companies using a new product based on an open-source software license.[89]

### Challenges in the Use of Software Copyrights

Although software copyrights do not face the same issues as software patents, copyrights are increasingly likely to be violated via unauthorized use, copying, and distribution.

Despite legislation in the United States such as the Digital Millenium Copyright Act[90], global treaties such as the Berne Convention and the GATT[91], and organizations such as the BSA and the International Intellectual Property Alliance, as noted earlier, software piracy is rampant in the software industry, and is especially on the rise in emerging markets.[92] In addition, criminal elements and organizations are becoming more and more sophisticated in their ability to copy, distribute, and sell pirated software over the Internet. Witness, for example, the sophistication of the counterfeiting operation in Guangdong, China, discussed earlier in this chapter. This organization manufactured and distributed pirated Microsoft software throughout the world for years, earning an estimated $2 billion in global sales.[93] Reportedly, even customs officials were fooled by the counterfeit software, which contained hologram markings and Microsoft's difficult-to-replicate certificates of authenticity.[94]

As a result, software companies have had to become more aggressive in protecting their copyrights against infringement. Some, like Microsoft, have put together antipiracy task forces and large legal teams, embedded technical identification and verification marks in their products that are difficult to replicate, and created online forums where users can report violations. Others rely on the courts and organizations like the BSA to help enforce software copyrights.

### The Future for Software Intellectual Property Protections

Looking ahead, defining what constitutes intellectual property and how to protect it, and determining what constitutes legitimate use of intellectual property protections are likely to become even more important and problematic issues in the software industry.

Despite efforts by firms, industry alliances and legislative bodies, copyrights will likely face ever more sophisticated attempts at infringement via organized software piracy. According to the BSA, over the last decade, the losses from software piracy have more than doubled, and this trend is likely to continue as the software industry expands into new markets and the opportunities for piracy increase.[95] As a result, additional legal and technical mechanisms to prevent and punish software piracy may need to be introduced, or firms' incentives to innovate and create new software products may be adversely affected.

Perhaps even more troubling for the software industry is the growing problem with how patents are being used by firms in the industry. Software patents have sometimes been called the gold dust in the industry and are frequently used in ways not intended by the law. Unless the USPTO and the courts come to agreement on whether software can be patented and what constitutes patent-eligible material in software programs, litigation over software patent claims is only likely to increase in the future.

This suggests that software firms may have to devote ever larger portions of their budgets to litigation rather than to R&D. Projecting into the future, some software industry analysts believe that buying and litigating patents will become normal for firms in the industry, and will be a major cash outflow in coming years.[96] The threat of litigation may inhibit entry into the software industry by startup firms with novel ideas and products. Eventually, patents and patent litigation costs may crowd out true innovation and competition in the software industry.

Some have even advocated doing away with intellectual property protections in the software industry altogether, given the difficulty of defining exactly what constitutes intellectual property in a fungible medium like software, the difficulty of enforcing protections, and the fast movement of the industry (which often advances to new products and ideas before legal claims for prior products can be resolved). The country of New Zealand, for example, recently outlawed software patents.[97] Perhaps this will be a new trend in the industry.

## Key Takeaways

This chapter discussed important regulatory and legal issues in the software industry.

Antitrust legislation can play a major role in preserving competition in the software industry and in influencing its products, services, and market structure. Although the software industry has features that tend to lead to natural monopolies, antitrust policies can limit the ability of a dominant firm in the software industry to compete in a way that hurts consumers.

There are many ways that software firms can protect their intellectual property. For example, a software product could be protected by patents, copyrights, and trademarks. The trademark uniquely identifies the company (source) of the product. The copyright protects the expression of the idea, that is the code itself. The patent protects the functional expression of the idea—for example using a single click to purchase a book online.

However, despite the protections offered to software intellectual property, because of the fungible nature of software, the law is not consistent in how it determines whether software can be patented and how it treats software intellectual property rights. Thus, it can be difficult for companies to present and defend claims of ownership to their software intellectual property. Certainly, significant resources must be devoted to intellectual property concerns in the software industry.

Software piracy—unauthorized copying of software—is a major problem in the software industry, particularly in emerging countries. Although there are several treaties that prohibit software piracy, firms in the software industry must be diligent in enforcing copyright protection of their software products.

Firms are increasingly using intellectual property protections not only to defend their intellectual property but also as strategic and competitive weapons. Some argue that the resources devoted to litigating software intellectual property would be better spent on research and development to continue innovation in the software industry. There are grassroot movements to do away with intellectual property protections such as patents.

# CHAPTER 7

# Challenges, Opportunities, and Trends in the Software Industry

There are a number of important challenges, opportunities, and trends that are facing the software industry.

The chapter starts with the challenges of ensuring software security and privacy in the industry. Breaches of networks and databases to obtain sensitive customer information and the source code for popular software products are becoming all-too-common. Given the mission-critical applications of software, such attacks can have significant and wide-ranging consequences. There are also heightened concerns about protecting privacy, given the vulnerability of software firms to attacks and exploitation by criminal elements, increased pressures by governments to reveal sensitive information, and the ubiquity of big data generated by the industry. Software firms can use various approaches to prevent attacks or mitigate the consequences of attacks.

The chapter then describes opportunities and trends in the industry including innovative pricing and delivery schemes and emerging software business models such as open source, software ecosystem and platform models, and software as a service.

Finally, the chapter concludes by considering what the future holds for the software industry.

## Software Security and Privacy Issues in the Software Industry

On October 3, 2013, Adobe Systems was the victim of a sophisticated cyber-attack. Hackers accessed Adobe customer IDs, encrypted passwords and data for over 38 million Adobe customers, and also stole the source code for Adobe Acrobat, ColdFusion, ColdFusion Builder, and other Adobe software products.[1]

KrebsOnSecurity, a cyber-security news site found the Adobe source code on the servers of hackers believed responsible for breaches at Dun and Bradstreet, Altegrity's Kroll Background America, and Reed Elsevier's LexisNexis.[2] The Adobe data accessed by the hackers included customer names, encrypted payment card numbers, expiration dates, and orders. Security experts argue that since the hackers accessed the source code for Adobe's products, they have the blueprints to exploit new vulnerabilities in the software and that Adobe's customers are vulnerable to future attacks.

In 2011, hackers attacked Sony's network, which provides PlayStation users with access to video game software, and compromised more than 77 million customer accounts. This was the second-largest online data breach in history, and cost Sony an estimated $155.4 million in lost revenues.[3] Claiming that Sony could have prevented the breach by keeping its software up-to-date and ensuring that passwords were secure, the company was also sued by the United Kingdom's privacy regulator, and paid a fine of U.S. $394,500.[4]

In a recent Internet Security Report, Symantec (the software firm that creates security and antivirus products like Norton 360) reported blocking more than 5.5 billion malware attacks (an 81 percent increase over the prior year) as well as reporting a 30 percent increase in Web-based attacks, a 41 percent increase in new variants of malware, and a 32 percent increase in the number of vulnerabilities reported in mobile operating systems.[5]

These examples highlight the growing problems with software security in the software industry.

*Software security* is building software to function properly even when under malicious attack.[6] As the cyber-attacks on Adobe Systems and Sony illustrate, software security has become a critically important issue in the software industry. Software security involves protecting assets (software source code, distributed systems, and sensitive data) that may be vulnerable to attack or exploitation by various threats. Countermeasures may be used to neutralize or eliminate threats.

The following sections examine why software products are under increasing attack and why these attacks have more serious consequences. The major types of software security problems and causes of these problems are identified. Finally, the chapter considers different approaches that can be used to increase the security of software products, ranging from technical solutions to standards and legislation.

### Attacks on Software Are Escalating

As highlighted in Symantec's Internet Security report, software is under increasing attack from a variety of threats. The connectivity of the Internet has made it relatively easy to launch attacks and to reach a large number of users. Social media can also be used to spread the range and scope of an attack. Mobile devices have been enthusiastically adopted worldwide but mobile software appears to be an increasingly attractive target and is vulnerable to attack.

Software is also updated frequently. Every update to software affords an opportunity for attackers to embed malicious code. Software is also very complex. Many of the popular software products—Microsoft Office, Adobe Acrobat, Oracle database software—have been around for decades, and some of the products have become large and unwieldy over years of patches and upgrades, containing spaghetti code. For example, Adobe has been criticized for the poor quality of its core code which renders its key products vulnerable to attack.[7] Adobe's Flash Player was at the top of Symantec's list of vulnerable plug-in software in 2012, 2010, and 2009.[8] Complex and fragile code increases the risk of flaws that leave the software open to attack.

Unfortunately, while it is easier than ever before to launch attacks on software, the consequences of the attacks are also becoming more significant. Today, software is both ubiquitous and mission critical—embedded not only in mobile phones but also in airplanes, cars, homes, medical devices, point-of-sale (POS) terminals, nuclear power plants, energy grids, and transportation networks. For example, the U.S. military's F-35 fighter jet has 130 subsystems, hundreds of thousands of interfaces, and millions of lines of software code; more than 90 percent of its functions are managed by software.[9] Hacks of embedded software in military weapons could have disastrous consequences.

From November 27, 2013, to December 15, 2013, malicious software embedded in Target Store's POS devices stole credit and debit card information from up to 110 million customers who shopped at Target during that time period.[10] What is unusual about this attack is that the malicious software did not target databases over the Internet, but was apparently planted on physical POS devices in Target stores by a compromised server and sent sensitive customer information directly from Target's cash registers to the hackers. The organization, sophistication, and scope of the attack were exceptional—this is largest theft to date of card accounts in U.S. history, surpassing the scam involving the retailer TJX that affected at least 45.7 million card users.

When critical software fails due to security problems, the consequences could be catastrophic—such as software-based failures in air traffic control or medical device usage, or financial market flash crashes.

### Why Software Is Vulnerable

Software is vulnerable for a variety of reasons. For the most part, software vulnerabilities are caused by coding errors. Software security researchers have identified the types of flaws that make software susceptible to attack. Major types of flaws are shown in Table 7.1.[11] As suggested in this table, many of the errors that make software vulnerable have to do with poor validation of user input, poor password validation and control, and just plain old sloppy programming.

Software with the problems described in Table 7.1 is susceptible to a variety of attacks. These include malware (viruses, worms, and Trojan horses), spam and phishing; denial of service attacks, data breaches, cyber warfare, and industrial espionage. More recently, attacks are launched using social networks and mobile devices. *Botnets* are also used to initiate attacks. Botnets (or robot networks) are a collection of Internet-connected programs that communicate with other similar programs in order to perform tasks. These tasks can include legal activities such as helping to control communications on the Internet or illegal activities such as sending spam e-mail or participating in distributed denial-of-service attack attacks.

Table 7.2 identifies the key ways that software can be attacked and provides examples of each type of attack.

*Table 7.1  A taxonomy of software coding flaws that increase its vulnerability to attack*

| Type of software flaw | Brief description | Examples of how the flaw can be abused by an attacker |
|---|---|---|
| 1. Poor input validation and representation | Software program trusts input that is incorrect or corrupted | • "Buffer overflow"—writing outside the bounds of the program's memory can corrupt data<br>• "Cross-site scripting"—sending nonvalidated data to a Web browser can result in the browser executing malicious code<br>• "Injection errors"—allowing a hacker to inject a command into the code |
| 2. Application programming interface (API) abuse | There is a problem between a call to a program and the response to the call via the API | • "Exception handling"—program can crash due to unexpected data<br>• "Unchecked return value"—program can overlook unexpected states and conditions |
| 3. Inadequate security features | Authentication, confidentiality and access control problems. Usually relates to password handling. | • "Privacy violation"—Mishandling private information, such as customer passwords or social security numbers, can compromise user privacy and is often illegal<br>• "Poor password management"—using a hard-coded password, empty password, or an all-text password can risk system compromise |
| 4. Issues with time and state | Unexpected interactions between data and processing | • Creating and using insecure temporary files can leave the system and data vulnerable to attack<br>• Too long of a delay between authenticating access to a file and actually using the file can be exploited to launch an attack |
| 5. Errors | Improper error handling | • Ignoring exceptions and other error conditions may allow an attacker to induce unexpected behavior unnoticed.<br>• Overly complex error handling code is likely to contain security vulnerabilities |
| 6. Poor code quality | Poor code quality from complex logic or improper data handling | • Overly complex code can cause system crashes by branching outside the bounds of the session<br>• Poorly written code can allow a back door into the code to permit denial of service attacks |
| 7. Lack of encapsulation | Weak boundaries between programs, data, or systems | • Debugging code left in the software can create unintended access points<br>• Data can leak between uses |
| 8. Environmental issues | Issues outside of the program | • Insecure configuration management can enable hackers to gain access |

*Source:* Tsipenyuk, Chess, and McGraw (2005).

Table 7.2 *Types of software attacks*

| Type of software attack | What it is | An example |
|---|---|---|
| Virus | A piece of code that is capable of copying itself and typically has a detrimental effect, such as corrupting the system or destroying data | The *Creeper Virus* in the 1970s traveled over the Internet to a remote system and displayed the message "I'm the creeper, catch me if you can!" It was one of the first computer viruses and was relatively innocuous.[12] |
| Worm | Standalone malware computer program that replicates itself in order to spread to other computers | The *Code Red* worm in 2001 exploited a vulnerability in Microsoft's IIS web server software. The worm replicated and spread by using the buffer overflow vulnerability (described earlier in Table 7.1). The worm used a long string of the letter "N" to overflow a software program buffer, allowing the worm to execute arbitrary code and infect the machine. It displayed the message: "HELLO! Welcome to http://www.worm.com! Hacked By Chinese!"[13] |
| Trojan Horse | A program in which malicious or harmful code is contained inside an apparently harmless program or data in such a way that it can get control of a computer and do its chosen form of damage | The *Sub7* or *SubSeven* or *Backdoor. SubSeven* trojan horse deposited a program via a downloaded .exe file sent by e-mail that allowed hackers to take 'virtually complete control' over a computer. It affected users of Windows software.[14] |
| Spam | Junk electronic mail or junk e-newsgroup postings. Note: can be sent to mobile phones as well as computers. Note: can be done using social media (like Twitter) Note: can be sent by a zombie computer (a compromised computer connected to the Internet) | Unsolicited advertisements for phone service, travel, books, and other products. Requests for donations from spammers posing as stranded travelers or entrepreneurs who are often purportedly located in countries in Eastern Europe or Africa. |

| Phishing | The act of sending an e-mail to a user falsely claiming to be an established legitimate enterprise in an attempt to scam the user into surrendering private information that will be used for identity theft. The e-mail directs the user to visit a bogus website where they are asked to update personal information, such as passwords and credit card, social security, and bank account numbers, etc. | The eBay phishing scam of 2003 sent e-mails to eBay users informing them that their accounts were compromised and asking them to click on a link to set up another account. The link directed users to a fake website, not eBay.[15] |
|---|---|---|
| (Distributed) Denial of Service (DDoS) | An attempt to make a computer or network resource unavailable to its intended users by temporarily or indefinitely interrupting or suspending services of a host connected to the Internet. | Operation Payback, organized by the group Anonymous launched DDoS attacks on websites of banks and financial institutions (e.g., Mastercard, Visa, PayPal) who had withdrawn banking facilities from WikiLeaks in 2010 after the Julian Assange affair.[16] |
| Data Breach | The intentional or unintentional release of secure information to an untrusted environment | In August 2013, US Airways' frequent flyer database was breached. 7,700 customers with Dividend Miles accounts may have had their information compromised, including deleting frequent flier miles. Dates of birth, security question answers, the last four digits of credit card numbers, and frequent-flier miles were accessed and compromised.[17] |
| Cyber warfare or Espionage | Politically motivated hacking to conduct sabotage and espionage | In 2010, a software worm by the name of Stuxnet attacked Iran's nuclear facilities, causing them to go offline.[18] Stuxnet spread via Microsoft Windows, and targeted Siemens industrial control system software. Stuxnet was the first discovered malware that disrupted industrial systems. In addition to Iran, Stuxnet also infected computers in Indonesia and India. |

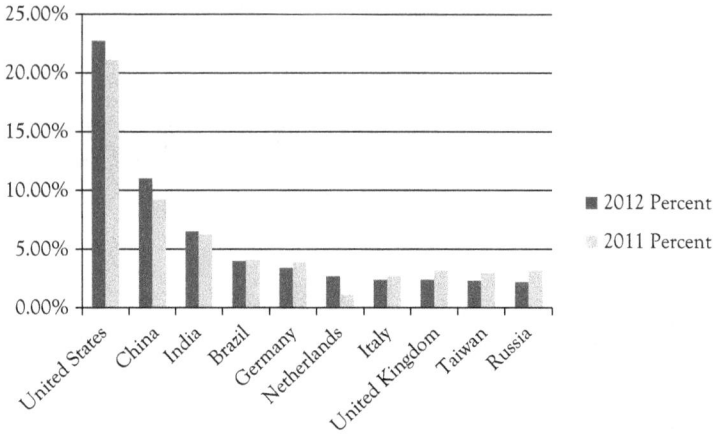

*Figure 7.1  Top 10 countries for malicious software activity (all types) in 2012 and 2011*

*Source:* Symantec (2013).

According to Symantec, in 2012 there was a 42 percent increase in targeted software attacks, 60 percent of global e-mails were spam, and the average number of identities exposed per data breach was 604,826 at a cost of almost $200 per breach to fix.[19] Symantec also noted a significant increase in mobile device malware families, which increased 58 percent from 2011.[20]

Figure 7.1 shows the source of malicious software activity of all types in the last 2 years, ranking the top ten countries on a percentage basis as a source for malicious software attacks.[21] As shown in Figure 7.1, the United States is ranked first as a source of malicious software activity, closely followed by China. The top 10 countries accounted for almost 60 percent of all malicious software activity in 2012.

Within specific categories of malicious activity in 2012, most phishing attacks (50 percent), botnet attacks (15.3 percent), and web-based attacks (34.4 percent) originated in the United States. Most network attacks originated in China (29.2 percent), and most spam zombies originated in India (17.1 percent).[22]

## How to Increase Software Security

There are a variety of approaches that firms can take to increase the security of their software products. These approaches include technical

*Table 7.3 Best practices for building in software security*

| Best practice | Description |
|---|---|
| Code review | Analyzes the software code to detect bugs and flaws, usually using automated tools. Estimated to catch about 50 percent of security problems. |
| Architectural risk analysis | Evaluates the design and specifications of the architecture (e.g., user interface, network, data, server, etc.) in which the software is embedded, for risks that could impact the software. |
| Penetration testing | Tests the software in its environment for security flaws and defects, based upon the security risks identified. Differs from traditional functional tests which evaluate whether the software works as planned. Penetration tests evaluate whether the software will work when attacked, based on the likely attacks identified in the architectural risk analysis. |
| Risk-based security testing | Tests security functionality of the software to make sure security features work. Also, tests the software based on attack patterns, risks analysis results, and abuse cases. |
| Abuse cases | Defines use cases that describe the system's behavior under attack. Details what needs to be protected, from whom, and for how long. Useful as input to testing. |
| Security requirements | Identifies requirements for security of the software, including functional security (e.g., use of encryption) as well as for abuse cases and attack patterns. |
| Security operations | Evaluates software security in the field. Includes network security. Also involves security monitoring of the operation of the software. |
| External analysis | Examination of the software by someone outside of the software product design team. |

*Source*: McGraw (2006).

solutions, methodologies, improved testing, and code verification as well as market forces and regulation.

There are a number of best practices (touch points) for building in software security.[23] Table 7.3 summarizes these best practices.

An essential concept that underlies software security practices is that of risk management. Risk management involves identifying risks, performing qualitative and quantitative analyses to evaluate the probability of a risk occurring and its severity of impact, ranking and prioritizing risks, planning risk responses and contingency plans, and controlling and managing risks.[24]

The security approaches described here apply to software in general.

Mobile applications are a special case and require additional security processes. More and more people are using smartphones and are storing sensitive information on the devices. Smartphones are also being used in the workplace and in society at large. Given the increasing use of smartphones, their availability (up 24 × 7), their frequent connection to payment systems (which makes them an attractive target), and the many points of contact to them (often not protected), securing mobile applications is of growing concern.

According to Symantec, mobile vulnerabilities increased 32 percent from 2011 to 2012.[25] Attacks on mobile applications can arise from various sources. Users are often naïve and can be easily tricked by malware. Attacks can exploit weaknesses from means of communication like unsecured wifi networks. Attacks can also exploit software vulnerabilities from the Web browser and operating system. Android was the most frequently attacked mobile platform in 2012, accounting for 95 percent of the unique mobile threats; however, most mobile vulnerabilities (93 percent) are on the Apple iOS platform.[26] Symantec reasons that while Apple iOS is more vulnerable, Android is actually attacked more because it is easier to install apps on the Android platform from unofficial markets and because it is relatively difficult for Google to roll out fixes to the complex Android ecosystem.

Most mobile malware has the goal of stealing information from smartphone users. Another popular attack involves premium number fraud in which malicious apps send expensive text messages. Mobile phones have also been harnessed into linked networks of mobile botnets that send out spam and other malicious e-mails.

Different security countermeasures are being developed and applied to smartphones. Such measures can include security software for mobile operating systems, such as firewalls and antivirus software. Biometrics (such as facial recognition, fingerprints, etc.) can also be used for more secure authentication to limit access to the smartphone. One other tactic involves creating a sandbox or compartments in the mobile phone's operating system. Creating compartments can segment and protect vulnerable applications and data on the system from outside attacks. For example, the Apple iOS uses defines a sandbox by limiting access to its API for applications from the App Store.

Beyond technical solutions to improve software security, organizations, regulations, and standards are important to address or mitigate threats in the software industry.

There are a number of laws that are directed at increasing the security of information. For example, parts of the Health Insurance Portability and Accountability Act (HIPAA) focus on rules to protect and safeguard the privacy of individuals' medical information.[27] Other laws may lead to improved software security by focusing on control of the software development process. The Sarbanes-Oxley Act (SOX) of 2002[28] set new or enhanced standards for all U.S. public company boards, management, and financial institutions. The Act defines a variety of control processes and standards. In the context of software security, financial institutions that are compliant with SOX are likely to stress control of the software development lifecycle, with auditing of processes, including those for user security of software applications.

Standards such as IEEE P1074 require that security be incorporated throughout the software development life cycle. According to the authors of the standard: "it is the first IEEE software process standard to embed dedicated, mandatory, security-related activities in the software development life cycle that specifically address how to determine your project security objectives at the top of a project, and how to validate they were achieved at the end of a project."[29]

There are also a number of standards defined by the International Organization for Standardization (ISO) and by the International Electrotechnical Commission (IEC), for information security (such as the ISO/IEC 27000 series of standards which provide best practice guidelines on information security management, risks and controls).[30]

Legislation and software liability laws may be one way to motivate firms to improve the security of their software products. As software performs important functions and reaches into many aspects of society, software failures can have serious consequences such as economic loss, property damage, or personal injury. Software firms may face lawsuits (both criminal and civil) when their products do not work as expected.

For example, in November 2000, 28 patients at the National Cancer Institute in Panama were jolted with massive overdoses of gamma rays due to defects in the software of a radiation therapy machine.[31] At least five patients died from radiation poisoning. Three Panamanian medical technicians were charged with second-degree murder for introducing changes into the software that led directly to the patients' deaths.[32]

The software manufacturer (Multidata Systems—a company based in the United States in St. Louis) was sued for damages totaling as much as $28 million. In 2004, the U.S. court in which the case was filed dismissed the case, indicating that Panama would be a more appropriate venue. The plaintiffs complied with the U.S. court order and re-filed their case in Panama. However, in 2006, the Panamanian District Court dismissed the case due to lack of jurisdiction and competence. Defendants appealed this ruling. In 2009, the Panamanian Appellate Court affirmed the lower court's decision. In 2010, the Panamanian Supreme Court affirmed the Appellate Court's decision, dismissed the Defendants' challenge, and determined the amount of costs to be 200 Balboas (U.S. $200).[33]

This case illustrates the lack of clarity on and courts' treatment of software liability. Plaintiffs have had difficulty in prevailing in lawsuits against software firms. Generally, when software is considered a product (mass produced) rather than a service (custom developed under contract), it may be appropriate to apply product liability laws. Firms producing software products may thus be subject to the damages and warranty provisions of the Uniform Commercial Code (UCC).[34]

However, it should be noted that there is still no specific software liability law in place today in the United States. There is much discussion and debate on the topic. Recently the European Commission has been considering introducing laws to extend consumer protection rules to software products.

Finally, there are organizations focused on managing software security at a country level such as the U.S. Computer Emergency Readiness Team (US-CERT) in the U.S. Department of Homeland Security, and the CERT® Coordination Center (CERT/CC), housed in the Software Engineering Institute at Carnegie Mellon University.[35]

The US-CERT leads efforts to improve the U.S. cyber security posture, coordinate cyber information sharing, and manage cyber security risks.[36] The CERT/CC at Carnegie Mellon focuses on risks at the software and system level, identifying and addressing existing and potential threats, notifying system administrators and other technical personnel of these threats, and coordinating with vendors and incident response teams

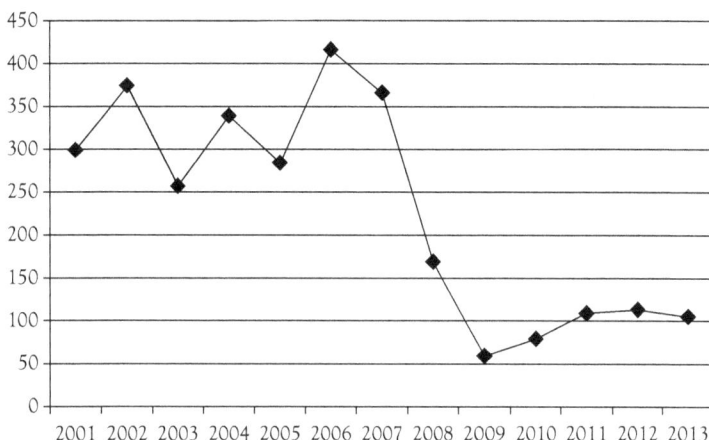

*Figure 7.2  Number of software vulnerabilities reported to the CERT®
coordination center*

*Source*: CERT Coordination Center (2013).

worldwide to address the threats. The CERT/CC keeps a database that
tracks all software vulnerabilities reported to the center.

Figure 7.2 shows the number of software vulnerabilities reported to
the CERT/CC from 2001 to 2013 (projected). The number of distinct
software vulnerabilities reported peaked in 2006 and 2007 (at the height
of U.S. economic boom) and has dropped sharply thereafter. While the
number of unique software vulnerabilities reported may have decreased
in recent years, the number of malicious attacks (based on Symantec's
data reported earlier in the chapter) has not.

In addition to the CERTs located in the United States, there are cyber
security CERTs located throughout the world, such as in Denmark, Brazil,
Austria, Ireland, Belgium, and Japan.[37] These CERTs communicate and
coordinate to help address global software security threats and incidents.

### The Future for Software Security

Looking ahead, software security is likely to continue to increase in
importance as more software products and services are adopted around
the world and as software plays an increasingly critical role in running the
global economy and society. In particular, effectively addressing mobile
threats will be an important next frontier for software security. Given

the amount of data collected on individuals and their social and economic behaviors, and the vulnerability of data to attacks, data breaches of increasing size, scope, and impact are also likely. Finally, as the consequences of software failures become more severe, new laws and regulations may need to be introduced.

## Trends and Opportunities in the Software Industry

As described in Chapter 3, companies in the software industry have traditionally sold their products to customers using perpetual license agreements. Under such licenses, the customer acquires rights to the product for its entire life. Note that these are rights to use the product. As described in Chapter 6, generally, software companies do not transfer ownership of intellectual property to the customer, nor do they provide the customer with the source code for the product.

In terms of distribution, software companies have typically sold software products using direct sales forces, telemarketing, bundled with hardware, or via mail-order catalogs, traditional retail stores, and warehouse superstores.

The Internet has been, of course, dramatically changing this by opening up innovative delivery, licensing, and pricing schemes. Online distribution (downloads of software products to customers via the Internet) has become a very popular channel in the software industry that is increasingly dominating software sales. On-demand usage is also becoming popular. In terms of licensing schemes, there are now free software licenses which grant the customer extensive rights to modify and redistribute the software. Other emergent software pricing arrangements include subscription-based pricing such as a monthly fee for use of the software or pricing based on various units of consumption, for example per CPU, user, time period of use, or transaction. In advertising-based (indirect) pricing schemes, the software is free to the customer, but the software firm makes money from advertisers (Google is an example).

The sections below discuss emerging pricing and distribution models in the software industry, including freemium business models, cloud computing and software as a service, open-source software, service-oriented architectures, and software ecosystems and platforms.

### Freemium Business Models

A freemium business model is a pricing strategy in which a certain tier of software product or service is offered free to the customer, but a fee (a premium) is charged for other tiers of the software product or service. Variants of this tiered business model have actually been present in the software industry for some time. In the 1980s and 1990s it was not uncommon for software firms to provide free samples of their products involving limited feature sets or limited time availability of features. For example, in 1988, Microsoft released Microsoft Works—a limited functionality version of Microsoft Office for as little as $2 to Original Equipment Manufacturers (OEMs). Given the low price, the software often was offered free to customers who purchased computer hardware as OEMs preinstalled it on the hardware. In the late 1990s Microsoft offered free trials of MS Office, and Lotus Development Corporation offered free trials of Lotus Notes. Makers of statistical software such as SAS offered free versions of their products with limited functionality (for example, limiting the number of observations that could be analyzed or the types of commands that could be executed) or allowed access to full features for a limited time period of availability (for example, a free trial ending in 30 or 90 days).

While the tiered business model has been present in the software industry for some time, the use of the term "freemium" ("free" plus "premium") to describe it is more recent.[38] A book entitled "Free: The Future of a Radical Price" examined the popularity of this business model in 2009.[39] Freemium business models offer a number of benefits to software firms. For example, allowing free samples of full products to a limited number of customers (seeding) can generate word-of-mouth advertising that helps to jump-start the market for the product.[40] Seeding is effective when customers cannot properly value the product's functionality. In contrast, allowing customers to sample a feature of the product (for example, providing Adobe Acrobat Reader for free) but charging customers for premium features (for example, charging for Adobe Distiller) may be more effective when exposing customers to some basic functionality can lead them to increase their valuation of the premium features.[41] On the other hand, it can be difficult for software firms to recover the costs of developing products and reach sales goals if the freemium model is not applied appropriately.

Freemium business models are often used by mobile app providers and by cloud service providers. Cloud computing and software as a service are described in the next section.

### Cloud Computing and Software as a Service

Cloud computing is an innovative delivery mechanism for computer-related products and services. It involves providing access to a shared pool of resources (such as applications, servers, storage, and services) that can be rapidly provided and scaled to match demand.[42] It uses a network of remote servers hosted on the Internet to store, manage, and process data, rather than performing the information processing locally. The model relies on the use of shared computing resources, such as software applications, services, and computing infrastructure, to achieve economies of scale. Essential characteristics of cloud computing include on-demand self-service, broad network access, resource pooling, rapid scaling of capabilities, and an ability to meter and measure the services consumed.[43] The model is similar in concept to a utility.

Cloud computing enables on-demand access to software applications and other technical resources, affording the delivery of distinct types of services: software-as-a-service (SAAS), platform-as-a-service (PAAS) and infrastructure-as-a-service (IAAS).[44] Given the primary focus of this book, SAAS is most relevant segment.

SAAS refers to business or consumer software applications that are accessed on-demand via the Internet. The software applications are hosted and maintained on third-party servers and in third-party data centers. Access to the applications is typically offered using a seat-based or usage-based pricing scheme. Ideally all on-demand customers are using the same version of the software application. This makes customer support more cost effective for the vendor. For the customer, SAAS allows access to sophisticated software applications which customers do not need to purchase, install, and maintain. Customers can use the applications when, where, and as much as needed, depending on the particular service they have purchased.

Customer Relationship Management (CRM), and in particular, sales automation applications are among the most popular SAAS offerings. Salesforce.com is the largest SAAS company. The company was founded in 1999 by a former Oracle executive—Mark Benioff—who serves as its current Chairman and CEO. The company provides CRM applications for rent over the Internet, the most popular of which is the sales automation application. The sales automation application provides sales representatives with a customer profile and account history, allows the user to manage marketing campaign spending and performance across a variety of channels, and keeps track of information unique to a company's sales process.[45] According to IDC, in 2012, Salesforce.com accounted for 28.1 percent of the market share in sales automation software, and the company's sales are projected to reach $3 billion in 2013.[46] Oracle and SAP also represent significant market share in this segment.

Looking ahead, SAAS business models are projected to grow strongly at a compound average growth rate ranging from 20 to 30 percent, with projected revenues of $67.3 billion by 2016.[47] However, it is important to note that SAAS does not suit all users—there is a limited ability to customize an application and there are concerns about migrating sensitive data to a third-party control, performance, security, and availability. For example, recent revelations by Edward Snowden about the surveillance tactics used by the U.S. National Security Agency (NSA) may have heightened concerns about the ability of cloud vendors to protect sensitive client data stored in the cloud. Among other things, Snowden revealed that the NSA was secretly tapping into Yahoo and Google data centers to collect information from hundreds of millions of account holders through a program called MUSCULAR.[48] Such concerns may prevent certain types of applications from moving to the cloud. Nevertheless, the SAAS delivery model is likely to grow in popularity in the foreseeable future.

### Open Source Software

Chapter 2 defined and described open-source software: software source code that is freely available for download and use via the Internet. As described in Chapter 6, open-source software is typically licensed using a free licensing scheme. Under this scheme the license holder has the right to study, change, and distribute the software to anyone and for any purpose. The copyleft provision requires that any derived software based on the code is released under the compatible copyleft scheme.

From a business model perspective, open-source software is a variant of the packaged software and software services models, in which the packaged software is offered for free, but the vendor makes money by selling a variety of services around the software. For example, the company Red Hat, Inc. offers a free version of the Linux open-source operating system, but charges for a variety of support services, such as customization, integration, installation, operations, documentation, maintenance, training, and technical support. Red Hat's revenues passed the $1 billion mark for the first time in 2012.[49]

Open-source software provides a low-cost option to customers. Although (as noted in Chapter 2) Linux' share of the open-source software desktop segment is still a very tiny portion of the overall software market (less than one percent), the segment is growing strongly at an estimated rate of 22 percent through 2016.[50]

The open-source software business model is projected to impact the software industry in several ways. First, open-source software will increase price pressures on traditional software companies to offer their customers a better return on investment.[51] Second, open-source software represents a movement toward open architecture and standards in the industry. Industry analysts expect that open-source software and other open-architecture software business models will experience significant growth in the future given their low-cost profiles.[52]

### Service Oriented Architectures

A service-oriented architecture (SOA) is a design in which the functions performed by the software are broken down into discrete pieces of functionality which are provided as services to other applications.[53] For example, retrieving a customer account and paying a bill are services. Because the design is generally based on Internet standards, the service can exchange information with any other service in the network without human interaction and without the need to make changes to the underlying program itself. Services can be combined by other software applications to provide the complete functionality of a large software application.

Potential benefits of SOA include increased flexibility, reuse, faster cycle time, and responsiveness to change. However, there are significant challenges in implementing SOA such as defining standards and metadata, testing, security, and managing the architecture.

Some of the major software companies that offer software infrastructure and middleware products, like IBM, Sun Microsystems, Oracle, and Red Hat, have architectures with attributes of SOA.[54] However, although analysts consider the potential impacts of SOA on the software industry to be significant, there has not been a large movement of software companies to SOA deployments.

Some researchers envision an internet of services and service marketplaces enabled by SOAs in which the Internet will be used to offer services for all areas of life and business, such as virtual insurance, online banking, and online healthcare benefits distribution.[55] If such visions come to fruition, SOAs may permeate the software industry in the future.

## Software Ecosystems or Platforms

Software platform ecosystems are an interesting software business model. When one thinks of ecosystems in the natural world, images of rainforests and deserts come to mind. In the business world, an *ecosystem* is "an economic community supported by a foundation of interacting organizations and individuals—the organisms of the business world."[56] A *software* ecosystem includes the software products and services that enable, support, and automate the activities and transactions of the actors in the associated business ecosystem and the firms that provide these software solutions.[57]

Software ecosystems form around platforms. Platforms are infrastructure and rules that enable connections between the actors in an ecosystem. In the software industry, examples of platforms include Microsoft's Windows, Apple's iPhone, and Facebook. In these examples, a common platform supports interactions between key actors such as the platform owner (e.g., Apple), developers (independent software vendors), and end users (customers).[58] Platforms can be open or closed. In closed platforms (such as the three examples provided), the platform owner controls how the platform is used and releases limited details of the underlying architecture. In contrast, open platforms (such as the Linux operating system or Google's Android mobile device operating system) feature open standards, such as a fully documented application program interface (API) or open-source software code.[59]

From a business perspective, platform ecosystems provide an effective and efficient way for companies (platform owners) to satisfy the needs of many or all of their customers, without having to invest the time and R&D needed to develop the solutions themselves. Specifically, a company creates a software ecosystem around its platform and a set of initial product or service offerings. Independent software vendors participate in the company's ecosystem and create complementary product and service offerings that are compatible with that platform. Such offerings can effectively address the needs of small customer segments or even individual customers. For example, the company SAP has created a platform ecosystem around its enterprise software. In the ecosystem, SAP partners with solution providers, value-added resellers, distributors, and technology and service partners. Becoming designated as an SAP-certified partner means that the external firms' products or services are compatible with SAP's enterprise computing platform. SAP offers a range of supporting services and technologies (such as a development portal, help portal, training, newsletters, and a service marketplace) to foster its partner networks, and currently has more than 20,000 partners.[60] It is one of the industry's largest enterprise software platform ecosystems.

Platform ecosystems in the software industry typically form around operating systems, such as for the desktop, web, video game console, or mobile device. Platform ecosystems can also form around applications— like SAP's enterprise software or the CRM application of Salesforce.com. Salesforce.com offers a partner program in which independent software vendors can create applications compatible with the company's application and can market them on Salesforce.com's AppExchange.[61]

Given the trends in the software industry toward Internet-based business models such as SAAS and SOA, and the advantages of ecosystems for platform owners, software platform ecosystems are likely to increase in popularity. Platforms will be especially important in the high-growth mobile device software segment of the industry.

## The Future of the Software Industry

The software industry is vibrant and constantly evolving. This book has told the story of the industry and how it works, reviewed its history and structure, profiled the key countries and firms participating in the industry, examined workforce issues and trends, identified important legal and regulatory concerns, and explored the challenges, opportunities, and trends in the industry.

What does the future hold for the software industry?

Although certain niches in the software industry, such as mobile software and security software are experiencing high growth, the packaged software industry as a whole has been growing modestly since the days of the dot.com bust in the early 2000s, averaging about six percent growth per year.[62] In particular, the enterprise software segment, traditionally one of the largest segments in the industry, is considered mature, with projected growth only in the five percent range.[63] Some analysts consider that, without a new killer app, growth for the enterprise segment and for the software industry overall will continue in the single-digit range.[64]

Are the glory days over for the software industry?

Consider computer hardware. In its early days, computer hardware was specific to a vendor or even to a customer. However, over the last 50 years, hardware has become a commodity. As a result, profit margins in the computer hardware business have become unattractive. Many of the large computer hardware vendors (e.g., IBM, Hewlett Packard) have been shifting their focus instead to services. At one time, most of IBM's revenues came from the different mainframe and personal computers it produced. Today, most of IBM's revenues derive from technology services.

The same trend may be occurring in the software industry, with a similar impact. At least in some segments of the industry, software is becoming a commodity. There are more and more low-cost or free alternatives to software applications. As a result, the software industry may see a shift from a product-focus to a service-focus.

A typical concern with a services-based business is profit margin. For example, consider two large software firms profiled in Chapter 4: Cap Gemini, one of the largest software and professional services firms in the world and Dassault Systèmes, one of the largest software product companies in the world. In 2012, Cap Gemini had an operating margin[65] of 7.7 percent.[66] Dassault Systèmes had an operating margin of 31.6 percent.[67]

One other example is Salesforce.com. Salesforce.com, considered a pure SAAS firm, had an operating margin ranging from two to eight percent from 2004 to 2011, but in 2012 the company's operating margin dropped below zero to –0.5 percent, and it has continued its downward trend in 2013.[68]

Traditionally, services in the software industry are labor intensive, requiring highly skilled software engineers and support staff to develop customized software and to provide training, integration, installation, and maintenance of the software. It is difficult to build up the scale and expertise needed to be efficient in service delivery. For that reason, a services-based business may not be as attractive to a software products company.

However, as discussed earlier in this chapter, the Internet may be changing the cost dynamics of software services, by automating activities such as software support and by enabling innovative service delivery models such as SAAS and platform ecosystems. As a result, even traditional software products firms such as Oracle and SAP are making more of their revenues from services than from their software products.

An interesting study suggests that the optimal mix of products and services in the software industry seems to be at 70 percent products and 30 percent services; however, there are sweet spots at the very low level of services and at the very high level of services.[69] Companies at the low end of services are pure product companies such as video game software firms that make most of their revenues from their products. Companies at the high end of services, such as SAP and Oracle, make money from services as they have the scale and experience to perform services efficiently; they also use innovative service delivery schemes like software platform ecosystems.

If the packaged software products market is mature and becoming commoditized, and the Internet can be leveraged to offer services in a cost-effective way, more software product firms may move to services to increase revenues and profits.

Thus, in the next few years, one may see more and more software services firms in the software industry. Certainly, as discussed in Chapter 5, most of the growth in the workforce in the software industry is in the software services segment.

Software firms can servitize products (offer complementary services around their primary products).[70] Software firms can also productize services (leverage the Internet to implement innovative and cost effective service delivery schemes). Both trends are likely to occur in the software industry.

Given these trends, how will the software industry of tomorrow look? Over the last 50 years, the industry has undergone several major transformations. As described in Chapter 2, the original structure of the software industry was vertical, dominated by a handful of mainframe hardware vendors (for example, IBM, DEC). In the 1980s the introduction of the PC transformed the software industry into a horizontal structure in which the hardware, operating systems, and applications were de-coupled.

Given the unfolding impacts of the Internet on software development and distribution, the software industry of the future may not be vertical or horizontal. Instead it may be structured as a network—a network of ecosystems or clusters of companies around platforms that look a lot like Oracle or SAP or Salesforce. Figure 7.3 illustrates a possible future structure of the software industry. In this structure, software product firms (the large nodes) are platform owners and form ecosystems for their platforms. Platforms (P1 through P6 in the figure) are built for key products—such as an enterprise application (like SAP), an operating system (like Android), or an end-user application (like Yahoo! Pipes). Platforms could be open (such as the Linux operating system) or closed (such as SAP). Independent software vendors (the small dark gray nodes) could cluster around one or more platforms and provide complementary software products and services for them. Users (the small light gray nodes) could consume the products and services but also could participate in co-creating them.

The software industry of the future may thus shift from a product focus to more of a software services business, enabled by Internet-based

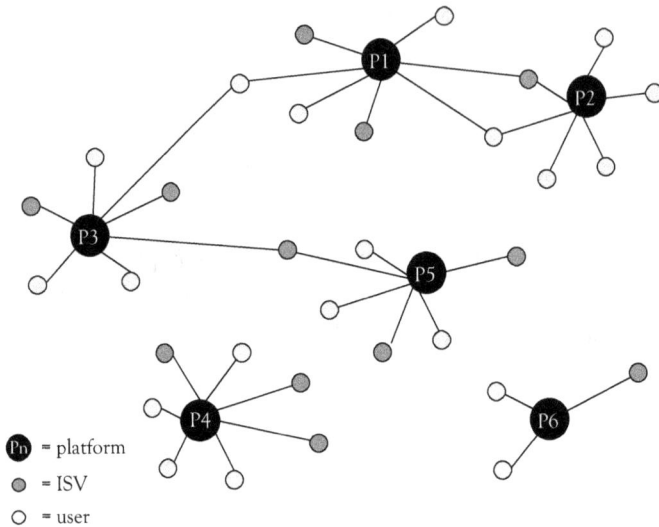

**Figure 7.3 A possible future structure of the software industry**

software delivery models. The industry may eventually become organized into clusters of platform ecosystems.

Only time will tell, however, if the industry will move to this structure or some other, as the software industry is nothing if not unpredictable!

## Key Takeaways

This chapter has explored challenges, trends, and opportunities in the software industry.

Software security is a major concern that plagues the industry, and there is no sign that attacks on software systems are abating. Instead, new segments, such as mobile software and other types of embedded software, appear to be especially vulnerable. Given the ubiquity of software, the rate of attacks and their scope and impact are likely to increase. As a result, there will likely be more pressure for improved software development processes and for legislation to hold firms liable for security breaches due to poor software code.

This chapter also has explored emerging software business models. The Internet has significantly changed the dynamics of the software business and has contributed to disruptive software delivery models, such as

SAAS and SOA which rely on on-demand service delivery. Innovative pricing schemes such as freemium models are replacing traditional software licenses. There is also a shift in customer preference to low-cost or free software such as open-source software. These trends could hasten the commoditization of certain elements of the software industry.

With the commoditization of the industry and the ability to leverage the Internet to enable innovative business models, more software product firms may shift to services to increase revenues and profits.

# Suggestions for Further Reading

For readers interested to learn more about the software industry, below are key resources and references organized by major topic. Some of the resources noted below have been cited in this book, and some have been added for those who seek additional information. This is followed by a glossary of key terms. Finally, there is the complete list of all references cited in this book, in alphabetical order, by author last name.

## Selected Resources by Topic

### History of the Software Industry

Books and Journal Articles on the History of the Software Industry

- IEEE Computer Society. January–March 2014. *Annals of the History of Computing, IEEE* (series of journal articles on various topics relating to software history.) See the Journal's website at: http://www.computer.org/portal/web/computingnow/annals
- Beyer, K.W. 2009. *Grace Hopper and the Invention of the Information Age*. Cambridge, MA: MIT Press.
- Campbell-Kelly, M. Winter 1995. "Development and Structure of the International Software Industry, 1950–1990," *Business and Economic History* 24, no. 2, pp. 73–110.
- Campbell-Kelly, M. 2003. *From Airline Reservations to Sonic the Hedgehog: A History of the Software Industry*. Cambridge, MA: MIT Press.
- Halacy, D.S. 1970. *Charles Babbage, Father of the Computer*. New York, NY: MacMillan.
- Hamilton, T.W. 1969. *IBM's Unbundling Decision: Consequences for Users and the Industry*. Programming Sciences Corporation.
- Toole, B.A. 1998. *Ada, the Enchantress of Numbers: Prophet of the Computer Age, A pathway to the 21st Century*. Mill Valley, CA: Strawberry Press.

- Philipson, G. 2005. "A Short History of Software." In *Management, Labour Process and Software Development: Reality Bites*, eds. R. Barrett, 13–45. New York, NY: Routledge.
- Steinmueller, W.E. 1996. "The U.S. Software Industry: An Analysis and Interpretive History." In *The International Computer Software Industry: A Comparative Study of Industry Evolution and Structure*, ed. D.C. Mowery, 15–52. UK: Oxford University Press.

Web Resources on Computing History

- Computer History Museum: http://www.computerhistory.org/

## Profiles of the Software Industry and Companies

Software Industry Profiles: Encyclopedias and Industry References

- *Business Insights: Global Software Publishers*. Gale Group: Cengage Learning.
- *Encyclopedia of Global Industries*. Ed. Lynn M. Pearce. Detroit: Gale.
- *Encyclopedia for Business*, 2nd ed., SIC 7372, Prepackaged Software.
- *Highbeam Industry Reports*: Computer Programming Services. Gale Group.
- *Standard & Poor's Capital IQ Industry Surveys:* Industry Surveys, Computers: Software.
- Wetfeet. December 3, 2012. *Industry Overview: Computer Software*, https://www.wetfeet.com/articles/industry-overview-computer-software (accessed January 3, 2014).
- Wikipedia: www.wikipedia.org

Software Industry Data

- International Data Corporation (IDC). n.d. A business intelligence firm that collects data on the Software industry, www.idc.com
- Compustat, S&P Capital IQ, McGraw-Hill Financial. n.d. Provides financial data on publicly held companies based on

annual reports and filings with the U.S. Government, https://www.capitaliq.com

- PricewaterhouseCoopers. n.d. Provides an Analysis of Revenues for the Top 100 Software Companies and Countries. *PWC Global 100 Software Leaders*,www.pwc.com/globalsoftware100 (accessed September 30, 2013).
- Truffle Capital. n.d. Provides an Analysis of Revenues for the Top 100 European Software Companies, with a Breakdown by Country. *Top 100 European Software Vendors by Truffle Capital*, http://www.truffle100.com/2012/countries.php (accessed September 9, 2013).

Company Profiles: Articles and Data

- *International Directory of Company Histories*, Gale Group, Cengage Learning.
- Hoovers.n.d. *Hoover's Company Profiles,* www.hoovers.com
- The Million Dollar Database: http://www.mergentmddi.com/
- EDGAR U.S. Securities and Exchange Commission. n.d. Provides a Database of Public Company SEC Filings, Financial and Company Reports, http://www.sec.gov/edgar.shtml
- Individual companies.
  - Company history. (Look up a company's website as the company history is typically summarized there.) (Example: Agilent Company History. See http://www.agilent.com/about/companyinfo/history )
  - Company financial report. Some companies (especially U.S. based publicly held companies) also report their financial performance often with annual reports on their websites (Example: Microsoft Corp. See http://www.microsoft.com/investor/AnnualReports/default.aspx )

### The Software Industry in Different Countries

Profiles and Data on Software Industry in Different Countries

- Arora, A.; and A. Gambardella. 2005. *From Underdogs to Tigers: The Rise and Growth of the Software Industry in Brazil, China, India, Ireland and Israel*. Oxford, UK: Oxford University Press.

- Aspray, W.; F. Mayadas; and M.Y. Vardi. 2006. "Globalization and Offshoring of Software: A Report of the ACM Job Migration Task Force." *Association for Computing Machinery.* http://www. acm.org/globalizationreport/
- Keller, K. and B. Mack. 2013. Maturity Profile Reports, *CMMI Institute*, March 2013, http://cmmiinstitute.com/resource/ process-maturity-profiles/ (accessed September 14, 2013).
- Organization for Economic Cooperation and Development (OECD). (OECD provides an analysis and comparative data on the Information and Communications Technology (ICT) industry for OECD and non-OECD nations.) See: OECD Science, Technology and Industry Scoreboard 2013, Retrieved January 3, 2014, from http://www.oecd-ilibrary.org/ science-and-technology/oecd-science-technology-and-industry-scoreboard-2013_sti_scoreboard-2013-en )
- Economic or trade associations for software or information technology in different countries. May report information about the industry. See, for example:
  - Brazilian Association of Software Companies. 2013. http:// www.abes.org.br/ (accessed September 22, 2013).
  - Chinese Software Industry Association. 2008. *China Software Industry Annual Report 2008*, http://www.csia.org.cn/chinese_ en/index/csiaintro.html (accessed September 14, 2013).
  - Department of Trade and Industry—South Africa. 2013. *The South African Software Development Industry.* http://www. suedafrika-wirtschaft.org/index.php?&pageID=45 (accessed December 29, 2013).

## Profiles and Data on Software Companies in Different Countries

- Company history. (Look up a company's website as the company history is typically summarized there.) (Examples: Consinco, Brazil, Company History. See http://www.consinco.com.br/ or Celtech, Ireland. See http://www.celtech.ie/company/history)
- Company financial report. Some foreign companies (especially multinational companies) also report their financial performance

often with annual reports on their websites. (Example: Capgemini. See http://www.capgemini.com/investors )

### Workforce Issues in the Software Industry

- U.S. Bureau of Labor Statistics (reports data on employment by industry by occupation)
  - Occupational Employment Survey Statistics, http://stat.bls.gov/oes/home.htm
  - Labor Force Statistics from the Current Population Survey, http://www.bls.gov/cps/tables.htm
  - Consumer Price Inflation Tables, http://www.bls.gov/cpi/tables.htm
  - Occupational Outlook Handbook, Computer and Information Technology, http://www.bls.gov/ooh/Computer-and-Information-Technology/
- National Science Foundation. 2012. "Science and Engineering Indicators 2012." *National Science Board* 12-01. (Data on enrollment in science and engineering degree programs across the U.S.). http://www.nsf.gov/statistics/seind12/c2/c2s3.htm (accessed November 3, 2013).
- Occupational Information Network (O*NET). 2013. *U.S. Department of Labor/Employment and Training Administration (USDOL/ETA)*, (Database of occupations—describes job requirements, training and average salary). http://www.onetonline.org/ (November 5, 2013).

### Software Regulation and Intellectual Property

Antitrust in the Software Industry

- Katz, M.L.; and C. Shapiro. 1999. "Antitrust in Software Markets." In *Competition, Innovation and the Microsoft Monopoly: Antitrust in the Digital Marketplace*, eds. Eisenach, J.; and T. Lenard. Norwell, MA: Kluwer Academic Publishers.
- Liebowitz, S.; S. Margolis; and J. Hirshleifer. 2001. *Winners, Losers & Microsoft: Competition and Antitrust in High Technology.* Oakland, CA: The Independent Institute.

Intellectual Property Articles and Data

- Bessen, J.; and R. Hunt. 2007. "An Empirical Look at Software Patents." *Journal of Economics and Management Strategy* 16, no. 1, pp. 157–189.
- Closa, D.; A. Gardiner; F. Giemsa; and J. Machek. 2010. *Patent Law for Computer Scientists: Steps to Protect Computer-Implemented Inventions.* Springer.
- Digital Millennium Copyright Act of 1998. (1998). Pub. L. No. 105-304, 112 Stat. 2860 (October 28, 1998).
- Free Software Foundation. 2007. *GNU General Public License.* http://www.gnu.org/copyleft/gpl.html (accessed October 1, 2013).
- International Intellectual Property Alliance, IIPA. 2013. *Copyright & Trade Issues, IIPA.* http://www.iipa.com/copyrighttrade_issues. html (accessed October 6, 2013).
- Lawmart.com. 2013. "Copyright vs. Trademark vs. Patent." *Lawmart.* http://www.lawmart.com/forms/difference.htm (accessed September 30, 2013).
- U.S. Patent and Trademark Office, USPTO
  - General Information Concerning Patents, USPTO, Retrieved September 30, 2013, from http://www.uspto.gov/patents/ resources/general_info_concerning_patents.jsp
  - Basic Facts about Trademarks, USPTO, Retrieved October 1, 2013, from http://www.uspto.gov/trademarks/basics/Basic_ Facts_Trademarks.jsp
  - Searchable database of Patents and Trademarks issued by the USPTO: http://patft.uspto.gov/
- U.S. Copyright Office. 2013. *Information about copyrights.* www. copyright.gov
- World Intellectual Property Organization, WIPO
  - PCT Resources, *WIPO*, Retrieved October 2, 2013, from http://www.wipo.int/pct/en/
  - WIPO Copyright Treaty, *WIPO*, Retrieved October 6, 2013, from http://www.wipo.int/treaties/en/ip/wct/
  - Berne Convention for the Protection of Literary and Artistic Works, *WIPO*, Retrieved October 6, 2013, from http://www. wipo.int/treaties/en/ip/berne/

### Software Security

Articles and Data on Software Piracy and Security

- Business Software Alliance. 2011. "Global Software Piracy." *9th Annual BSA Global Software Piracy Study*. http://globalstudy. bsa.org/2011/ (accessed October 6, 2013).
- CERT® Coordination Center (2013). *CERT-CC, Software Engineering Institute, Carnegie Mellon University.* http://www.cert. org/certcc.html (accessed October 16, 2013).
- McGraw, G. 2006. *Software Security: Building Security in.* Addison-Wesley.
- Smith, M.D.; and R. Telang. August 19, 2012. *Assessing the Academic Literature Regarding the Impact of Media Piracy on Sales.* SSRN: http://ssrn.com/abstract=2132153 or http://dx.doi. org/10.2139/ssrn.2132153 (accessed January 1, 2014).
- Software and Information Industry Association. 2013. "SIIA Anti-Piracy 2012 Year in Review." *SIIA.* www.siia.net (accessed October 6, 2013).
- Symantec.2013. "2013 Internet Security Threat Report." *Symantec Corporation* 18. http://www.symantec.com/security_ response/publications/threatreport.jsp (October 11, 2013).

### Emerging Software Business Models

Articles and Books on Emerging Software Business Models

- Buxman, P.H. Diefenback; and T. Hess. 2012. *The Software Industry: Economic Principles, Strategies and Perspectives.* Springer.
- Cusumano, M.A. 2004. *The Business of Software: What Every Manager, Programmer and Entrepreneur Must Know to Thrive in Good Times and Bad.* New York, NY: Free Press.
- Cusumano, M.A. (2008). "The Changing Software Business: Moving from Products to Services." *IEEE Computer* 41, no. 1, pp. 20–27.
- Eisenmann, T.G. Parker; and M.W. Van Alstyne. 2006. "Strategies for Two-sided Markets." *Harvard Business Review* 84, no. 10, p. 92.

- Messerschmitt, D.; and C. Szyperski. 2005. *Software Ecosystem: Understanding an Indispensable Technology and Industry.* The MIT Press.
- Raymond, E. 2001. *The Cathedral & the Bazaar: Musings on Linux and Open Source by an Accidental Revolutionary.* Sebastopol, CA: O'Reilly Media, Inc.

### Resources on Software Engineering

Articles and Books on Software Engineering Concepts and Methodologies

- Brooks, F. 1995. *The Mythical Man Month: Essays on Software Engineering.* Addison-Wesley.
- Boehm, B. 1981. *Software Engineering Economics.* Englewood Cliffs, NJ: Prentice-Hall.
- Beck, K. 1999. *Extreme Programming Explained: Embrace Change.* Addison-Wesley.
- Dennis, A.B. Wixom; and D. Tegarden. 2009. *Systems Analysis and Design with UML Version 2.0*, 3rd ed. Wiley.
- Gabbrielli, M.; and S. Martini. 2010. *Programming Languages: Principles and Paradigms.* New York, NY: Springer.
- Schwaber, K.; and M. Beedle. 2002. *Agile Software Development with Scrum.* Princeton, NJ: Prentice-Hall.

Articles and Resources on the Capability Maturity Model

- Paulk, M. 2009. "A History of the Capability Maturity Model for Software." *Software Quality & Productivity, American Society for Quality* 12, no. 1, pp. 5–19.
- Software Engineering Institute's Capability Maturity Model Integration: See http://www.sei.cmu.edu/cmmi/

# Glossary of Key Terms

**Agile development**   An approach to developing software in which software development is broken down into small increments that can be completed within a short time frame (time boxes) that typically last from one to four weeks. A small, cross-functional team works on an increment and at the end of the iteration, a working product results. Types of agile development include Scrum and eXtreme Programming (XP).

**Application or "App"**   A single software program that performs a specific function using a computer, such as verifying a credit card number or allowing a user to play a game. Also called an app.

**Application programming interface (API)**   A set of rules or specifications that serve as an interface between different software programs or components and define how they can interact with each other.

**Applications software**   Applications software is used to accomplish specific end-user tasks (such as inventory management, playing a game, tracking product sales, or creating an architectural drawing) beyond just running the computer system.

**Applications software system**   A larger grouping of application software is a collection of fundamental programs that may provide some service to a variety of other independent applications. An example is an accounts receivable system.

**Biometrics**   Use of biological means such as facial recognition, fingerprints, and so forth, to provide authentication and allow access to a system or data.

**Botnet**   Robot networks are a collection of Internet-connected programs that communicate with other similar programs in order to perform tasks (legal or illegal).

**Browser**   A software program that retrieves, displays, and prints information and documents from the Internet.

**Capability maturity model (CMM)**   A framework of best practices or methodology that can be used to improve a company's software development processes. There are different levels of sophistication and maturity of processes, ranging from ad-hoc (level 1) to optimizing (level 5). The Software Engineering Institute at Carnegie Mellon University created the CMM, originally for software development (now called CMM-SW). The current version of the CMM is the CMMI (Capability Maturity Model Integration).

**Cloud computing**    Using a network of remote servers hosted on the Internet to providing access to a shared pool of resources (such as applications, servers, data, storage and services) that can be rapidly provided and scaled to match demand.

**Compatibility**    Products which can communicate with each other or can be used with the same complementary components. In the software industry, compatibility exists when software products—such as a spreadsheet program and a word processing program—can exchange or share files in a common format. It also exists when a particular software application can run on a particular operating system.

**Compiler**    Computer instructions that translate human-understandable software source code into machine-understandable object code that can be executed by the computer processor.

**Component**    A small piece or unit of software code that includes a set of related functions or data.

**Component-based development (CBD)**    An approach to developing software in which the functions of the system are divided into small units or components. Development includes defining, implementing, and composing the loosely coupled independent components into systems.

**Computer-aided software engineering (CASE)**    A set of software programs and tools that help automate design, development, and implementation of a software system. CASE can include tools to create visual diagrams and representations of the system, an information repository of software designs and components that can be reused, tools to design, generate and test software code, and other management tools.

**Copyright**    Protects the form of expression of "original works of authorship" including literary, dramatic, musical, artistic, and certain other intellectual works, both published and unpublished. Copyrights are registered by the Copyright Office of the Library of Congress.

**Custom software**    Software programs or systems that are specifically designed to meet the needs of a particular user.

**Cyberwarfare/espionage**   Politically motivated hacking to conduct sabotage and espionage.

**Data breach**   The intentional or unintentional release of secure information to an untrusted environment.

**Distributed denial of service (DDoS)**   An attempt to make a computer or network resource unavailable to its intended users by temporarily or indefinitely interrupting or suspending services of a host connected to the Internet.

**Economies of scale**   An economic term describing a business model in which it costs a company less to produce each product the more it produces and sells. Technically, it refers to a situation in which the long-run average cost curve for producing something declines as production increases as there are low marginal costs to replicate and distribute the product relative to average costs to produce the first copy.

**Enterprise resource planning systems**   Enterprise Resource Planning (ERP) Systems are very large systems that connect what were, heretofore, largely independent applications (e.g., order management, inventory management, accounting, human resource management), under a common interface.

**Firewall**   A software barrier or gateway that separates the Internet from a private network or local area network. It restricts certain internal data from passing to these external networks and screens incoming traffic.

**Global delivery network**   Units, centers, or divisions of a company located in different parts of the world that together produce or deliver a product or service. Different centers may specialize in different activities in the value chain such as software design or software quality assurance or documentation.

**Graphic artist**   An occupation in the software industry that creates graphic designs for a software product or brand, or designs the website for a software product.

**H1-B work visa**   A temporary work visa in the United States that is issued to employers to hire workers in occupations requiring at least a bachelor's degree and highly specialized knowledge and skills.

**Hacking**   Using programming skills to gain access (legally or illegally) to a computer system.

**Incremental development**    A method to develop software in which a system is delivered in increments, versions, or releases. The initial release is the core product. Updates and extensions to the core product are made in subsequent increments, versions, or releases

**Internet**    The global network of computers that grew out of ARPAnet, a project funded by the U.S. Department of Defense. The network is supported by a large national backbone and regional networks around the world.

**Linux**    An open-source operating system inspired by Unix.

**Mainframe computer**    A very large computer that serves hundreds or thousands of users in an organization.

**Malware**    Malicious software that disrupts computer processing or gains unauthorized access to data or other sensitive information.

**Middleware**    Software designed to promote interoperability between diverse software applications and infrastructure across a network.

**Mini- or microcomputer**    Mid-range computers that are less powerful than mainframe computers but more powerful than personal computers and may serve one or more users.

**Model-driven architecture (MDA)**    An approach to developing software that attempts to separate the design of the software from its physical implementation. It involves creating design models of the functions and features to be implemented in the software and includes tools and techniques to help produce software code from those design models and diagrams.

**Network effects**    The effects that one consumer of a good or service has on the value of that product to other people. A product that has network effects is more valuable to consumers when more consumers use it.

**Object-oriented development (OOD)**    An approach to designing and developing software by building self-contained modules (objects) that can be easily replaced, modified, and reused.

**Offshoring**    The outsourcing of software development and other activities to countries outside the "home" country.

**Open source software**    Software source code that is posted on the Internet and is freely available to the public to read, use, and modify.

**Operating system**   The software system that supports and manages the basic functions of a computer, such as scheduling tasks, executing application software, and controlling hardware devices.

**Outsourcing**   The hiring of another firm to provide services such as custom programming, testing, and integration.

**Package**   A small group of programs that work closely together to accomplish a task, such as an architectural rendering (e.g., the software package AutoCAD).

**Packaged or prepackaged software industry**   Includes companies that design, develop, and produce software products for sale in the mass market.

**Patent**   The grant of a property right to the inventor, issued by the U.S. Patent and Trademark Office. Generally good for up to 20 years.

**Patent pool**   Involves a consortium of at least two companies that agree to cross-license patents relating to a particular technology.

**Patent thicket**   Overlapping sets of patent rights that require innovators to negotiate licensing deals for multiple patents from multiple sources.

**Patent troll**   A firm that buys patents for products and services. The firm makes money by litigating to enforce patent rights against accused infringers.

**Personal computer**   A small computer that serves an individual user. Less powerful than mainframe, minicomputers, or microcomputers.

**Phishing**   The act of sending an e-mail to a user falsely claiming to be an established legitimate enterprise in an attempt to scam the user into surrendering private information that will be used for identity theft. The e-mail directs the user to visit a bogus website where they are asked to update personal information, such as passwords and credit card, social security, and bank account numbers.

**Platform**   Infrastructure and rules that enable connections between the actors in an ecosystem. An example software platform is Microsoft's Windows operating system.

**Product line**   A set of software programs which share common features that satisfy the needs of a particular market segment. The programs are developed using a common or shared set of software functions and tools. An example is a software product line of software security products aimed at corporate users versus another product line aimed at individual users.

**Product maintenance engineer**    An occupation in the software industry that debugs and fixes software product problems and monitors and improves technical performance of the software product.

**Program**    A group or sequence of instructions written to perform a specific task with a computer, such as balancing one's checkbook.

**Programming language**    A specific set of notations for instructions used to write a software program. Examples of programming languages include JAVA, COBOL, FORTRAN, and C++.

**Prototyping**    A method to develop software which creates a "mock up" version of a system that is not fully functional, but can be developed quickly.

**Rapid application development (RAD)**    A method to develop software which creates "components" or small pieces of software systems that are fully functional, and that can be built and installed within 60–90 days.

**Sandbox**    Creating compartments in a system to segment and protect vulnerable applications and data on the system from outside attacks

**Service**    The different tasks associated with producing a software product, such as design, programming, testing, documentation, integration, installation, training, and support.

**Service oriented architecture (SOA)**    A design in which the functions performed by the software are broken down into discrete pieces of functionality which are provided as services to other applications.

**Software**    The computer instructions that control the functioning of computer hardware and direct its operations. Includes two types of instructions: machine instructions (the binary code that turns certain electronic pulses on and off to communicate with the computer processor) and source code (human-understandable instructions).

**Software architect**    An occupation in the software industry that designs software architecture and platforms and defines technical standards.

**Software client manager**    An occupation in the software industry that develops and sustains relationships with clients.

**Software designer or content engineer**    An occupation in the software industry that designs the user experience and provides content for software products.

**Software developer/engineer**    An occupation in the software industry that writes and implements software code for products.

**Software ecosystem**    The software products and services that enable, support, and automate the activities and transactions of the actors in the associated business community and the firms that provide these software solutions.

**Software integration engineer**    An occupation in the software industry that manages integration of the software components for a product and ensures that software components work together.

**Software packaging engineer**    An occupation in the software industry that designs and develops packages for software products that are physically distributed

**Software piracy**    The unauthorized copying of computer software.

**Software product**    A set of one or more computer software programs that a company offers for sale. Examples of software products include a spreadsheet or an antivirus software tool.

**Software product/project manager**    An occupation in the software industry that manages the software product over its life cycle (from initiation to retirement).

**Software product marketer**    An occupation in the software industry that develops product marketing, sales, and pricing strategies.

**Software product sales representative**    An occupation in the software industry that sells software products to customers.

**Software quality assurance engineer**    An occupation in the software industry that assures that the software product conforms to company's quality standards; tests software products for usability and functionality; and develops software quality standards.

**Software R&D engineer**    An occupation in the software industry that conducts basic and applied research on computer science and translates research to new product ideas.

**Software security**    Building software to function properly even when under malicious attack. Also involves protecting assets (software source code, distributed systems, and sensitive data) that may be vulnerable to attack or exploitation by various threats.

**Software tester/test engineer**    An occupation in the software industry that tests software products to make sure they work properly and satisfy requirements.

**Software value chain**    The different activities that are needed to produce and market software products, such as research and development, coding, testing, marketing and advertising, documentation, and distribution.

**Software-as-a-service (SAAS)**    Refers to business or consumer software applications that are accessed on-demand via the Internet.

**Spam**    Junk electronic mail or junk e-newsgroup postings.

**Standards**    Define an explicit or an implicit agreement to do certain things in a certain way. In software, standards exist for file formats, user interface designs, or other interfaces.

**Suite**    A larger group of programs which includes related but independent programs and packages that have a common user interface or shared data format, such as Microsoft Office. The Microsoft Office suite consists of an integrated word processor, spreadsheet, database, presentation software, and other programs.

**Switching costs**    The one-time costs of switching from the product of one firm to another product of that firm or to a product of another firm.

**Systems of systems**    The largest grouping of application software which represents a collection of interdependent systems. An example is enterprise resource planning systems.

**Systems software**    Software that controls, integrates, and manages the individual hardware components of a computer system. Generally, system software consists of an operating system and utilities such as file managers, display managers, text editors, user authentication (login), security and systems management tools, and networking and device control software.

**Technical support specialist**    An occupation in the software industry that provides assistance and communicates technical solutions to customers

**Technical writer/documentation specialist**    An occupation in the software industry that develops software product documentation, help guides, manuals, and white papers.

**Trademark**    A word, name, symbol, or device that is used to indicate the source of a product and to distinguish it from the products of others.

A servicemark is the same as a trademark except that it identifies and distinguishes the source of a service rather than a product.

**Trojan horse**    A program in which malicious or harmful code is contained inside an apparently harmless program or data in such a way that it can get control of a computer and do damage.

**Virus**    A piece of code that is capable of copying itself and typically has a detrimental effect, such as corrupting the system or destroying data.

**Waterfall development**    A step-by-step process for developing a software system in stages by first understanding requirements, then designing the system, then coding it, then testing it, and finally implementing it.

**Worm**    A standalone malware computer program that replicates itself in order to spread to other computers.

**Y2K**    The Y2K (or Year 2000) problem occurred at the rollover from 1999 to 2000, for computer systems that abbreviated and stored the year in a date as 2 digits instead of 4 digits. Storing only 2 digits could cause problems with date sequencing, leap year calculation, and other issues.

# Notes

## Preface

1. Kostier (2013).
2. Cox (1990), p. 26.
3. McAfee (2013a).
4. McAfee (2013b).
5. U.S. Securities and Exchange Commission (2006).
6. Wikipedia (2013e).
7. Swartz (2013b).
8. Swartz (2013b).
9. Kaplan (2013).
10. Swartz (2013a).

## Chapter 1

1. O'Reilly Media (2013).
2. Happy Codings (2013b).
3. Daily Free Code (2012).
4. Happy Codings (2013c).
5. Jones (1996).
6. Jones (1996).
7. Toomey (2011).
8. Windows (2014).
9. Bricklin (2009).
10. Jones (2012).
11. Hurwitz (2007).
12. Newcomb (2012).
13. Brown et al. (1994).
14. Frankel (2003).
15. Dennis et al. (2009).
16. Dennis et al. (2009).
17. Boehm (1988).
18. Unified Modeling Language (2014).
19. Beck (1999).
20. Schwaber and Beedle (2002).
21. Microsoft (January 7, 2000).
22. Lunden (2013).

23. U.S. Census Bureau (1997).
24. Lunden (2013).
25. Lunden (2013).

# Chapter 2

1. Philipson (2005).
2. Toole (1998), pp. 240–261.
3. Toole (1998).
4. Halacy (1970).
5. Computer History Museum (2008).
6. Copeland (2006).
7. Copeland (2005). Note also that Turing's other major contribution to computing is the famous Turing Test, which states that a computer can be said to "think" if a person cannot tell it apart from a human being in talking with it. This test has been very influential in the field of artificial intelligence. A reversed form of the Turing test is widely used today on the Internet—it is called a CAPTCHA test, which is used to determine whether a user is a human or a computer.
8. Weik (1961).
9. The idea of using vacuum tubes was inspired by John Atanasoff's earlier computer called the ABC. Atanasoff's recognition as the designer and developer of first fully electronic computer was granted by the U.S. Court in 1973 when the court voided ENIAC's patent.
10. The women included Jean Jennings Bartik, Frances "Betty" Snyder Holberton, Kathleen McNulty Mauchly Antonelli, Marlyn Wescoff Meltzer, Ruth Lichterman Teitelbaum, and Frances Bilas Spence. Retrieved July 18, 2013, from http://www.columbia.edu/cu/computinghistory/eniac.html
11. Goldstine and Goldstine (1946).
12. John von Neumann, a mathematician working on the hydrogen bomb at Los Alamos, became aware of the ENIAC and influenced its development.
13. Hoyle (2006).
14. Alfred (2008).
15. Note that the requirements of SAGE were beyond IBM's capabilities, and the software part of the contract was awarded to Rand Corporation in 1955.
16. Tukey (1958), p. 1.
17. Bellis (2013).
18. Beyer (2009).
19. Pugh et al. (1991).
20. Brooks (1995).
21. Fisher, McKie, and Mancke (1983), p. 322.

22. Smith (2007).
23. Cusumano (2004), p. 91.
24. Naur and Randell (1969).
25. Randell and Buxton (1970).
26. Codd (1970).
27. Smith (1970). Prices adjusted for inflation to 2013 dollars using the inflation calculator provided by the U.S. Bureau of Labor Statistics (n.d.).
28. Steinmueller (1996), p. 23.
29. Grove (1996).
30. Steinmueller (1996). Table 2. Prices adjusted for inflation to 1970 dollars using the inflation calculator provided by the U.S. Bureau of Labor Statistics. Bureau of Labor Statistics (n.d.).
31. Kahney (2003). According to the Guinness Book of World Records, more than 30 million of the Commodore 64 were sold during its lifetime.
32. Coventry (2006).
33. Steinmueller (1996).
34. Philipson (2005).
35. Wikipedia. (n.d. a)
36. Reference for Business (n.d.).
37. Reference for Business (n.d.).
38. Power (2004).
39. Sigel (1985), p. 126.
40. Steinmueller (1996).
41. Campbell-Kelly (1995).
42. OECD report on the Software Industry (1998). Prices adjusted for inflation to 1970 dollars using the inflation calculator provided by the U.S. Bureau of Labor Statistics. Bureau of Labor Statistics (n.d.).
43. Paulk (2009).
44. Banker, Davis, and Slaughter (1998).
45. Wikipedia. (n.d. b).
46. Baum (1981).
47. Grove (1996).
48. Corr (1992).
49. Wikipedia (n.d. c).
50. Gross (2013).
51. Wikipedia (n.d. d).
52. Reference for Business (n.d.).
53. Wikipedia (n.d. e).
54. Netmarketshare (n.d.).
55. Raymond (2001).
56. IDC (2004, December).

57. Leonard (2001).
58. Netmarketshare (n.d.).
59. Netmarketshare (n.d.).
60. Netmarketshare (n.d.). Note that the company counts usage market share in terms of unique visitors. According to the company's website, it collects data from the browsers of site visitors to its exclusive on-demand network of HitsLink Analytics and SharePost clients. The network includes over 40,000 websites and spans the globe. The company counts unique visitors to its network sites, and only counts one unique visit to each network site per day. The data is compiled from approximately 160 million unique visits per month.
61. Kaspersky (2012).
62. Gale Group (2013b).
63. Gale Group (2013b). Prices adjusted for inflation to 1970 dollars using the inflation calculator provided by the U.S. Bureau of Labor Statistics. Bureau of Labor Statistics (n.d.).

# Chapter 3

1. Li, Shang, and Slaughter (2010 September), p. 632.
2. Rumelt (2003).
3. Based on data in Li, Shang, and Slaughter (2010).
4. Kessler (2012), p. 5.
5. Based on data from CBEMA reported in Steinmueller (1996). Table 2, and OECD (2002). Adjusted for inflation to 1970 dollars using the U.S. Bureau of Labor Statistics inflation calculator. US Bureau of Labour Statistics (n.d.).
6. Coffey (2013), p. 8. Source of revenue data reported is from IDC.
7. Wikipedia (n.d.g).
8. Wikipedia (n.d.h).
9. Wikipedia (n.d.i).
10. Wikipedia (n.d.j).
11. Kessler (2012).
12. Wikipedia (2013).
13. Bednarz (2011).
14. Bednarz (2011).
15. IBM (n.d.).
16. HP (n.d.a).
17. HP (n.d.b).
18. HP (n.d.c).
19. Agilent Technologies (n.d.).

20. HP (n.d. d).
21. Porter (1996, November–December).
22. Vaughan (2004).
23. Williams (2011).
24. Williams (2011).
25. Kessler (2012).
26. Li, Shang, and Slaughter (2010).
27. Fayad, Laitimen, and Ward (2000).
28. Kessler (2012).
29. Based on data reported by Forrester Research, Inc., in Lunden (2013).
30. Kessler (2012).
31. Shapiro and Varian (1998).
32. Crossley (2010).
33. Banker and Slaughter (1997).
34. Liu, Kemerer, Slaughter, and Smith (2012, September).
35. POSIX (2011).
36. Brynjolfsson and Kemerer (1996, December).
37. Katz and Shapiro (1999).
38. Brynjolfsson and Kemerer (1996, December).
39. Porter (1979, March–April).
40. Bruce (2011).
41. Data from IDC, U.S. Black Book reported by Business Software Alliance (2009).
42. Wheelen and Hunger (2000), p. 125.
43. Jacobini and McCreary (1994).
44. Kerravala (2009).
45. Kessler (2012).

# Chapter 4

1. Campbell-Kelly (1995).
2. Campbell-Kelly (1995).
3. Cusumano and Kemerer (1990 November).
4. Balatchandirane et al. (2004).
5. According to data retrieved December 29, 2013, from www.payscale.com the median annual salary for a software engineer with 2 to 4 years of experience working in Bangalore, India is about 400,000 Rupees ($6,500) while the median annual salary for a software engineer with 2 to 4 years of experience working in the United States is about $76,500.
6. Bansal, Kaka, Kejriwal, and Sharma (2001).
7. Aggarwal, Berry, Kenney, Lenway, and Taylor (2006).

8. PricewaterhouseCoopers (2013) and Gale Group (2013a). PwC reports data from the top 100 global firms and countries and notes that the data originate from IDC and from company annual reports. For Sweden, the company Ericsson is the source of software sales, and the numbers, according to PwC are obtained from Ericsson's annual reports. The data for all countries are from 2011, which are the most complete. Gale Group (2013a) provides a source for the total sales from NAICS 511210 for packaged software of $359M for 2011 which is used to compute the total global software sales.

9. Sweden's presence in the list is due to Ericsson—the large telecommunications company—which is headquartered in Sweden. Although Ericsson primarily produces telecommunications equipment, it also (like many computer hardware vendors) produces software for sale.

10. PricewaterhouseCoopers (2013). Sweden, Belgium, the United Kingdom, France, Germany, the Netherlands and Norway are among the top 20 countries in the world for software revenues in 2011–2012. Retrieved December 29, 2013, from http://www.pwc.com/gx/en/technology/publications/global-software-100-leaders/compare-results.jhtml

11. Jaeger (2012).

12. Jaeger (2012).

13. Leimbach (2008 October–December).

14. Leimbach (2008 October–December).

15. Gale Group (2013a).

16. Gale Group (2013a).

17. Gale Group (2013a).

18. Jaeger (2012).

19. Jaeger (2012).

20. Jaeger (2012).

21. Jaeger (2012).

22. International Directory of Company Histories (1997).

23. Kessler (2012).

24. The Associated Press (2011).

25. Siemens (2012).

26. Siemens (2013).

27. Wikipedia (2013b).

28. Bourn (2006).

29. Wikipedia (2013a).

30. Gale Group (2013a).

31. Truffle Capital (2013).

32. Gale Group (2013a).

33. Gale Group (2013a).

34. Truffle Capital (2013).

35. Capgemini (2013).
36. Capgemini (2013).
37. Capgemini (2013).
38. Berthiaume (2013).
39. Berthiaume (2013).
40. Dassault Systemes (2013).
41. International Directory of Company Histories (1999).
42. Bernard (2013).
43. Bernard (2013).
44. Dassault Systemes (2013).
45. Truffle Capital (2013).
46. Microsoft (2008).
47. Sage Group (2013).
48. Vaughan-Adams (2003).
49. Sage Group (2013).
50. Sage Group (2013).
51. Industrial Development Agency (2013).
52. Drew (1994).
53. Moynihan (2013).
54. Moynihan (2013).
55. Organization for Economic Cooperation and Development (2002).
56. Moynihan (2013).
57. Moynihan (2013).
58. Moynihan (2013).
59. Irish Exporters Association (2013).
60. Irish Software Association (n.d.).
61. Irish Software Association (n.d.).
62. CR2 (2013).
63. Celtech (2013).
64. Sands (2005).
65. Conduit (n.d.a).
66. Conduit (n.d.b).
67. Breznitz (2005).
68. Breznitz (2005).
69. Breznitz (2005).
70. Breznitz (2005).
71. Israel Export and International Cooperation Institute (2010).
72. Israel Export and International Cooperation Institute (2010).
73. Breznitz (2005).
74. International Directory of Company Histories (2002).
75. Amdocs (n.d).

76. Check Point (n.d).
77. Yahoo! Inc. (2013a).
78. Breznitz (2007).
79. Breznitz (2007).
80. Dow Jones News Service (2005).
81. Breznitz (2007).
82. Ferzinger (2006 August, 31).
83. Davidoff (2013).
84. Yahoo! Inc. (2013b).
85. Yahoo! Inc. (2013b).
86. Datamonitor (2011 August, 30).
87. Department of Trade and Industry—South Africa (2013).
88. Datamonitor (2011 August, 30).
89. South Africa (n.d.).
90. South Africa (n.d.).
91. Nortje (2008).
92. Dimension Data (n.d.).
93. Dimension Data (n.d.).
94. Online Innovations (n.d).
95. Bardhan and Kroll (2006).
96. Bardhan and Kroll (2006).
97. Software Russia (2012).
98. Auriga (2013).
99. Auriga (2013).
100. Artezio (2013).
101. EPAM (2013).
102. EPAM (2013).
103. EPAM (2013).
104. EPAM (2013).
105. Devexperts (2013).
106. Russoft Vendors Directory (2012).
107. Kaspersky (2013).
108. Zetter (2012).
109. Zetter (2012).
110. Zetter (2012).
111. International Data Corporation (2013).
112. Kaspersky (2013).
113. Chinese Software Industry Association (2008). Note that there is a significant discrepancy between the sales numbers provided by the Chinese Software Industry Association and by the IDC (the primary source of global software industry data). IDC estimates Chinese software industry revenue

in 2000 at U.S. $1 billion (1/7 the number provided by the Chinese Software Industry Association).

114. Gale Group (2013a).
115. Tschang and Xue (2005).
116. Tschang and Xue (2005).
117. Tschang and Xue (2005).
118. Gale Group (2013a).
119. Gale Group (2013a).
120. Tschang and Xue (2005).
121. Keller and Mack (2013).
122. Neusoft Corporation (2013a).
123. Neusoft Corporation (2013b).
124. Neusoft Corporation (2013b).
125. Neusoft Corporation (2013b).
126. Neusoft Corporation (2013a).
127. Wikipedia (2013g).
128. Wikipedia (2013g).
129. Edgar SEC Filing (2013).
130. Edgar SEC Filing (2013).
131. The statistics reported in this paragraph are from Shanda's SEC Filing report. Edgar SEC Filing (2013).
132. Chan and Pei (2013).
133. Microsoft (2013).
134. Chan and Pei (2013).
135. Ministry of Economy, Trade and Industry (2012).
136. Ministry of Economy, Trade and Industry (2012).
137. Ministry of Economy, Trade and Industry (2012).
138. Cole and Shinya (2010).
139. Cusumano (1991a).
140. Cusumano (1991b).
141. Cole and Shinya (2010).
142. Gale Group (2013a).
143. Cole and Shinya (2010).
144. Fujitsu (n.d.).
145. Fujitsu (n.d.).
146. Hitachi (n.d.).
147. Hitachi (n.d.).
148. Hitachi (n.d.).
149. Hitachi (n.d.).
150. NEC Corporation (1984).
151. NEC Corporation (1984).

152. Lenovo (2011).
153. Athreye (2005).
154. NASSCOM (2013).
155. NASSCOM (2013).
156. Athreye (2005).
157. Equity Master Agora Research (2013).
158. Equity Master Agora Research (2013).
159. Equity Master Agora Research (2013).
160. Keller and Mack (2013).
161. Gopal and Gao (2009).
162. Landon (2002).
163. Tata Consultancy Services (2013).
164. Tata Consultancy Services (2013).
165. Wipro (2013).
166. Wipro (2013).
167. Wipro (2013).
168. Equity Master Agora Research (2013).
169. Infosys (2013).
170. Infosys (2013).
171. Infosys (2013).
172. Mysore Samachar (2013).
173. Infosys (2013).
174. Infosys Press Release (2013).
175. Invest in Australia (2013).
176. Invest in Australia (2013).
177. Earl (2013).
178. Australian Bureau of Statistics (2006–2007).
179. Wikipedia (n.d.k).
180. Atlassian (n.d.a).
181. Atlassian (n.d.b).
182. Atlassian (n.d.b).
183. Atlassian (n.d.c).
184. Wikipedia (n.d.l).
185. Redtribe (n.d).
186. Botelho, Stefanuto, and Veloso (2005).
187. Softex (2013).
188. Botelho, Stefanuto, and Veloso(2005).
189. Botelho, Stefanuto, and Veloso(2005).
190. U.S. Department of Commerce's International Trade Administration (2013).
191. U.S. Department of Commerce's International Trade Administration (2013).

192. Pacheco (2012).
193. U.S. Department of Commerce's International Trade Administration (2013).
194. Brazilian Association of Software Companies (2013).
195. Totvs (2013).
196. Totvs (2013).
197. Pacheco (2012).
198. Consinco (2013).
199. Consinco (2013).
200. Pacheco (2012).
201. Syhunt (2013).
202. Syhunt (2013).
203. Technology Executives Club (2013).
204. Technology Executives Club (2013).
205. Bujarski (2012).
206. Mexico (n.d.).
207. Flannery (2012).
208. Mexico (n.d.).
209. Mexico (n.d.).
210. Pro Mexico (n.d).
211. Flannery (2012).
212. Flannery (2012).
213. Keller and Mack (2013).
214. Softtek (n.d.).
215. Mexico (n.d.).

# Chapter 5

1. Gruber (2010).
2. Sarno (2010).
3. Zuckerberg (2010).
4. Segall (2012).
5. PricewaterhouseCoopers (2013), p. 3.
6. The material in this section draws from the occupational handbook published by the U.S. Bureau of Labor Statistics (2013d) and the occupational database of O*NET (2013).
7. Lomanto (2011) provides an excellent description of the occupation of software product marketers and their job functions.
8. Wetfeet (2012).
9. Wikipedia (2013f).
10. Ang, Slaughter, and Ng (2002); Mithas and Krishnan (2008 March).

11. Lockard and Wolf (2012 January).
12. National Science Foundation (2012).
13. U.S. Bureau of Labor Statistics (2013a). Note that the number of workers includes only those in computer-related occupations who work for software publishers (NAICS 511200) or for software services (NAICS 541500). The count of workers does not include managers and other noncomputer-related workers, nor does it include computer workers in other industries.
14. Ang, Slaughter and Ng (2002).
15. Mithas and Krishnan (2008 March).
16. U.S. Bureau of Labor Statistics (2013c).
17. U.S. Bureau of Labor Statistics (2013b).
18. Information Technology Association of America (2005).
19. U.S. Department of Labor (2010).
20. Ashcraft and Blithe (2010).
21. National Science Foundation (2012).
22. National Science Foundation (2012).
23. Ahuja (2002 March).
24. Schafer and Trautlein (2007).
25. Levina and Xin (2007 June).
26. Joseph, Ang and Slaughter (2008).
27. Musio (2009).
28. Thibodeau (2012).
29. Musio (2009).
30. Thibodeau (2012).
31. Mithas and Lucas (2010 May) provide an excellent discussion of U.S. visa policies and the IT industry. This section draws from their article.
32. U.S. Citizenship and Immigration Services (USCIS) (2013).
33. Park (2007).
34. Saxenian (2002 Winter).
35. Kerr and Lincoln (2010 February).
36. Schechtman (2013).
37. The National Science Foundation indicators stop at 2009. There are anecdotal reports of sharp increases in enrollment in computer science programs in more recent years.

# Chapter 6

1. A query (written by the author) of software patents vs. total patents in the USPTO database indicates that more than one-third of total patents awarded in 2012 were for software-related patents. See Figure 6.2 and the note to this Figure for more details on how software patents were recognized.

2. Hart (1998), p. 75.
3. Letwin (1956).
4. Letwin (1956).
5. Hamilton (1969).
6. AT&T (n.d.).
7. AT&T (n.d.).
8. AT&T (n.d.).
9. Lasar (2011).
10. For readers interested in the story of UNIX, see the book on UNIX history by Salus (1994).
11. Lasar (2011).
12. Salus (1994) and Lasar (2011).
13. Sugawara (1993).
14. Etro (2008).
15. Lohr and Brinkley (1998).
16. Etro (2008).
17. Etro (2008).
18. Etro (2008).
19. Castle and Jolly (2008).
20. Liebowitz, Margolis, and Hirshleifer (2001) and Page and Lopatka (2009).
21. Katz and Shapiro (1999).
22. Hemphill and Vonortas (2005).
23. *Addamax vs. Open Software Foundation, Inc.* (1995).
24. Katz and Shapiro (1999).
25. Katz and Shapiro (1999).
26. Cordeiro (2010).
27. Cooley (2011).
28. Cooley (2011).
29. The HHI is a commonly used measure of market concentration. It is calculated by squaring the market share of each firm competing in a market, and then summing the resulting amount. The HHI can range from close to zero to 10,000. The closer a market is to being a single-firm monopoly (HHI of 10,000), the higher the market's concentration (and the lower its competition). If there were perfect competition with thousands of firms competing, each would have nearly zero percent market share, and the HHI would be close to zero.
30. Cooley (2011).
31. Greene (2011).
32. Greene (2011).
33. U.S. Patent and Trademark Office (2013b).
34. U.S. Copyright Office (2013).

35. Copyright Act of 1976 (1976).
36. Computer Software Copyright Act of 1980 (1980).
37. *Lotus Development vs. Borland International* (2003).
38. Digital Millenium Copyright Act of 1998 (1998, October).
39. World Intellectual Property Organization (2013b).
40. Free Software Foundation (2007).
41. U.S. Patent and Trademark Office (2013a).
42. U.S. Patent and Trademark Office (2013a).
43. A third type of patent is a "plant" patent. Plant patents may be granted to anyone who invents or discovers and asexually reproduces any distinct and new variety of plant. Plant patents are not relevant to the software industry.
44. Smith (2007).
45. Smith (2007).
46. Closa, Gardiner, Giemsa, and Machek (2010).
47. *Diamond vs. Diehr* (1981).
48. Federal Circuit Court (1998).
49. *Bilski vs. Kappos* (2010).
50. U.S. Patent and Trademark Office (2013c).
51. Bessen and Hunt (2007).
52. WIPO (n.d.).
53. Kerr (2013).
54. Kerr (2012).
55. Software and Information Industry Association (2013).
56. Software and Information Industry Association (2013).
57. Software and Information Industry Association (2013).
58. Business Software Alliance (2011).
59. Business Software Alliance (2011).
60. Smith and Telang (2012).
61. Business Software Alliance (2011).
62. Business Software Alliance (2011).
63. International Intellectual Property Alliance (2013).
64. European Union Directives (2009).
65. World Intellectual Property Organization (2013b).
66. World Intellectual Property Organization (2013a).
67. Finn (2011).
68. Finn (2011).
69. Thurott (2007).
70. Barbosa (2008).
71. Womack (2012).
72. Raustiala and Sprigman (2013).
73. Allison, Lemley, and Walker (2010).

74. Lodsys (2013).
75. Wikipedia (2013c).
76. Nazier (2013).
77. The material in the next paragraphs draws upon the summary of the *Apple vs. Samsung* patent battles provided by Pepitone (2013).
78. Pepitone (2013).
79. Pepitone (2013).
80. Decker and Wingfield (2013).
81. Pepitone (2013).
82. Raustiala and Sprigman (2013).
83. Bessen (2013).
84. Allison, Lemley, and Walker (2010).
85. Lee (2013).
86. Ballardini (2009).
87. Vakili (2012).
88. Vakili (2012).
89. Wen, Ceccagnoli, and Forman (2013).
90. Digital Millenium Copyright Act of 1998 (1998 October, 28).
91. World Intellectual Property Organization (2013b).
92. Business Software Alliance (2011).
93. Barboza (2009).
94. Barboza (2009).
95. Business Software Alliance (2011).
96. Kessler (2012).
97. Lee (2013).

# Chapter 7

1. Finkle (2013).
2. Finkle (2013).
3. Bodoni (2013).
4. Bodoni (2013).
5. Symantec (2013).
6. McGraw (2006).
7. Paglieri (2013).
8. Symantec (2013).
9. Arena, Younossi, Brancato, and Grammich (2008).
10. Kitten (2013) and Wagstaff (2014).
11. Tsipenyuk, Chess, and McGraw (2005 November–December).
12. Schantz (2006 January–March).
13. Moore and Shannon (2001).

14. Symantec (2007).
15. Kay (2004).
16. Mackey (2010).
17. Surane (2013).
18. BBC News (2010).
19. Symantec (2013).
20. Symantec (2013).
21. Symantec (2013).
22. Symantec (2013).
23. McGraw (2006).
24. McGraw (2006).
25. Symantec (2013).
26. Symantec (2013).
27. Health Insurance Portability and Accountability Act (1996).
28. Sarbanes-Oxley (2002).
29. Software Engineering Standards Committee (2006).
30. Wikipedia (2013d) provides a list of these standards.
31. Gage and McCormack (2004).
32. Gage and McCormack (2004).
33. Cuniberti (2010).
34. Levy and Bell (1990).
35. CERT® Coordination Center (2013).
36. U.S. Computer Emergency Readiness Team (2013).
37. CERT® Coordination Center (n.d.).
38. The term "freemium" was created by Jarid Lukin of Alacra in response to a 2006 blog post by venture capitalist Fred Wilson summarizing the model.
39. Anderson (2009).
40. Niculescu and Wu (2014).
41. Niculescu and Wu (2014).
42. Mell and Grance (2011).
43. Mell and Grance (2011).
44. Kessler (2012).
45. Salesforce.com (2013a).
46. Coffey (2013 August).
47. Coffey (2013 August).
48. Gellman and Soltani (2013).
49. Red Hat (2013).
50. Coffey (2013).
51. Kessler (2012).
52. Coffey (2013 August).
53. The Open Group (2013).

54. Cardoso, Barros, May, and Kylau (2010).
55. Cardoso, Barros, May, and Kylau (2010).
56. Moore (1993 May–June).
57. Bosch (2009).
58. Frutiger, Slaughter, and Narasimhan (2014).
59. Frutiger, Slaughter, and Narasimhan (2014).
60. SAP (2013).
61. Salesforce.com (2013b).
62. Coffey (2013).
63. Kessler (2012).
64. Kessler (2012).
65. Operating margin equals Operating Income divided by Net Sales. Operating margin is the proportion of revenues remaining after paying the costs of running the business.
66. Berthiaume (2013).
67. DassaultSystemes (2013).
68. Salesforce.com (2013a, b, c).
69. Cusumano (2008 January).
70. Cusumano (2008 January).

# References

*Addamax Corporation v. Open Software Foundation.* 1995. 888 F. Supp. 274 (D. Mass).

Aggarwal, A.;O. Berry; M. Kenney; S. Lenway; and V. Taylor. 2006. "Corporate Strategies for Software Globalization." In *Globalization and Offshoring of Software: A Report of the ACM Job Migration Task Force*, eds. W. Aspray; F. Mayadas; and M.Y. Vardi. Association for Computing Machinery. http://www.acm.org/globalizationreport/ (accessed August 23, 2013).

Agilent Technologies. n.d. *Agilent Company History*, http://www.agilent.com/about/companyinfo/history/index.html?cmpid=4491 (accessed August 4, 2013).

Ahuja, M.K. March 2002. "Women in the Information Technology Profession: A Literature Review, Synthesis and Research Agenda." *European Journal of Information Systems* 11, no. 1, pp. 20–34.

Alfred, R. November 4, 2008. "November 4, 1952: Univac Gets Election Right, But CBS Balks." *WiredMagazine*, http://www.wired.com/science/discoveries/news/2008/11/dayintech_1104 (accessed December 27, 2013).

Allison, J.R.; M.A. Lemley; and J. Walker. 2010. "Patent Quality and Settlement Among Repeat Patent Litigants." *Georgetown Law Journal* 99, no. 3, p. 677.

Amdocs. n.d. *Amdocs Home Page*, www.amdocs.com (accessed September 12, 2013).

Anderson C. 2009. *Free: The Future of a Radical Price*, New York: Hyperion.

Ang, S.; S. Slaughter; and K.Y. Ng. November 2002. "Human Capital and Institutional Determinants of Information Technology Compensation: Modeling Multilevel and Cross-Level Interactions." *Management Science* 48, no. 11, pp. 1427–1445.

Arena, M.; O. Younossi; K. Brancato; I. Blickstein; and C. Grammich. 2008. "Why Has the Cost of Fixed-Wing Aircraft Risen? A Macroscopic Examination of Trends in U.S. Military Aircraft Costs Over the Past Several Decades." *RAND Corporation*, Monograph MG-696, http://www.rand.org/pubs/monographs/MG696.html (accessed October 26, 2013).

Artezio. 2013. *Artezio: Company*, http://www.artezio.com/company (accessed September 21, 2013).

Ashcraft, C.; and S. Blithe. 2010. "Women in IT: The Facts." *National Centre for Women & Information Technology Report*, http://www.ncwit.org/sites/default/files/legacy/pdf/NCWIT_TheFacts_rev2010.pdf, (accessed November 5, 2013).

AT&T. n.d. *History*, http://www.corp.att.com/history/milestones.html (accessed January 1, 2014).

Athreye, S. 2005. "The Indian Software Industry." In *From Underdogs to Tigers: The Rise and Growth of the Software Industry in Brazil, China, India, Ireland, and Israel*, eds. A. Arora; and A. Gambardella. Oxford, UK: Oxford University Press.

Atlassian. n.d.(a). *About Us*, www.atlassian.com/company/about (accessed December 30, 2013).

Atlassian. n.d.(b). *Atlassian Home Page*, www.atlassian.com (accessed December 30, 2013).

Atlassian. n.d.(c). *ShipIt Days At Atlassian*, https://www.atlassian.com/company/about/shipit (accessed December 30, 2013).

Auriga. 2013. *Auriga: About Us*, http://www.auriga.com/about/ (accessed September 21, 2013).

Australian Bureau of Statistics. 2006–2007. Cat. No. 8515.0, *Digital Game Development Services*, Australia.

Balatchandirane, G.; M. Blasgen; A. Bode; C.H. House; M. Kenney; V. Mansingh; G Marklund; B. Shah; and T. Umezawa. 2006. "The Country Perspective." In *Globalization and Offshoring of Software: A Report of the ACM Job Migration Task Force*, eds. W. Aspray; F. Mayadas; and M.Y. Vardi. Association for Computing Machinery, http://www.acm.org/globalizationreport/ (accessed August 23, 2013).

Ballardini, R.M. 2009. "The Software Patent Thicket: A Matter of Disclosure." *SCRIPTed* 6, no. 2, pp. 207–233, http://www.law.ed.ac.uk/ahrc/script-ed/vol6-2/ballardini.asp (accessed October 5, 2013).

Banker, R.D.; and S.A. Slaughter. December 1997. "A Field Study of Scale Economies in Software Maintenance." *Management Science* 43, no. 12, pp. 1709–1725.

Banker, R.D.; G.B. Davis; and S.A. Slaughter. April 1998. "Software Development Practices, Software Complexity, and Software Maintenance Performance: A Field Study." *Management Science* 44, no. 4, pp. 433–450.

Bansal, A.; N. Kaka; M. Kejriwal; and S. Sharma. 2001. *Offshoring Software Product Development to India*, McKinsey & Co., http://www.palnar.com/resource/off_sw_mck_study.pdf (accessed August 23, 2013).

Barboza, D. December 31, 2008. "Chinese Court Convicts 11 in Microsoft Piracy Case." *The New York Times*, http://www.nytimes.com/2009/01/01/business/worldbusiness/01soft.html (accessed October 6, 2013).

Bardhan, A.; and C. Kroll. March 2006. "Competitiveness and an Emerging Sector: The Russian Software Industry and Its Global Linkages." *Industry and Innovation* 13, no. 1, pp. 69–95.

Baum, C. 1981. *The System Builders: The Story of SDC*. Santa Monica, CA: System Development Corporation.

BBC News. September 26, 2010. "Stuxnet Worm Hits Iran Nuclear Plant Staff Computers." *BBC News Middle East*, http://www.bbc.co.uk/news/world-middle-east-11414483 (accessed October 12, 2013).

Beck, K. 1999. *Extreme Programming Explained: Embrace Change*. Boston, MA: Addison-Wesley.

Bednarz, A. January 10, 2011. "IBM Snares 5,896 Patents, Apple Debuts Among Top 50 Patent Winners." *Network World*, http://www.networkworld.com/news/2011/011011-patent-winners-ibm-apple.html (accessed August 4, 2013).

Bellis, M. 2013. "Fortran: The First Successful High Level Programming Language." *About.com Inventors*, http://inventors.about.com/od/computers oftware/a/Fortran.htm (accessed December 27, 2013).

Bernard, F. 2013. *The Dassault Systemes Success Story*, ed. D. Menezes, www.deelip.com (accessed August 29, 2013).

Berthiaume, D. 2013. "Capgemini Year-End Results Show Encouraging Signs for BPO." *BPO Outcomes, Next Coast Media and Marketing Services*, http://bpooutcomes.com/capgemini-2012-results/ (accessed August 28, 2013).

Bessen, J. September 3, 2013. "The Patent Troll Crisis Is Really a Software Patent Crisis." *The Washington Post*, http://www.washingtonpost.com/blogs/the-switch/wp/2013/09/03/the-patent-troll-crisis-is-really-a-software-patent-crisis/ (accessed September 6, 2013).

Bessen, J.; and R. Hunt. Spring 2007. "An Empirical Look at Software Patents." *Journal of Economics and Management Strategy* 16, no. 1, pp. 157–189.

Beyer, K.W. 2009. *Grace Hopper and the Invention of the Information Age*. Cambridge, MA: MIT Press.

Bilski V. Kappos. 2010. No. 08-964. U.S. Supreme Court, June 28, 2010.

Bodoni, S. January 24, 2013. "Sony Fined $394,500 Over Hacker Attack on Playstation Data." *Bloomberg News*, http://www.bloomberg.com/news/2013-01-24/sony-fined-394-000-over-2011-hacker-attack-on-playstation-data.html (accessed October 12, 2013).

Boehm, B. 1981. *Software Engineering Economics*. Englewood Cliffs, NJ: Prentice-Hall.

Boehm, B.W. May 1988. "A Spiral Model of Software Development and Enhancement." *IEEE Computer* 21, no. 5, pp. 61–72.

Bosch, J. 2009. "From Software Product Lines to Software Ecosystems." In *Proceedings of the 13th International Software Product Line Conference*, 111–119. Pittsburgh, PA: Carnegie Mellon University.

Botelho, A.J.J.; G. Stefanuto; and F. Veloso. 2005. "The Brazilian Software Industry." In *From Underdogs to Tigers: The Rise and Growth of the Software Industry in Brazil, China, India, Ireland and Israel*, eds. A. Arora; and A. Gambardella. Oxford, UK: Oxford University Press.

Bourn, J. 2006. *BBC Outsourcing: The Contract Between the BBC and Siemens Business Services for the Provision of Technology Services.* London, UK: National Audit Office.

Brazilian Association of Software Companies. 2013. *ABES,* http://www.abessoftware.com.br/ (accessed September 22, 2013).

Breznitz, D. 2005. "The Israeli Software Industry." In *From Underdogs to Tigers: The Rise and Growth of the Software Industry in Brazil, China, India, Ireland and Israel,* eds. A. Arora; and A. Gambardella. Oxford, UK: Oxford University Press.

Breznitz, D. 2007. *Innovation and the State: Political Choice and Strategies for Growth in Israel, Taiwan, and Ireland* (Revised ed.). New Haven, CT: Yale University Press.

Bricklin, D. 2009. *VisiCalc Executable for the IBM PC,* www.bricklin.comhttp://www.danbricklin.com/history/vcexecutable.htm (accessed October 26, 2013).

Brooks, F. 1995. *The Mythical Man Month: Essays on Software Engineering.* Boston, MA: Addison-Wesley.

Brown, A.W.; D.J. Carney; E.J. Morris; D.B. Smith; and P.F. Zarrella. 1994. *Principles of CASE Tool Integration.* Oxford, UK: Oxford University Press.

Bruce, B. January 21, 2011. *Teen's 'Bubble Ball' Game is Top Free iPhone App,* http://www.ksl.com/?nid=148&sid=14034658&autostart=y (accessed August 20, 2013).

Brynjolfsson, E.; and C. Kemerer. December 1996. "Network Externalities in Microcomputer Software: An Econometric Analysis of the Spreadsheet Market." *Management Science* 42, no. 12, pp. 1627–1647.

Bujarski, L.M. 2012. "The 2012 Investor's Guide to Mexico's Business and Technology Services." *Nearshore Americas,* http://nearshoreamericas.com/wp-content/uploads/2012/05/Mexico-investment-guide-business-technology-services-2012.pdf (accessed December 30, 2013).

Business Software Alliance. 2009. *Software Facts and Figures,* www.bsa.org (accessed July 17, 2013).

Business Software Alliance. 2011. Global Software Piracy." *9th Annual BSA Global Software Piracy Study,* http://globalstudy.bsa.org/2011/ (accessed October 6, 2013).

Campbell-Kelly, M. 1995. "Development and Structure of the International Software Industry, 1950–1990." *Business and Economic History, Business History Conference* 24, no. 2, pp. 73–110.

Capgemini. 2013. *Capgemini Company History,* http://www.capgemini.com/about/group/history, (August 28, 2013).

Cardoso, J.; A. Barros; N. May; and U. Kylau. 2010. "Towards a Unified Service Description Language for the Internet of Services: Requirements and First

Developments." In *2010 IEEE International Conference on Services Computing*, 602–609. Washington, DC: IEEE Computer Society.

Castle, S.; and D. Jolly. February 28, 2008. "Europe Fines Microsoft $1.3 Billion." *The New York Times*, http://www.nytimes.com/2008/02/28/ business/worldbusiness/28msoft.html?_r=0 (accessed October 26, 2013).

Celtech. 2013. *Celtech Company History*, http://www.celtech.ie/company/history (accessed September 9, 2013).

CERT® Coordination Center (CERT-CC). 2013. *CERT-CC*, Software Engineering Institute, Carnegie Mellon University, http://www.cert.org (accessed October 16, 2013).

CERT® Coordination Center (CERT-CC). n.d. *List of CERTs Around the World*, http://www.cert.org/csirts/cert_authorized.html (accessed December 1, 2013).

Chan, V.; and A. Pei. January 2013. "China Management Software." *Credit Suisse Securities Research & Analytics: Sector Forecast*, 10.

CheckPoint. n.d. *Checkpoint,* www.checkpoint.com (accessed September 12, 2013).

Chinese Software Industry Association. 2008. *China Software Industry Annual Report 2008*, http://www.csia.org.cn/chinese_en/index/csiaintro.html (accessed 14 September, 2013).

Closa, D.; A. Gardiner; F. Giemsa; and J. Machek. 2010. *Patent Law for Computer Scientists: Steps to Protect Computer-Implemented Inventions.* Berlin, NY: Springer.

Codd, E.F. June 1970. "A Relational Model of Data for Large Shared Data Banks." *Communications of the ACM,* 13, no. 6, pp. 377–387.

Coffey, B. August 2013. Industry Surveys, Computers: Software, *Standard & Poor's Capital IQ Industry Surveys*, New York: McGraw-Hill Financial.

Cole, R.; and Shinya, F. 2010. "An Evolutionary and Comparative Perspective on the Japanese Enterprise Software Industry." In *Have Japanese Firms Changed: The Lost Decade,* eds. Y. Nakata. Hampshire, UK: Palgrave MacMillan's Asian Business Series.

Computer History Museum. 2008. *The Babbage Engine*, http://www. computerhistory.org/babbage/henrybabbage/ (accessed July 14, 2013).

Computer Software Copyright Act of 1980. 1980 Pub. L. No. 96-517, 94 Stat. 3015, 3028.

Conduit. n.d.(a). *Conduit Home Page,* www.conduit.ie (accessed September 12, 2013).

Conduit. n.d.(b). *Conduit About Us,* http://www.conduit.ie/conduit_about_us_ our_history.aspx (accessed September 12, 2013).

Consinco. 2013. *Consinco: History*, http://www.consinco.com.br/ (accessed September 22, 2013).

Cooley LLP. December 5, 2011. "Government Prevails in Antitrust Challenge to Software Merger." *Cooley LLP*, http://www.cooley.com/showalert.aspx?Show=65839 (accessed September 30, 2013).

Copeland B.J. 2005. *Alan Turing's Automatic Computing Engine*. Oxford, UK: Oxford University Press.

Copeland, B.J. 2006. *Colossus: The Secrets of Bletchley Park's Code-Breaking Computers*. Oxford, UK: Oxford University Press.

Copyright Act of 1976. 1976. Pub. L. 94-553 (Oct. 19, 1976).

Cordeiro, B. October 13, 2010. "H&R Block to Buy TaxACT Maker 2SS Holdings for $288 Million." *Reuters*, http://www.reuters.com/article/2010/10/13/us-hrblock-idUSTRE69C68U20101013 (accessed September 30, 2013).

Corr, O.C. 1992. "IBM vs. Microsoft—Software Superbowl—IBM to Kick Off New Version of OS/2, but Will Microsoft Make Winning Goal?" *The Seattle Times*, http://community.seattletimes.nwsource.com/archive/?date=19920329&slug=1483527 (accessed August 23, 2013).

Coventry, J. 2006. "Interview with Dan Bricklin: Inventor of the Electronic Spreadsheet." *Low End Mac*, http://lowendmac.com/coventry/06/dan-bricklin-visicalc.html (accessed July 16, 2013).

Cox, B.J. November 1990. "Planning the Software Industrial Revolution." *IEEE Software* 7, no. 6, pp. 25–33.

CR2. 2013. "Who We Are." *CR2*, http://www.cr2.com/company/who-we-are.html (accessed September 9, 2013).

Crossley, R. 2010. "Study: Average Dev Costs as High as $28m." *Develop Online*, http://www.develop-online.net/news/33625/Study-Average-dev-cost-as-high-as-28m#after_ad (accessed August 5, 2013).

Cuniberti, G. August 16, 2010. "Panamanian Conflict Rules Trump Forum Non Conveniens." *Conflict of Laws*, http://conflictoflaws.net/2010/panamanian-conflict-rules-trump-forum-non-conveniens/(accessed October 16, 2013).

Cusumano, M.A. 1991a. *Japan's Software Factories: A Challenge to US Management*. New York, NY: Oxford University Press, Inc.

Cusumano, M.A. 2004. *The Business of Software: What every Manager, Programmer and Entrepreneur Must Know to Thrive in Good Times and Bad*. New York, NY: Free Press.

Cusumano, M.A. January 2008. "The Changing Software Business: Moving from Products to Services." *IEEE Computer* 41, no. 1, pp. 20–27.

Cusumano, M.A. January–March 1991b. "Factory Concepts and Practices in Software Development." *Annals of the History of Computing, IEEE* 13, no. 1, pp. 3–32.

Cusumano, M.A.; and C.F. Kemerer. November 1990. "A Quantitative Analysis of US and Japanese Practice and Performance in Software Development." *Management Science* 36, no. 11, pp. 1384–1406.

Daily Free Code. n.d. *Code for Program for Generating Date and Time in Cobol,* http://www.dailyfreecode.com/code/generating-date-time-1835.aspx (accessed December 24, 2013).

Dassault Systemes. 2013. *3DS at a Glance,* http://www.3ds.com/about-3ds/ (accessed August 29, 2013).

Datamonitor. August 30, 2011. "Software in South Africa: Industry and Country Analysis." *Datamonitor,* Report No. 1FD6D8B4-830D-49BC-83C1-C670EF9343F5.

Davidoff, S.M. March 26, 2013. "In a Faded Wall Street Scandal, Lessons for a Current One." *New York Times,* http://dealbook.nytimes.com/2013/03/26/in-a-faded-wall-st-scandal-lessons-for-a-current-one/?_r=0 (accessed September 12, 2013).

Decker, S.; and B. Wingfield. October 8, 2013. "Samsung Loses Bid for Obama Veto of Apple-Won Import Ban." *Bloomberg News,* http://www.bloomberg.com/news/2013-10-08/samsung-loses-bid-for-presidential-veto-of-apple-won-import-ban.html (accessed October 9, 2013).

Dennis, A.; B. Wixom; and D. Tegarden. 2009. *Systems Analysis and Design with UML Version 2.0,* 3rd ed. Hoboken, NJ: Wiley.

Department of Trade and Industry—South Africa. 2013. *The South African Software Development Industry,* http://www.suedafrika-wirtschaft.org/index.php?&pageID=45 (accessed December 29, 2013).

DevExperts. 2013. *DevExperts: About Us,* http://www.devexperts.com/en/company/a/about.html (accessed September 21, 2013).

Diamond v. Diehr. 1981. *Diamond v. Diehr,* 450 U.S. 175—Supreme Court.

Digital Millennium Copyright Act of 1998. October 28, 1998. Pub. L. No. 105-304, 112 Stat. 2860.

Dimension Data. n.d. *About Us,* http://www.dimensiondata.com/en-US/AboutUs#.UsDTz7Sovls, (accessed December 29, 2013).

Dow Jones News Service. April 25, 1995. Security Company's Stock Rises. *Newsday,* A33.

Drew, E.P. 1994. *Information Technology in Selected Countries: Reports from Ireland, Ethiopia, Nigeria, and Tanzania.* Tokyo, Japan: United Nations University.

Earl, R. July 27, 2013. "What Ever Happened to Australia's Software Industry?" *Sydney Morning Herald: IT Pro,* http://www.smh.com.au/it-pro/it-opinion/whatever-happened-to-australias-software-industry-20130727-hv0na.html (accessed December 29, 2013).

Edgar SEC Filings. 2013. *Shanda Games Ltd.,* http://www.nasdaq.com/symbol/game (accessed September 15, 2013).

EPAM. 2013. *EPAM: Company,* http://www.epam.com/company.html (accessed September 21, 2013).

EquityMaster Agora Research. 2013. *Indian Software Company Results for June 2013 Quarter*, http://www.equitymaster.com/research-it/sector-info/software/Software-Sector-Analysis-Report.asp (accessed September 23, 2013).

Etro, F. 2008. "Market Leaders, Antitrust Policy and the Software Market." *The ICFAI Journal of Industrial Economics* 5, no. 1, pp. 1–24.

European Union Directives. 2009. *Directive 2009/24/EC of 23 April 2009 on the Legal Protection of Computer Programs*. The European Parliament and the Council of the European Union.

Fayad, M.E.; M. Laitimen; and R.P. Ward. March 2000. "Software Engineering in the Small." *Communications of the ACM* 43, no. 3, pp. 115–118.

Federal Circuit Court. 1998. 149 F. 3d 1368 (Fed.Cir. 1998).

Ferzinger, J. August 31, 2006. "Kobi Alexander, Once Wooed by World Leaders, Now Chased by FBI." *Bloomberg News*.

Finkle, J. October 3, 2013. *Adobe: Customer Data, Source Code Accessed in Cyber-Attack, Reuters News Service*, http://news.yahoo.com/adobe-says-customer-data-source-code-accessed-cyber-213737576--sector.html (accessed October 11, 2013).

Finn, D. 2011. "Software Piracy: The Risks Are Greater Than Ever." *Microsoft on the Issues: Microsoft Corporation*, http://blogs.technet.com/b/microsoft_on_the_issues/archive/2011/02/03/software-piracy-the-risks-are-greater-than-ever.aspx (accessed October 6, 2013).

Flannery, N.P. March 7, 2012. "Mexico's Silicon Valley." *Americas Quarterly*, http://www.americasquarterly.org/mexicos-silicon-valley (accessed December 30, 2013).

Frankel, D.S. 2003. *Model Driven Architecture: Applying MDA to Enterprise Computing*. Indianapolis, IN: John Wiley & Sons.

Free Software Foundation. 2007. *GNU General Public License*, http://www.gnu.org/copyleft/gpl.html (accessed October 1, 2013).

Freetutes.com (2011). Visual Basic Tutorials, Advanced VB6 Tutorial, Chapter 17, http://visualbasic.freetutes.com/learn-vb6-advanced/lesson17/p6.html Retrieved March 16, 2014.

Frutiger, M.; S. Slaughter; and S. Narasimhan. 2014. "A Business Ecosystem Perspective on Open Platforms and Outsourcing Relationships: A Software Industry Case Study," Working Paper, Georgia Institute of Technology.

Fujitsu. n.d. *About Us*, http://www.fujitsu.com/global/about/profile/info/ (August 23, 2013).

Gage, D.; and J. McCormack. 2004. *We Did Nothing Wrong: Why Software Quality Matters, Panama's National Cancer Institute: Case 109—A Dissection*, http://www.iaea.org/newscenter/features/radiotherapy/dissection109.pdf (accessed October 16, 2013).

Gale Group. 2013a. *Business Insights: Global Software Publishers*. Stanford, CT: Cengage Learning.

Gale Group. 2013b. *Highbeam Industry Reports: Computer Programming Services*, http://business.highbeam.com/industry-reports/business/computer-programming-services (accessed July 26, 2013).

Gellman, B.; and A. Soltani. October 30, 2013. "NSA Infiltrates Links to Yahoo, Google Data Centers Worldwide, Snowden Documents Say." *The Washington Post*, http://www.washingtonpost.com/world/national-security/nsa-infiltrates-links-to-yahoo-google-data-centers-worldwide-snowden-documents-say/2013/10/30/e51d661e-4166-11e3-8b74-d89d714ca4dd_story.html (accessed January 1, 2014).

Goldstine, H.; and A. Goldstine. 1946. "The Electronic Numerical Integrator and Computer (ENIAC)." *American Mathematical Society* 2, no. 15, pp. 97–110 (reprinted in 1982. *The Origins of Digital Computers: Selected Papers*, 359–373. New York, NY: Springer-Verlag).

Gopal, A.; and G.G. Gao. Summer 2009. "Certification in the Indian Offshore IT Services Industry." *Manufacturing & Service Operations Management* 11, no. 3, pp. 471–492.

Greene, J. April 8, 2011. "Google-ITA Merger Approved, with Conditions." *Blog of Legal Times—An ALM Publication*, http://legaltimes.typepad.com/blt/2011/04/google-ita-merger-approved-with-conditions.html (accessed September 30, 2013).

Gross, J. 2013. "A Case Study on Hershey's ERP Implementation Failure: The Importance of Testing and Scheduling." *Pemeco Consulting*, http://www.pemeco.com/wp-content/uploads/2013/09/Hershey_ERP_Case_Study.pdf (accessed December 27, 2013).

Grove, A.S. 1996. *Only the Paranoid Survive: How to Exploit the Crisis Points That Challenge Every Company*. New York: Doubleday.

Gruber, G. May 25, 2010. "The Fallacy of Software Factories and the Importance of Talent, Outsourcing: Travel Technology." *Software Industry Insights*, http://www.softwareindustryinsights.com/2010/05/the-fallacy-of-software-factories-and-the-importance-of-talent/ (accessed November 2, 2013).

Halacy, D.S. 1970. *Charles Babbage, Father of the Computer*. New York, NY: MacMillan.

Hamilton, T.W. 1969. *IBM's Unbundling Decision: Consequences for Users and the Industry*, New York: Programming Sciences Corporation.

Happy Codings. 2013a. *Program Code in Assembly and Java*, www.happycodings.com (accessed July 11, 2013).

Happy Codings. 2013b. *Assembly Code Example: Clock*, http://assembly.happycodings.com/code24.html (accessed October 26, 2013).

Happy Codings. 2013c. *C++ Algorithms Code Example: Realtime Clock*, http://cplusplus.happycodings.com/Algorithms/code20.html (accessed October 26, 2013).

Hart, D. Winter 1998. "Antitrust and Technological Innovation." *Issues in Science and Technology* 15, no. 2, pp. 75–82.

Health Insurance Portability and Accountability Act (HIPAA). 1996. "Public Law 104-191. 104th Congress." http://www.cms.gov/Regulations-and-Guidance/HIPAA-Administrative-Simplification/HIPAAGenInfo/Downloads/HIPAALaw.pdf (accessed October 16, 2013).

Hemphill, T.; and N. Vonortas. Summer 2005. "U.S. Antitrust Policy, Interface Compatibility Standards, and Information Technology." *Knowledge, Technology & Policy* 18, no. 2, pp. 126–147.

Hitachi. n.d. *About Us*, http://hitachi.com/about/corporate/history/ (accessed August 23, 2013).

Hoyle, M.A. 2006. *The History of Computer Science; Computers: From the Past to the Present, John von Neumann*, http://lecture.eingang.org/neumann.html (accessed December 26, 2013).

HP (Hewlett Packard). n.d.(a). *HP History*, http://www8.hp.com/us/en/hp-information/about-hp/history/history.html (accessed August 4, 2013).

HP (Hewlett Packard). n.d.(b). *Early Instruments*, http://www.hp.com/hpinfo/abouthp/histnfacts/museum/personalsystems/0021/ (accessed August 4, 2013).

HP (Hewlett Packard). n.d.(c). *Personal Systems*, http://www.hp.com/hpinfo/abouthp/histnfacts/museum/personalsystems/0021/ (accessed August 4, 2013).

HP (Hewlett Packard). n.d.(d). *HP Fast Facts*, http://www8.hp.com/us/en/hp-information/facts.html (accessed August 4, 2013).

Hurwitz, J. 2007. "How Does SAP Turn 250 Million Lines of Code into Modular Services?" *Judith's Balancing Act, Hurwitz,& Associates*, http://hurwitz.com/blogs/judith-balancing-act/entry/how-does-sap-turn-250-million-lines-of-code-into-modular-services (accessed October 26, 2013).

IBM. n.d. *IBM Research*, Research.ibm.com (accessed August 4, 2013).

Industrial Development Agency (IDA-Ireland). 2013. *Industrial Development Agency*, http://www.idaireland.us/ida-ireland/ (accessed September 9, 2013).

Information Technology Association of America. 2005. ITAA Diversity Study: Numbers of Women, Minorities in Tech Too Low. *Information Technology Association of America, Report*. http://www.internetnews.com/stats/article.php/3515001 (accessed June 23, 2013).

Infosys Press Release. 2013. *Infosys to Expand Its Operations with New Delivery Center in Wisconsin*, http://www.infosys.com/newsroom/press-releases/Documents/2012/delivery-center-wisconsin.pdf (accessed September 24, 2013).

Infosys. 2013. *Infosys: About Us*, http://www.infosys.com/about/Pages/history. aspx

International Data Corporation (IDC). August 2013. *Worldwide Endpoint Security 2013–2017: Forecast and 2012 Vendor Shares*, IDC #242618.

International Data Corporation (IDC). December 2004. *Worldwide Linux 2004-2008 Forecast: Moving from Niche to Mainstream*, IDC #32424.

International Directory of Company Histories. 1997. *SAP History* (Vol. 16). Farmington Hills, MI: St. James Press.

International Directory of Company Histories. 1999. Groupe Dassault Aviation SA History (Vol. 26). Farmington Hills, MI: St. James Press.

International Directory of Company Histories. 2002. *Amdocs Ltd. History* (Vol. 47). Farmington Hills, MI: St. James Press.

International Intellectual Property Alliance (IIPA). 2013. "Copyright & Trade Issues," *IIPA*, http://www.iipa.com/copyrighttrade_issues.html (accessed October 6, 2013).

Invest In Australia. 2013. *The ICT Industry in Australia, Essential Guide for International Investors*, http://www.investinaustralia.com/industry/ict/ict-industry-australia (accessed December 29, 2013).

Irish Exporters Association. 2013. *Top 250 Exporters: An Analysis of the Top 50 ISFC Companies and Top 50 Northern Ireland Exporters*, Irish Exporters Association.

Irish Software Association. n.d. *ISA,* www.software.ie (accessed September 12, 2013).

Israel Export and International Cooperation Institute. 2010. *Israel, Inspired by Innovation, Software Industry*, The Israel Export and International Cooperation Institute.

Jacobini, S.; and K. McCreary. July 1994. "Strategic Alliances in High Technology." *The Red Herring* 6, no. 2, p. 12.

Jaeger, M. 2012. "One-third of Europe's Software Industry is SAP." *The German View*, http://www.zdnet.com/one-third-of-europes-software-industry-is-sap-7000007106/ (accessed August 25, 2013).

Jones, A. May 31, 2012. "Angry Birds Code Used for Flame Cyber Weapon." *Infowars*, http://www.infowars.com/angry-birds-code-used-for-flame-cyber-weapon/ (accessed October 26, 2013).

Jones, C. 1996. *Applied Software Measurement: Assuring Productivity and Quality*, 2nd ed. Desoto, TX: McGraw-Hill.

Joseph, D.; S. Ang; and S. Slaughter. 2008. "Relative Wage Differences and the Career Transitions of IT Professionals, Organizational Communications and Information Systems Division (OCIS), Academy of Management." *Academy of Management Best Paper Proceedings*. Best Interactive Paper Award, Academy of Management.

Kahney, L. 2003. Grandiose Price for a Modest PC. *Wired Magazine*, http:// archive.wired.com/culture/lifestyle/news/2003/09/60349 (accessed July 16, 2013).

Kaplan, T. September 28, 2013. "John McAfee Reveals Details on Gadget to Thwart NSA." *San Jose Mercury News*, http://www.mercurynews.com/bay-area-news/ci_24198989/john-mcafee-reveals-details-gadget-thwart-nsa (accessed October 29, 2013).

Kaspersky. 2012. "2012 By the Numbers: Kaspersky Lab Now Detects 200,000 New Malicious Programs Every Day." *Kaspersky Lab*, http://www.kaspersky.com/about/news/virus/2012/2012_by_the_numbers_Kaspersky_Lab_now_detects_200000_new_malicious_programs_every_day (accessed July 19, 2013).

Kaspersky. 2013. "About Kaspersky Lab." *Kaspersky Lab*, http://www.kaspersky.com/about (accessed September 21, 2013).

Katz, M.L.; and C. Shapiro. 1999. "Antitrust in Software Markets." In *Competition, Innovation and the Microsoft Monopoly: Antitrust in the Digital Marketplace*, eds. J. Eisenach; and T. Lenard. Norwell, MA: Kluwer Academic Publishers.

Kay, R. January 19, 2004. "QuickStudy: Phishing." *Computerworld*, http://www.computerworld.com/s/article/89096/Phishing (accessed October 14, 2013).

Keller, K.; and B. Mack. March 2013. "Maturity Profile Reports." *CMMI Institute*, http://cmmiinstitute.com/resource/process-maturity-profiles/ (accessed September 14, 2013).

Kerr, D. July 9, 2013. "Microsoft Settles Thousands of Software Piracy Cases." *CNET*, http://news.cnet.com/news/microsoft-settles-thousands-of-software-piracy-cases/ (accessed October 6, 2013).

Kerr, D. May 24, 2012. "Google Tackles Piracy by Removing Millions of URLs." *CNET*, http://news.cnet.com/8301-1023_3-57441333-93/google-tackles-piracy-by-removing-millions-of-urls/ (accessed October 6, 2013).

Kerr, W.R.; and W.F. Lincoln. February 2010. "The Supply Side of Innovation: H-1B Visa Reforms and US Ethnic Invention." *Journal of Labor Economics* 28, no. 3, pp. 473–508.

Kerravala, Z. 2009. "Strategic Alliances: The Value of Partners." *Cisco Corporation*, www.cisco.com/c/dam/en/us/products/collateral/unified-communications/unified-communications-manager-callmanager/c22-558396-00_value_partners_so.pdf (accessed August 21, 2013).

Kessler, S. April 19, 2012. "Industry Surveys, Computers: Software." *Standard & Poor's Capital IQ Industry Surveys*.

Kitten, T. December 20, 2013. "Target Breach: What Happened?" *Bank Info Security*, http://www.bankinfosecurity.com/target-breach-what-happened-a-6312 /op-1 (accessed January 1, 2014).

Kostier, J. August 14, 2013. "This 12-Year-Old Kid Learned to Code on Code Academy, Built 5 Apps, and is Speaking at SXSW." *VentureBeat*, http://venturebeat.com/2013/08/14/this-12-year-old-kid-learned-to-code-on-codecademy-built-5-apps-and-is-speaking-at-sxsw/ (accessed December 24, 2013).

Landon, V. 2002. "Indian Software Keeps Swiss Securities Safe." *Swissinfo. International Service of the Swiss Broadcasting Corporation,* http://www.swissinfo.ch/eng/archive/Indian_software_keeps_Swiss_securities_safe.html?cid=2440972 (accessed September 23, 2013).

Lasar, M. July 19, 2011. "The UNIX Revolution—Thank You, Uncle Sam?" *ArsTechnica*, http://arstechnica.com/tech-policy/2011/07/should-we-thank-for-feds-for-the-success-of-unix/ (accessed January 1, 2014).

Lee, T. August 29, 2013. "New Zealand Just Abolished Software Patents: Here's Why We Should Too." *The Washington Post*, http://www.washingtonpost.com/blogs/the-switch/wp/2013/08/29/new-zealand-just-abolished-software-patents-heres-why-we-should-too/ (accessed October 10, 2013).

Leimbach, T. October–December 2008. "The SAP Story: Evolution of SAP within the German Software Industry." *Annals of the History of Computing, IEEE* 30, no. 4, pp. 60–76.

Lenovo. July 4, 2011. *NEC Lenovo Finalize Joint Venture and Launch Japan's #1 PC Company,* http://news.lenovo.com/article_display.cfm?article_id=1464 (accessed August 23, 2013).

Leonard, A. 2001. "Life, Liberty and the Pursuit of Free Software." *Salon Media Group,* http://www.salon.com/2001/02/15/unamerican/ (accessed July 19, 2013).

Letwin, W. 1956. "Congress and the Sherman Antitrust Law: 1887–1890." *University of Chicago Law Review*, 23, pp. 221–258.

Levina, N.; and M. Xin. June 2007. "Comparing IT Workers' Compensation Across Country Contexts: Demographic, Human Capital and Institutional Factors." *Information Systems Research* 18, no. 2, pp. 193–210.

Levy, L.; and S. Bell. 1990. "Software Product Liability: Understanding and Minimizing the Risks." *Berkeley Technology Law Journal* 5, 112.

Li, S.; J. Shang; and S. Slaughter. September 2010. "Why Do Software Firms Fail? Capabilities, Competitive Actions, and Firm Survival in the Software Industry from 1995 to 2007." *Information Systems Research* 21, no. 3, pp. 631–654.

Liebowitz, S.; S. Margolis; and J. Hirshleifer. 2001. *Winners, Losers & Microsoft: Competition and Antitrust in High Technology.* Oakland, CA: The Independent Institute.

Liu, C.; C. Kemerer; S. Slaughter; and M. Smith. September 2012. "Information Technology Standards Competition in the Presence of Conversion

Technology: An Empirical Analysis of the Flash Memory Card Market." *MIS Quarterly* 36, no. 3, pp. 921–942.

Lockard, C.B.; and M. Wolf. January 2012. "Occupational Employment Projections to 2020." *Monthly Labor Review* 135, no. 1, pp. 84–108.

Lodsys. 2013. *About Lodsys*, www.lodsys.com (accessed October 5, 2013).

Lohr, S.; and J. Brinkley. May 18, 1998. "Antitrust Talks Founder on Microsoft's 'Desktop'." *The New York Times*, http://www.nytimes. com/1998/05/18/business/antitrust-talks-founder-on-microsoft-s-desktop. html?pagewanted=all&src=pm (accessed October 26, 2013).

Lomanto, G. October 17, 2011. "So What Is Product Marketing Anyways." *WordPress*, http://whatisproductmarketing.com/so-what-is-product-market ing-anyways/ (accessed November 2, 2013).

*Lotus Development Corporation vs. Borland International, Inc.* 2003. *The Oyez Project at IIT, Chicago-Kent College of Law,* http://www.oyez.org/ cases/1990-1999/1995/1995_94_2003 (accessed October 1, 2013).

Lunden, I. 2013. "Forrester: $2.1 Trillion Will Go into IT Spend in 2013— Apps and The U.S. Lead the Charge." *Forrester*, http://techcrunch. com/2013/07/15/forrester-2-1-trillion-will-go-into-it-spend-in-2013-apps- and-the-u-s-lead-the-charge/ (accessed July 15, 2013).

Mackey, R. December 6, 2010. "Updates on Leak of U.S. Cables, Day 9." The Lede Blogs, *The New York Times*, http://thelede.blogs.nytimes.com/2010/12/06/ latest-updates-on-leak-of-u-s-cables-day-9/?_r=0#operation-payback-plans- attacks-on-paypal (accessed October 14, 2013).

McAfee. 2013b. "McAfee: About Us." *McAfee*, http://www.mcafee.com/us/ about-us.aspx (accessed October 29, 2013).

McAfee. February 28, 2013a. "Intel Completes Acquisition of McAfee." *McAfee News*, http://www.mcafee.com/us/about/news/2011/q1/20110228-01.aspx (accessed October 29, 2013).

McGraw, G. 2006. *Software Security: Building Security In*. Boston, MA: Addison- Wesley.

Mell, T.; and P. Grance. September 2011. "The NIST Definition of Cloud Computing." *National Institute of Standards and Technology, (NIST)*, Special Publication 800-145. U.S. Department of Commerce.

Mexico. n.d. *Home Page,* www.mexico-it.net (accessed December 30, 2013).

Microsoft. 2000. "Microsoft Completes Acquisition of Visio." *Microsoft*, http:// www.microsoft.com/en-us/news/press/2000/Jan00/DealPR.aspx (accessed July 18, 2013).

Microsoft. 2008. "Developing the Future: Challenges and Opportunities Facing the UK Software Development Industry, Summary Findings and Recommendations." *Microsoft*, http://www.computerweekly.com/ blogs/editors-blog/Developing_The_Future_08_Summary.pdf (accessed September 7, 2013).

Microsoft. 2013. "Yonyou Software Co. Ltd., Case Study." *Microsoft*, http://www.microsoft.com/casestudies/Case_Study_Detail.aspx?casestudyid=710000000722 (accessed September 15, 2013).

Ministry of Economy, Trade and Industry (METI). October 31, 2012. "Preliminary Report on the Basic Survey on the Information and Communications Industry." Global ICT Strategy Bureau Ministry of Internal Affairs and Communications and Research and Statistics Department Minister's Secretariat of Ministry of Economy, Trade and Industry, Japan. http://www.meti.go.jp/english/press/2012/1031_03.html (accessed September 15, 2013).

Mithas, S.; and H.C. Lucas. May 2010. "Are Foreign IT Workers Cheaper? US Visa Policies and Compensation of Information Technology Professionals." *Management Science* 56, no. 5, pp. 745–765.

Mithas, S.; and M.S. Krishnan. March 2008. "Human Capital and Institutional Effects in the Compensation of Information Technology Professionals in the United States." *Management Science* 54, no. 3, pp. 415–428.

Moore, D.; and C. Shannon. 2001. "The Spread of the Code-Red Worm (CRv2)." *The Cooperative Association for Internet Data Analysis,* http://www.caida.org/research/security/code-red/coderedv2_analysis.xml (accessed October 14, 2013).

Moore, J.F. May–June 1993. "Predators and Prey: A New Ecology of Competition." *Harvard Business Review* 71, no. 3, pp. 75–86.

Moynihan, C. 2013. *The Irish Software Industry 1989-2008: An Overview of Its Development.* Master's Thesis, M.Sc. of Business Administration. Ronneby, Sweden: School of Management, Blekinge Institute of Technology.

Musio, I. 2009. "IBM Industry Practice: Challenges in Offshore Software Development from a Global Delivery Center." *Software Engineering Approaches for Offshore and Outsourced Development Lecture Notes in Business Information Processing* 35, pp. 4–13.

Mysore Samachar. 2013. *Infosys Builds World's Biggest Training Centre in Mysore*, http://www.mysoresamachar.com/info_trg_cent.htm (accessed September 24, 2013).

NASSCOM. 2013. Indian IT-BPO Industry, http://www.nasscom.in/indian-itbpo-industry (accessed September 23, 2013).

National Science Foundation. 2012. "Science and Engineering Indicators 2012." *National Science Board* 12-01, http://www.nsf.gov/statistics/seind12/c2/c2s3.htm (accessed November 3, 2013).

Naur, P.; and Randell, B., eds. 1969. *Software Engineering: Report of a Conference Sponsored by the NATO Science Committee*, Garmisch, Germany, October 7–11, 1968, Brussels, Scientific Affairs Division, NATO, p. 231.

Nazier, D. October 2, 2013. "Patent Troll Lodsys Settles for Nothing to Avoid Trial." *Electronic Frontier Foundation*, https://www.eff.org/deeplinks/2013/10/patent-troll-lodsys-settles-nothing-avoid-trial (accessed October 5, 2013).

NEC Corporation. 1984. "NEC Corporation: The First 80 Years." *The Corporation*, p. 103.

Netmarketshare. n.d. www.netmarketshare.com (accessed July 17, 2013).

Neusoft Corporation. 2013a. "Key Financial Data." *Neusoft*, http://www.neusoft.com/investor/1190/ (accessed September 15, 2013).

Neusoft Corporation. 2013b. "History." *Neusoft*, http://www.neusoft.com/about/1174/ (accessed September 15, 2013).

Newcomb, D. (2012). "The Next Big OS War Is in Your Dashboard," *Wired Magazine*, Retrieved on July 1, 2014 from http://www.wired.com/2012/12/automotive-os-war/all/ (accessed December 3, 2012).

Niculescu, M.F.; and Wu, D. J. 2014. "Economics of Free Under Perpetual Licensing: Implications for the Software Industry." *Information Systems Research* 25, no. 1, pp. 173-199.

Nortje, N. August 13, 2008. "South Africa Moves Towards Process Improvement." *Savant Press Release*, http://www.itweb.co.za/office/savant/PressRelease.php?StoryID=188229 (accessed December 29, 2013).

Occupational Information Network (O*NET). 2013. *U.S. Department of Labor/Employment and Training Administration (USDOL/ETA)*, http://www.onetonline.org/ (accessed November 5, 2013).

Ogden, J. 2013. "W163 [CC-BY-SA-3.0 (http://creativecommons.org/licenses/by-sa/3.0)]." *Wikimedia Commons*, http://commons.wikimedia.org/wiki/File%3AInternet_users_per_100_inhabitants_ITU.svg (accessed July 17, 2013).

Online Innovations. n.d. *Content Page of Online Innovation*, http://www.onlineinnovations.com/content.asp?pageid=123 (accessed December 29, 2013).

O'Reilly Media. 2013. "History of Programming Languages." *O'Reilly Media*, http://oreilly.com/news/graphics/prog_lang_poster.pdf (accessed July 11, 2013).

Organization for Economic Cooperation and Development (OECD). 1998. *The Software Sector: A Statistical Profile for Selected OECD Countries*, DSTI/ICCP/AH(97)4/REV1. Paris: OECD.

Organization for Economic Cooperation and Development (OECD). 2002. *OECD Information Technology Outlook 2002: ICTs and the Information Economy*. Paris: OECD.

Pacheco, F. October 2, 2012. "Brazil's Software Industry Diversifies: Expands to Far Corners of the Country" *Nearshore Americas*, http://www.nearshoreamericas.com/brazils-technology-innovation-software-expansion/ (accessed September 22, 2013).

Page, W.; and J. Lopatka. 2009. *The Microsoft Case: Antitrust, High Technology, and Consumer Welfare*, Reprint edition. Chicago, IL: The University of Chicago Press.

Paglieri, J. October 8, 2013. "Adobe Has an Epically Abysmal Security Record." *CNN Money*, http://money.cnn.com/2013/10/08/technology/security/ adobe-security/ (accessed October 13, 2013).

Park, E. 2007. "Unworthy of a Nation Built by Immigrants: The Political Mobilization of H-1B Workers." In *Movement of Global Talent: The Impact of High Skill Labor Flows from India and China*, ed. U. Tambar, 75–88. Princeton, NJ: Princeton University.

Paulk, M. 2009. "A History of the Capability Maturity Model for Software" *Software Quality & Productivity*, American Society for Quality 12, no. 1, pp. 5–19.

Pepitone, J. August 8, 2013. "Apple vs. Samsung Scorecard: A Timeline of the Patent Battle." *CNN Money*, http://money.cnn.com/2013/08/08/technology/ mobile/apple-samsung-timeline/index.html (accessed October 9, 2013).

Philipson, G. 2005. "A Short History of Software." In *Management, Labour Process and Software Development: Reality Bites*, ed. R. Barrett, 13–45. New York, NY: Routledge.

Porter, M.E. 1985. *Competitive Advantage*. New York, NY: Free Press.

Porter, M.E. March–April 1979. "How Competitive Forces Shape Strategy," *Harvard Business Review*, Reprint #79208.

Porter, M.E. November–December 1996. "What Is Strategy?" *Harvard Business Review*, Reprint #96608, pp. 61–78.

Posix 1003.1. 2011. "Frequently Asked Questions." *The Open Group*, http://www. opengroup.org/austin/papers/posix_faq.html (accessed August 5, 2013).

Power, J.D. August 30, 2004. "A Brief History of Spreadsheets." *DSSResources. COM*, World Wide Web, version 3.6, http://dssresources.com/history/ sshistory.html (accessed August 1, 2013).

PricewaterhouseCoopers. May 2013. *PWC Global 100 Software Leaders*, www. pwc.com/globalsoftware100 (accessed September 30, 2013).

Pro Mexico. n.d. "Mexico's Burgeoning IT Industry." *Prosoft*, http://negocios. promexico.gob.mx/english/04-2011/art01.html (accessed December 30, 2013).

Pugh, E.W.; L.R. Johnson; and J.H. Palmer. 1991. *IBM's 360 and Early 370 Systems*. Cambridge, MA: MIT Press.

Randell, B.; and J.N. Buxton. 1970. *Software Engineering Techniques: Report of a Conference Sponsored by the NATO Science Committee*, Rome, Italy, October 27–31, 1969, Brussels, Scientific Affairs Division, NATO, p. 164.

Raustiala, K.; and C.J. Sprigman. 2013. "How to Know a Patent Troll When You See One? You Can't." *Time Magazine: Business & Money Section*, http:// business.time.com/2013/07/08/how-to-know-a-patent-troll-when-you-see-one-you-cant/#ixzz2gsnu0Inj (accessed October 5, 2013).

Raymond, E. 2001. *The Cathedral & the Bazaar: Musings on Linux and Open Source by an Accidental Revolutionary*. Sebastopol, CA: O'Reilly Media, Inc.

Red Hat. 2013. "Red Hat Reports Fourth Quarter and Fiscal Year 2012 Results." *Red Hat*, http://www.redhat.com/about/news/press-archive/2012/3/red-hat-reports-fourth-quarter-and-fiscal-year-2012-results (accessed October 18, 2013).

Redtribe. n.d. *Home Page*, http://www.redtribe.com (accessed December 30, 2013).

Reference for Business. n.d. "Encyclopedia for Business, 2nd ed." *SIC 7372, Prepackaged Software*, http://www.referenceforbusiness.com/industries/Service/Prepackaged-Software.html (accessed July 16, 2013).

Rumelt, R.P. 2003. Visicorp 1978–1984 (Revised), UCLA, POL-2003-08.

Russoft Vendors Directory. 2012. *Devexperts: Company Profile*, http://www.russoft.org/directory/?profile=704 (accessed September 21, 2013).

Sage Group plc. 2013. "About Us." *Sage*, www.sage.com (accessed September 7, 2013).

Salesforce.com. 2013a. "Sales Cloud: Overview." *Salesforce.com*, http://www.salesforce.com/sales-cloud/overview/ (accessed October 18, 2013).

Salesforce.com. 2013b. "Partners: Partner with the Cloud Leader." *Salesforce.com*, http://www.salesforce.com/partners/overview/ (accessed October 19, 2013).

Salesforce.com. n.d. *Operating Margin*, http://www.wikinvest.com/stock/Salesforce.com_%28CRM%29/Data/Operating_Margin/2012 (accessed October 23, 2013).

Salus, P.H. 1994. *A Quarter Century of UNIX*. Boston, MA: Addison-Wesley.

Sands, A. 2005. "The Irish Software Industry." In *From Underdogs to Tigers: The Rise and Growth of the Software Industry in Brazil, China, India, Ireland and Israel*, eds. A. Arora; and A. Gambardella. Oxford, UK: Oxford University Press.

SAP. 2013. "The SAP Ecosystem in a Nutshell." *SAP*, http://www54.sap.com/partners/overview/find.html (accessed October 19, 2013).

Sarbanes-Oxley. 2002. An Act to Protect Investors by Improving the Accuracy and Reliability of Corporate Disclosures Made Pursuant to the Securities Laws, and for Other Purposes. Pub L107-204.116 Stat 745.*107th U.S. Congress*.

Sarno, D. September 7, 2010. "Hewlett-Packard Sues to Keep Former CEO from Going to Oracle." *Los Angeles Times*, http://articles.latimes.com/2010/sep/07/business/la-fi-hp-hurd-20100908 (accessed October 31, 2013).

Saxenian, A. Winter 2002. "Brain Circulation: How High-Skill Immigration Makes Everyone Better Off." *Brookings Review* 20, no. 1, pp. 28–31.

Schafer, P.; and B. Trautlein. 2007. "Women in Technology: 2007 Report." *Women in Technology International*, http://www.witi.com/center/webinar/WomenInTechnology07Report.pdf (accessed November 5, 2013).

Schantz, R. January–March 2006. "BBN's Network Computing Software Infrastructure and Distributed Applications (1970–1990)." *Annals of the History of Computing, IEEE*, 28, no. 1, pp. 72–88.

Schechtman, J. October 26, 2013. "Infosys Faces Largest U.S. Immigration Fine." *The Wall Street Journal, Morning Download*, ed. S. Rosenbush, http://blogs.wsj.com/cio/2013/10/29/the-morning-download-infosys-faces-largest-u-s-immigration-fine/ (accessed November 5, 2013).

Schwaber, K. 2004. *Agile Project Management with Scrum*. US: Microsoft Press.

Schwaber, K.; and M. Beedle. 2002. *Agile Software Development with Scrum*. Upper Saddle River, NY: Prentice-Hall.

Segall, L. March 20, 2012. "Google Nabs Digg Founder to Boost Google+" *CNN Money*, http://money.cnn.com/2012/03/20/technology/startups/Google-Digg-Milk/ (accessed October 31, 2013).

Shapiro, C.; and H. Varian. 1998. *Information Rules: A Strategic Guide to the Network Economy*, Boston, MA: Harvard Business School Press.

Siemens. 2012. *Siemens Annual Report for 2012*, http://www.siemens.com/investor/pool/en/investor_relations/siemens_ar_2012.pdf (accessed August 25, 2013).

Siemens. 2013. *Siemens History*, http://www.siemens.com/history/en/index.htm (accessed August 25, 2013).

Sigel, E. January 1985. "Alas Poor Visicorp." *Datamation* 31, no. 2, pp. 93–96.

Smith, G. December 3, 2007. "Unsung Innovators: Marty Goetz, Holder of First Software Patent." *Computerworld*, Data Center, http://www.computerworld.com/s/article/9046646/Unsung_innovators_Marty_Goetz_holder_of_first_software_patent (accessed July 18, 2013).

Smith, M.D.; and R. Telang. August 19, 2012. Assessing the Academic Literature Regarding the Impact of Media Piracy on Sales, SSRN: http://ssrn.com/abstract=2132153 or http://dx.doi.org/10.2139/ssrn.2132153 (accessed January 1, 2014).

Smith, W.D. April 5, 1970. "Maxi Computers Face Mini Conflict: Mini Trend Reaching Computers." *New York Times*.

Softex. 2013. *Softex Brazil*, www.softex.br (accessed September 22, 2013).

Softtek. n.d. *About Us*, http://www.softtek.com/en/about/fast-facts.

Software and Information Industry Association. 2013. "SIIA Anti-Piracy 2012 Year in Review." *SIIA*, www.siia.net (accessed October 6, 2013).

Software Engineering Standards Committee. 2006. Approved IEEE Draft Standard for Developing Software Life Cycle Processes (Revision of IEEE 1074-1997) Superseded by 1074-2006, *Institute for Electrical and Electronics Engineers*.

Software Russia. 2012. *Russia Software Industry Overview*, www.software-russia.com/why_russia/industry_overview (accessed September 17, 2013).

South Africa. n.d. *South Africa Info Home Page*, http://www.southafrica.info/ (accessed December 29, 2013).

Steinmueller, W.E. 1996. "The U.S. Software Industry: An Analysis and Interpretive History." In *The International Computer Software Industry: A Comparative Study of Industry Evolution and Structure*, ed. D.C. Mowery, 15–52. New York, NY: Oxford University Press.

Sugawara, S. August 21, 1993. "Justice to Launch Probe of Microsoft." *The Washington Post*, p. B01.

Surane, J. August 8, 2013. "US Airways Says Frequent-Flier Miles Deducted in Breach." *Bloomberg News*, http://www.bloomberg.com/news/2013-08-08/data-breach-may-have-erased-some-us-airways-frequent-flier-miles.html (accessed October 14, 2013).

Swartz, J. May 13, 2013b. "John McAfee Breaks Long Silence in Interview." *USA Today*, http://www.usatoday.com/story/tech/2013/05/12/john-mcafee-portland-belize-mysterious-murder/2135255/ (accessed October 29, 2013).

Swartz, J. October 24, 2013a. "McAfee Says He Spurned Request on HealthCare.gov." *USA Today*, http://www.usatoday.com/story/tech/2013/10/24/john-mcafee-says-he-turned-down-government-request/3178727/ (accessed October 29, 2013).

Syhunt. 2013. *Syhunt: About Us*, www.syhunt.com (accessed September 22, 2013).

Symantec. 2007. "Backdoor.SubSeven, Security Response." *Symantec Corporation*, http://www.symantec.com/security_response/writeup.jsp?docid=2001-020114-5445-99 (accessed October 14, 2013).

Symantec. 2013. "2013 Internet Security Threat Report." *Symantec Corporation*, 18, http://www.symantec.com/security_response/publications/threatreport.jsp (accessed October 11, 2013).

Tata Consultancy Services. 2013. *About TCS*, http://www.tcs.com/about/Pages/default.aspx (accessed September 23, 2013).

Technology Executives Club. 2013. *CPM Braxis*, http://www.technologyexecutivesclub.com/sponsorpages/cpmbraxis.php (accessed September 22, 2013).

The Associated Press. September 1, 2011. "Oracle Verdict Against SAP Is Overturned." *New York Times*, http://www.nytimes.com/2011/09/02/technology/oracle-verdict-against-sap-is-overturned.html?_r=0 (accessed August 25, 2013).

The Open Group. 2013. "Service Oriented Architecture: What Is SOA?" *The Open Group*, http://www.opengroup.org/soa/source-book/soa/soa.htm#soa_definition (accessed October 18, 2013).

Thibodeau, P. November 5, 2012. "In a Symbolic Shift, IBM's India Workforce Likely Exceeds U.S.: IT Salaries in India for All Firms Close to Minimum Wage in America." *Computerworld*, http://www.computerworld.com/s/article/9234101/In_a_symbolic_shift_IBM_s_India_workforce_likely_exceeds_U.S.?pageNumber=1 (accessed November 1, 2013).

Thurott, P. July 25, 2007. "China Makes Biggest Software Piracy Bust in History." *Windows IT Pro*, http://windowsitpro.com/windows-server/china-makes-biggest-software-piracy-bust-history (accessed October 6, 2013).

Toole, B.A. 1998. *Ada, the Enchantress of Numbers: Prophet of the Computer Age*. Mill Valley, CA: Strawberry Press.

Toomey, W. 2011. "The Strange Birth and Long Life of Unix." *Spectrum, IEEE* 48, no. 12, pp. 34–55.

Totvs. 2013. "Totvs: About *Totvs*" , http://www.totvs.com/sobre-a-totvs/nossa-historia (accessed September 22, 2013).

Truffle Capital. 2013. "The Top 100 European Software Vendors, Breakdown by Country." *Truffle Capital*, http://www.truffle100.com/2012/countries.php (accessed September 9, 2013).

Tschang, T.; and L. Xue. 2005. "The Chinese Software Industry" In *From Underdogs to Tigers: The Rise and Growth of the Software Industry in Brazil, China, India, Ireland and Israel*, eds. A. Arora; and A. Gambardella. Oxford, UK: Oxford University Press.

Tsipenyuk, K.; B. Chess; and G. McGraw. November–December 2005. "Seven Pernicious Kingdoms: A Taxonomy of Software Security Errors." *IEEE Security & Privacy* 3, no. 6, pp. 81–84.

Tukey, J.W. January 1958. "The Teaching of Concrete Mathematics." *American Mathematical Monthly* 65, no. 1, pp. 1–9.

U.S. Bureau of Labor Statistics. 2013a. *Occupational Employment Survey Statistics*, http://www.bls.gov/oes (accessed November 2, 2013).

U.S. Bureau of Labor Statistics. 2013b. *Labor Force Statistics from the Current Population Survey*, http://www.bls.gov/cps/tables.htm (accessed November 3, 2013).

U.S. Bureau of Labor Statistics. 2013c. *Consumer Price Inflation Tables*, http://www.bls.gov/cpi/tables.htm (accessed November 3, 2013).

U.S. Bureau of Labor Statistics. 2013d. *Occupational Outlook Handbook, Computer and Information Technology*, http://www.bls.gov/ooh/Computer-and-Information-Technology/ (accessed November 5, 2013).

U.S. Census Bureau. 1997. *SIC 73: Advertising Agencies*, http://www.census.gov/epcd/ec97brdg/E97B2_73.HTM (accessed October 26, 2013).

U.S. Citizenship and Immigration Services (USCIS). 2013. "H-1B Fiscal Year (FY) 2014 Cap Season." *Department of Homeland Security*, http://www.uscis.gov/working-united-states/temporary-workers/h-1b-specialty-occupations-and-fashion-models/h-1b-fiscal-year-fy-2014-cap-season (accessed November 5, 2013).

U.S. Computer Emergency Readiness Team (US-CERT). 2013. *US-CERT: About Us*, http://www.us-cert.gov/about-us (accessed October 16, 2013).

U.S. Copyright Office. 2013. *Copyrights*, www.copyright.gov (accessed October 2, 2013).

U.S. Department of Commerce's International Trade Administration. 2013. *Export: Brazil,* www.export.gov/brazil (accessed September 22, 2013).

U.S. Department of Labor. 2013. *Occupational Safety and Health Administration,* https://www.osha.gov/pls/imis/sic_manual.display?id=62&tab=group (accessed October 26, 2013).

U.S. Department of Labor. n.d. *Women in Labor Force,* http://www.dol.gov/wb/factsheets/Qf-laborforce-10.htm (accessed November 5, 2013).

U.S. Patent and Trademark Office (USPTO). 2013a. *General Information Concerning Patents USPTO,* http://www.uspto.gov/patents/resources/general_info_concerning_patents.jsp (accessed September 30, 2013).

U.S. Patent and Trademark Office (USPTO). 2013b. "Basic Facts about Trademarks." *USPTO,* http://www.uspto.gov/trademarks/basics/Basic_Facts_Trademarks.jsp (accessed October 1, 2013).

U.S. Patent and Trademark Office (USPTO). 2013c. *Searchable Database of Patents and Trademarks Issued by the USPTO,* http://patft.uspto.gov/

U.S. Securities and Exchange Commission. 2006. "SEC Charges McAfee, Inc. with Accounting Fraud; McAfee Agrees to Settle and Pay a $50 Million Penalty." *SEC News,* 2006, http://www.sec.gov/news/press/2006-3.htm (accessed October 29, 2013).

Unified Modeling Language (UML). n.d. www.uml.org

U.S. Bureau of Labor Statistics. n.d. *CPI Inflation Calculators,* www.bls.gov/data/inflation_calculator.htm (accessed December 29, 2013).

Vakili, K. 2012. *Competitive Effects of Collaborative Arrangements: Evidence from the Effect of the MPEG-2 Pool on Outsiders' Innovative Performance,* Working Paper. London, UK: London Business School, http://www.tiger.gatech.edu/REER%202012%20Papers/Vakili%20-%20Competitive%20Effects%20of%20Collaborative%20Arrangements.pdf (accessed October 9, 2013).

Vaughan, L. 2004. "The Reality of Video Games." *Stanford Graduate School of Business,* 2004, http://www.gsb.stanford.edu/news/headlines/2004futurentertainconf_videogames.shtml (accessed August 5, 2013).

Vaughan-Adams, L. 2003. "Sage Founder Retires at 43 to Get Married and Enjoy His £146m Fortune." *The Independent on Sunday* (London), http://www.highbeam.com/doc/1P2-1755383.html (accessed September 7, 2013).

Wagstaff, K. 2014. "Worst Breach in History Puts Data-Security Pressure on Retail Industry." *CNBC LLC,* http://www.cnbc.com/id/101328596 (accessed January 11, 2014).

Weik, M.H. 1961. *The ENIAC Story,* http://ftp.arl.mil/~mike/comphist/eniac-story.html (accessed October 26, 2013).

Wen, W.; M. Ceccagnoli; and C. Forman. August 2013. *Patent Commons, Thickets, and Open Source Software Entry by Start-Up Firms, NBER Working Paper 19394,* http://www.nber.org/papers/w19394 (accessed October 5, 2013).

Wetfeet. December 3, 2012. *Industry Overview: Computer Software*, https://www.wetfeet.com/articles/industry-overview-computer-software (accessed November 2, 2013).

Wheelen, T. L.; and Hunger, J. D. 2000. Strategic management and business policy: entering 21st century global society. 7th ed. London: Prentice Hall.

Wikipedia. 2013. *History of IBM,* http://en.wikipedia.org/wiki/History_of_IBM (accessed August 4, 2013).

Wikipedia. 2013a. "Siemens IT Solutions and Services." *Wikipedia,* http://en.wikipedia.org/wiki/Siemens_IT_Solutions_and_Services (accessed August 25, 2013).

Wikipedia. 2013b. "Siemens." *Wikipedia,* http://en.wikipedia.org/wiki/Siemens (accessed August 24, 2013).

Wikipedia. 2013c. "Lodsys." *Wikipedia,* http://en.wikipedia.org/wiki/Lodsys (accessed October 5, 2013).

Wikipedia. 2013d. "ISO/IEC 27000-Series." *Wikipedia,* http://en.wikipedia.org/wiki/ISO/IEC_27000-series (accessed October 16, 2013).

Wikipedia. 2013e. "McAfee." *Wikipedia,* http://en.wikipedia.org/wiki/McAfee (accessed October 29, 2013).

Wikipedia. 2013f. "Software Architect." *Wikipedia,* http://en.wikipedia.org/wiki/Software_architect (accessed November 2, 2013).

Wikipedia. 2013g. "Massively Multi-Player Online Role Playing Game (MMORPG)." *Wikipedia,* http://en.wikipedia.org/wiki/Massively_multiplayer_online_role-playing_game (accessed September 15, 2013).

Wikipedia. n.d.(a). *History of Microsoft,* http://en.wikipedia.org/wiki/History_of_Microsoft (accessed July 16, 2013).

Wikipedia. n.d.(b). *System Development Corporation,* http://en.wikipedia.org/wiki/System_Development_Corporation (accessed July 16, 2013).

Wikipedia. n.d.(c). *Windows NT,* http://en.wikipedia.org/wiki/Windows_NT (accessed July 17, 2013).

Wikipedia. n.d.(d). *History of the Internet,* http://en.wikipedia.org/wiki/History_of_the_Internet (accessed July 17, 2013).

Wikipedia. n.d.(e). *Market Adoption and Usage Share,* http://en.wikipedia.org/wiki/Internet_Explorer#Market_adoption_and_usage_share (accessed July 17, 2013).

Wikipedia. n.d.(g). *Oracle Corporation,* http://en.wikipedia.org/wiki/Oracle_Corporation (accessed July 26, 2013).

Wikipedia. n.d.(h). *Symantec,* http://en.wikipedia.org/wiki/Symantec (accessed July 26, 2013).

Wikipedia. n.d.(i). *Adobe Systems,* https://en.wikipedia.org/wiki/Adobe_Systems (accessed July 26, 2013).

Wikipedia. n.d.(j). *CATechnologies,* http://en.wikipedia.org/wiki/CA_Technologies (accessed July 26, 2013).

Wikipedia. n.d.(k). *Happy Feet,* http://en.wikipedia.org/wiki/Happy_Feet (accessed December 30, 2013).

Wikipedia. n.d.(l). *Redtribe,* http://en.wikipedia.org/wiki/Redtribe (accessed December 30, 2013).

Williams, M. November 15, 2011. "CIOs Seek Ways to Replace Legacy Systems." *Government Technology,* http://www.govtech.com/policy-management/CIOs-Seek-Ways-to-Replace-Legacy-Systems.html (accessed August 22, 2013).

Windows. n.d. *A History of Windows,* http://windows.microsoft.com/en-us/windows/history (accessed October 26, 2013).

WIPO. n.d. *PCT The International Patent System,* from http://www.wipo.int/pct/en/ (accessed October 2, 2013).

Wipro. 2013. *About Wipro,* www.wipro.com/about-wipro (accessed September 23, 2013).

Womack, C. July 24, 2012. "Google Says Almost Half of Motorola Purchase Price for Patents." *Bloomberg News,* http://www.bloomberg.com/news/2012-07-25/google-says-almost-half-of-motorola-purchase-price-for-patents.html (accessed October 9, 2013).

World Intellectual Property Organization (WIPO). 2013a. "WIPO Copyright Treaty." *WIPO,* http://www.wipo.int/treaties/en/ip/wct/ (accessed October 6, 2013).

World Intellectual Property Organization (WIPO). 2013b. "Berne Convention for the Protection of Literary and Artistic Works." *WIPO,* http://www.wipo.int/treaties/en/ip/berne/ (accessed October 6, 2013).

Yahoo! Inc. 2013a. *Profile: Check Point Software Technologies Ltd,* http://finance.yahoo.com/q/pr?s=CHKP (accessed September 12, 2013).

Yahoo! Inc. 2013b. *Profile: Comverse Inc,* http://biz.yahoo.com/ic/133/133217.html (accessed September 12, 2013).

Zetter, K. 2012. "Meet 'Flame,' The Massive Spy Malware Infiltrating Iranian Computers." *Wired Magazine,* http://www.wired.com/threatlevel/2012/05/flame/ (accessed September 21, 2013).

Zuckerberg, M. October 18, 2010. "Why Facebook Buys Startups." *YouTube,* http://www.youtube.com/watch?v=OlBDyItD0Ak (accessed October 31, 2013).

# Index

## OTHER TITLES IN OUR INDUSTRY PROFILES COLLECTION

Donald Stengel, California State University, Fresno, Editor

- *A Profile of the Electric Power Industry: Facing the Challenges of the 21st Century* by Charles Clark
- *A Profile of the Steel Industry: Global Reinvention for a New Economy* by Peter Warrian
- *A Profile of the United States Toy Industry: Serious Fun* by Christopher Byrne
- *A Profile of the Furniture Manufacturing Industry: Global Restructuring* by Susan M. Walcott
- *A Profile of the Oil and Gas Industry: Resources, Market Forces, Geopolitics, and Technology* by Linda Herkenhoff
- *A Profile of the Farm Machinery Industry: Helping Farmers Feed the World* by Dawn M. Drake
- *A Profile of the Automobile and Motor Vehicle Industry: Innovation, Transformation, Globalization* by James M. Rubenstein

## FORTHCOMING IN THIS COLLECTION

- *A Profile of the U.S. Film Industry: From Content to Media to the World* by John W. Clarry
- *A Profile of the Wine Industry: Global, Local, Earth, and Glitz* by Barbara Insel
- *A Profile of the Textile Manufacturing Industry* by Erin Parrish
- *A Profile of the Performing Arts Industry: Culture and Commerce* by David H. Gaylin
- *A Profile of the Global Airlines Industry* by Kent Gourdin

# Announcing the Business Expert Press Digital Library

*Concise E-books Business Students Need*
*for Classroom and Research*

This book can also be purchased in an e-book collection by your library as
- a one-time purchase,
- that is owned forever,
- allows for simultaneous readers,
- has no restrictions on printing, and
- can be downloaded as PDFs from within the library community.

Our digital library collections are a great solution to beat the rising cost of textbooks. E-books can be loaded into their course management systems or onto students' e-book readers.

The **Business Expert Press** digital libraries are very affordable, with no obligation to buy in future years. For more information, please visit **www.businessexpertpress.com/librarians**. To set up a trial in the United States, please email **sales@businessexpertpress.com**.

www.ingramcontent.com/pod-product-compliance
Lightning Source LLC
Chambersburg PA
CBHW061139220326
41599CB00025B/4293